AMERICA ONLINE'S GUIDE TO PERSONAL COMPUTING

Edited by Seth Godin

AOL
PRESS

America Online's Guide to Personal Computing

Editorial Director: Brad Schepp

Illustration on page 48 drawn by Penny Delaney.

© 1998 by America Online, Inc.

Printed in the United States of America

98 99 00 10 9 8 7 6 5 4 3 2 1

Library of Congress Cataloging-in-Publication Data

98-35339

ISBN 1-891556-53-3

GREETINGS FROM AMERICA ONLINE!

Welcome to *America Online's Guide to Personal Computing*.

AOL helps make using computers fun and productive. And that's really what this book is all about: getting the most out of your computer.

You'll learn about your computer's components, how to maintain it, upgrade it, and travel online as quickly as possible. We'll cover some things you probably didn't know about the software that's now available. We'll also show you how those cool multimedia and imaging components make computers come alive with sound, pictures, and video.

Throughout this book, you'll find many references to AOL areas that supplement what's covered. So feel free to hop online when the mood strikes.

If you check out AOL's Computing channel, you'll see it's a great resource for all AOL members—from novices to advanced users. You can explore all of your computing and technology interests, stay up on industry news and product information, find helpful software tools, and get reliable answers. And if you want to buy computers, software, and accessories, you can do that, too.

If there's one thing that AOL's 12 million members have in common, it's their interest in computers. Now, with this book and AOL's Computing channel, you can start making that computer earn its keep. And also have some fun along the way!

See you online,

Cheryl Davis

Director of Programming, AOL Computing

ACKNOWLEDGMENTS

With special thanks to Elizabeth Gardner, Trudi Reisner, and Mark Baven for their indispensable contributions to this book.

At AOL, thanks to Adam Rugel, Brad Schepp, John Tierny, Judy Karpinski, Cheryl Davis, John Dyn, Don Crowl, and Paul DiVito.

CONTENTS

INTRODUCTION

You're probably familiar with some of the basic things you can use your PC for, such as word processing, spreadsheets, personal information management, and getting online. But are you using it to its full potential? Probably not. All that high-tech bells-and-whistles hardware and software is great, but it can also overwhelm you. You'll get the most from your PC if you consider the many ways you can use it.

This book anticipates the most important questions you might have about what you can expect from your computer and your time online. You'll learn how to use the AOL service to answer any computer questions you have, shop for new components, and download great software.

Here's a brief synopsis of what you'll learn.

- **Chapter 1. Computer Resources on AOL.** Whether you're a novice, just savvy enough to be dangerous, or a certified expert, you'll be glad to discover Insiders' favorite computer resources on the AOL service. From tips at the Computing channel, to software from the Daily Download, to hardware from the AOL Store Hardware Shop, chapter 1 will help you find what you need.

- **Chapter 2. Understanding What You've Got.** Ever wonder what's inside your computer and how all the components work? Chapter 2 explains it all, from the motherboard to peripherals, from ROM to RAM, from mice to monitors, and more, with road signs pointing you to information on AOL.

- **Chapter 3. Linking Up and Communicating.** AOL makes surfing the Net painless. It comes with a built-in Web browser, so all you need is a modem—something your computer probably already has. In chapter 3 you'll learn how to cruise along with online communications—for example, how to troubleshoot modem problems, how to exchange e-mail and Instant Messages with anyone on the Internet, how to save time with Automatic AOL, and how to get free help at AOL Member Services.

- **Chapter 4. Multimedia: All Those Special Effects.** Exciting equipment like CD-ROM drives, sound cards, and scanners now comes standard with many computers. Chapter 4 will tell you how to evaluate what you have and how to maximize your computer's multimedia capabilities online and offline. Discover how much fun it can be to use stuff like scanners, as we introduce you to the new and exciting world of computer pictures.

- **Chapter 5. Maintaining and Repairing Your PC.** Hopefully you won't ever be faced with a system crash. But if it happens, chapter 5 can help you detect and diagnose the problem. You'll also learn how to clean your computer's components safely, how to make backups a no-sweat routine, and how to know when it's time to call for help.

- **Chapter 6. Upgrading Your PC.** The day inevitably will come when you outgrow one or more of your computer's components. Upgrading your PC can make your system faster and add desirable new features. Chapter 6 answers your questions about what, when, and how to upgrade.

- **Chapter 7. Buying a New PC.** Exciting new developments continuously arise in the PC industry. Chapter 7 helps you decide when it's time to buy a new PC and what new features to look for, and gives special emphasis to interpreting the abbreviations used in computer advertising.

- **Chapter 8. Your Computer as Your Personal Assistant: Making Software Work for You**. Software can make life easier. There are programs for word processing, desktop publishing, graphics, presentations, personal information management, database management, personal finance, Web publishing, utilities, games—you name it. Chapter 8 helps you decide which programs you need, and answers your questions about installing and upgrading software using the resources available on AOL.

The chapters follow a question-and-answer format, anticipating the many questions you probably have about computing and AOL. Appendix I is similarly organized, and answers FAQs (frequently asked questions) from AOL Member Services. Appendix II is a transcript from an online class held at the PC Hardware Forum, one of many ways AOL members can get live help. Rounding out the book is a comprehensive glossary of computer terms, an index of AOL keywords, and a general index.

What You Need to Know

You need to know something about how we wrote this book. With so many different computers available, we thought it would be best to keep the instructions simple. So we have assumed you are using a PC that has the Windows 95 operating system. But you can easily follow along if you've got another operating system, including Windows 98 and one created for the Macintosh. You should also know that this book was written to help you make the most of the features available in AOL version 4.0.

MINIMUM SYSTEM REQUIREMENTS FOR AOL 4.0

To take advantage of the features on AOL 4.0, make sure your PC meets the following specifications:

Windows 95 and Windows 98

- 16 megabytes RAM system configuration
- Pentium-class PC
- 45 megabytes available hard disk space
- 640 x 480, 256 colors screen resolution, or better
- 14.4 kbps modem, or faster

Windows 3.1

- 16 megabytes RAM system configuration
- 486-class PC, or better
- 30 megabytes available hard disk space
- 640 x 480, 256 colors screen resolution, or better
- 14.4 kbps modem, or faster

Macintosh

- 12 megabytes RAM system configuration
- System 7.1, or better
- 68040 or PowerPC Macintosh
- 640 x 480, 256 colors screen resolution, or better
- 14.4 kbps modem, or faster

If you need to upgrade any system components, be sure to visit the AOL Store's Hardware Shop at keyword **Hardware Center**. (See the Upgrade Tips section.) Users with Windows 95 machines that don't meet the AOL 4.0 for Windows 95 requirements can use the 16-bit version (which is normally used on Windows 3.x).

AOL keywords and Web addresses change over time. And your screen may look slightly different from the figures that illustrate this book. That's because the AOL service (and the Internet) is always changing and improving.

Yep, computing in the '90s is more exciting than ever! Hardware and software have dropped way down in price to give you more features for your money. Get ready to examine the many ways you can use PCs. Why not get started right now?

1

COMPUTER RESOURCES ON AOL

The questions and answers in this chapter provide a miniature navigational guide to the best computer information about hardware, software, the AOL service and other resources on the Net. With your mouse as your gearshift, you can easily cruise to sites where you'll read articles and reviews, contact the experts, converse with your peers, order any tools you need, and download the software you want.

You'll learn about all sorts of other useful and interesting sites throughout the book, but the ones introduced in this chapter will become your control center. You'll find yourself returning to them again and again.

Even if you're a total novice, you can dive right in. And if you're already familiar with computers, AOL, and the Net, this guide will speed you along so you don't waste time. There are no prerequisites, and we don't throw in any technical jargon or overly detailed explanations—just clear and helpful answers that will make you an expert at navigating America Online and understanding your computer.

The Computing Channel

The more you understand what your computer can do for you, the better your AOL experience will be. That's why America Online has created so many sites designed to help you learn about your machine, acquire new hardware and software, and, most important, network with other computer users.

The first place to go is the AOL Computing channel (keyword: **Computing**) shown in figure 1.1. It's among America Online's most popular channels, and for good reason. Here's an overview of what you can find and do there:

- Get help, advice, and tips about every computer topic you can think of.

- Access online computer classes and information about software and hardware.

- Search large software libraries for files to download to your PC.

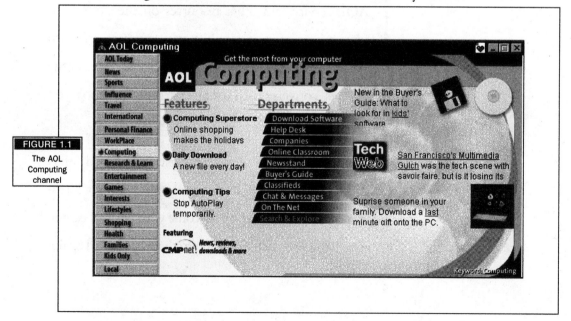

FIGURE 1.1
The AOL Computing channel

- Discover scads of computing forums where you can hook up with other AOL users interested in particular computing topics. You can join live discussions or just check out what other AOL members and experts have to say.

- Get free product support directly from the computer manufacturers at the AOL Industry Connection.

- Do your shopping at the AOL Store (keyword: **AOL Store**) and save yourself time and hassle. At the Hardware Shop (keyword: **Hardware Center**) and the Software Shop (keyword: **Software Shop**), you can buy the same new products you find at "real" stores.

- Pore over the Computing Newsstand (keyword: **Computing Newsstand**) and read all the articles you want from computer magazines without paying a single cover price.

If I have questions about using my PC, where can I get some quick tips?

When you want immediate help, go to Computing Tips (keyword: **Computing Tips**) shown in figure 1.2. It's organized by category, and will answer many of your computer questions or problems. You can also learn some basics—just check out PC Tips and AOL Tips.

Where do I go to learn about more specific computer topics like PC games, Windows 95, and music software?

Whatever computer area you're interested in, AOL has a forum that covers it. You'll find more information, tips, advice, and answers than you ever imagined! Most of these forums feature active message boards where you can post questions, review ready-made answers to frequently asked questions (FAQs), and read long lists of valuable information on the general topic and its subdivisions. And there's always a conference room where you can talk the talk with other online members who are drawn to the same subject.

The hardware and software forums are run by dedicated enthusiasts who are available nearly 'round the clock and on weekends. They often host conferences to feature new products or discuss specific computing topics. And they're happy to answer any questions you have, in plain English.

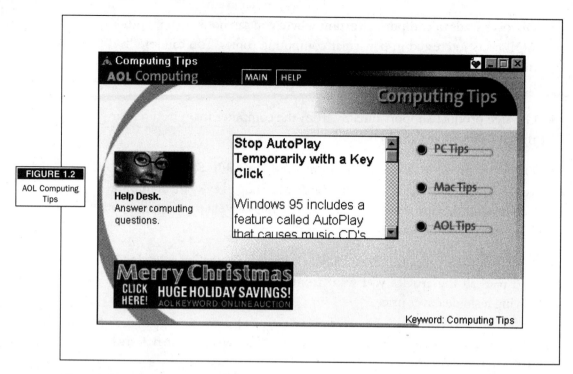

FIGURE 1.2
AOL Computing
Tips

10

Plus, AOL members are always looking to help each other out, regardless of anyone's level of expertise. Just post a question to the message board, and someone (or several people) will either provide you with an answer or point you to the AOL or Internet resources that will.

So whether you want fast info, deep background, or some friendly conversation about your chosen topic, the AOL sites listed below are the ticket. (In this chapter we'll cover about half of them in some detail.)

- PC Help Desk (keyword: **Help Desk**)

- PC Applications Forums (keyword: **APPS**)

- PC Hardware Forum (keyword: **PC Hardware** or **PHW**)

- PC Animation & Video Forum (keyword: **A&V Forum**)

- PC Music & Sound Forum (keyword: **PC Music**)

- PC Graphic Arts Forum (keyword: **PGR**)

- PC Telecom & Networking Forum (keyword: **PTC**)

To locate an area of interest on AOL, click the Find tool on the AOL toolbar and choose Find it on AOL. The Find Central window will open. From there, choose anything you want to get to the area you're interested in. Another way to find areas of interest is to use AOL keywords. Enter a keyword in the address box on the AOL toolbar and click the Go button on the AOL toolbar. AOL will bring you right to the area you want to explore. You will find keywords throughout this book, which take you to the computer areas on AOL. Don't know the right keyword to use? Use keyword: **Keyword** to review your options alphabetically or by channel.

- PC Windows Forum (keyword: **WIN**)

- DOS Forum (keyword: **DOS**)

- The OS/2 Forum (keyword: **OS2**)

- PC Development Forum (keyword: **PDV**)

- Personal Digital Assistants Forum (keyword: **PDA**)

- The User Group Network (keyword: **UGF**)

- PC Games Forum (keyword: **PC Games**)

And if you're a Mac user, you'll find a hearty selection of Mac forums, which we'll tell you about later in this chapter.

Before I buy software, I'd like to make sure it's useful to me. Is it possible to test-drive it first?

Quite possibly, yes. In fact, the try-before-you-buy concept is the basis of a huge category of programs known as shareware. Plus you can take demo versions of regular commercial programs out for a spin as well.

Here's how it works. Just check in at the AOL Daily Download (keyword: **Daily Download**) shown in figure 1.3, where a different software demo or shareware package is offered each day. If you're already on the Computing channel, just click on the

Daily Download option button to see what's on the software menu that day.

The daily special isn't the type of software you're seeking? Not to worry: There is other downloadable software at More Files. And if you need a little help downloading any software, you'll find step-by-step instructions in the How to Download area.

With trial periods of generally between 10 and 30 days, you get to take a program for a nice long spin. If it passes muster, just go to the AOL Store Software Shop to plunk down your money.

From everything I hear, it seems I'm going to want to upgrade my PC sometime. Where can I buy computer components?

A comprehensive selection of new wares is sold at the AOL Store (keyword: **AOL Store**). You'll find virtually any type of computer hardware or software at one of its shops:

- Software Shop (keyword: **Software Shop**)

- Hardware Shop (keyword: **Hardware Center**)

- Modem Shop (keyword: **Modem Shop**)

- Digital Shop (keyword: **Digital Shop**)

The deals on imaging stuff like scanners and digital cameras are among the best. And when you're in the market for used goods, or looking for a bargain price for something new, the place to go is AOL Computing Classifieds (keyword: **Classifieds**). Flea markets won't have the same appeal anymore.

Where can I get Mac software online?

Go to the Mac Software File Search area (keyword: **Filesearch**). Choose Brand Name if you are interested in purchasing retail software, or Shareware if you want to try stuff out, then click on the MacSearch button. Fill in the MacSearch form and AOL will display a list of Mac software and shareware file categories with the week ending date for each category. If you want to purchase the software, go to the Software Shop at the AOL Store.

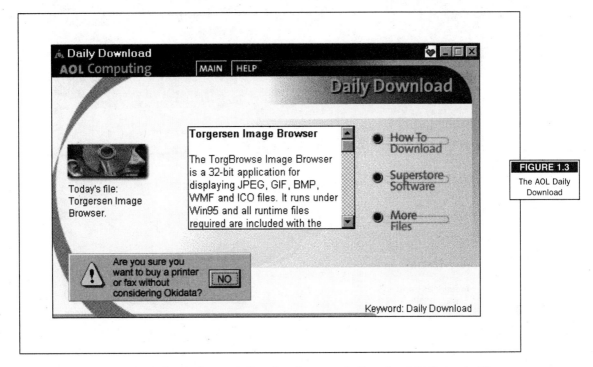

FIGURE 1.3

The AOL Daily Download

Another area to visit is the Software Libraries (keyword: **Download Software**). Choose a Software Category, and an appropriate Software Library to see a list of Mac software that's right for you.

13

Online Classroom

Until recently, if you really wanted to learn about new computer technology it meant signing up for computer classes at your local college or high school's adult ed program. Working with a textbook can be fine—until you come across something that you have trouble understanding. Besides, few of us have the determination to work through all the exercises in a book, and that hands-on practice is what makes new knowledge stick.

But now, an entirely new educational concept is at your fingertips: online computing classes. An extensive curriculum of hardware and software courses is available, with real teachers and scheduled sessions. Your admissions center is the AOL Online Classroom (keyword: **Online Classroom**) shown in figure 1.4. That's where you'll find the listings.

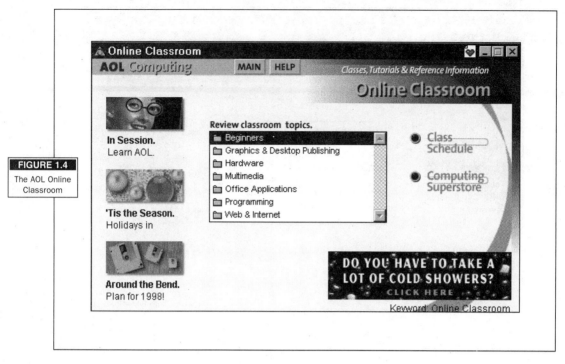

FIGURE 1.4

The AOL Online Classroom

Here's a sample of course topics offered:

- Beginners

- Graphics & Desktop Publishing

- Hardware

- Multimedia

- Office Applications

- Programming

- Web & Internet

I'm just a beginner. Can I find a course on computer basics?

The Online Classroom offers classes across the spectrum, from answers to basic questions like "How do I turn this thing off?" to advanced programming. If you're totally green, the Beginners class is a perfect place to start. You'll be amazed at how quickly you'll shorten the learning curve.

Some people find that their slow typing holds them back from using their computers efficiently. If you're a hunt-and-peck typist and you want to improve your skills, check out the Typing Programs area in the Online Classroom.

Is there a simple way to find out when these classes meet?

It's all there at the Online Classroom. Check there anytime for class dates, times, teachers, and brief descriptions.

I know a little bit about computers, but I meet loads of people who can talk tech circles around me. How do I know I won't feel dumb in these classes?

Most of the classes are geared to people at all levels. Classes designed especially for beginners or for advanced users are marked as such on the schedule.

What if I miss a class?

No problem. (And don't worry, the teachers don't take attendance.) Transcripts for every class are available at the Online Classroom. In fact, it's a good idea to print out the transcripts and keep them in a binder near your computer for easy reference. Appendix II features a sample transcript.

Other than the transcripts, are there recommended instruction or reference books I should buy to help with the online classes?

Yes, although they're not mandatory. Go to Tutorials & Books in the Online Classroom to see a list of the relevant materials you can buy and sources for buying them. Note, the AOL Store's Book Shop (keyword: **Book Shop**) also carries a lot of these computing books.

PC Help Desk

Everybody bumps up against a problem once in a while when learning how to use computers. There's no reason to feel embarrassed or to waste precious time trying to solve a problem by yourself. It's much easier to get a quick, clear answer immediately. The place for this is the PC Help Desk (keyword: **Help Desk**) shown in figure 1.5. Here you get access to the AOL computing staff, a list of AOL keywords, AOL Member Services, help on downloading files, and answers to frequently asked questions (FAQs).

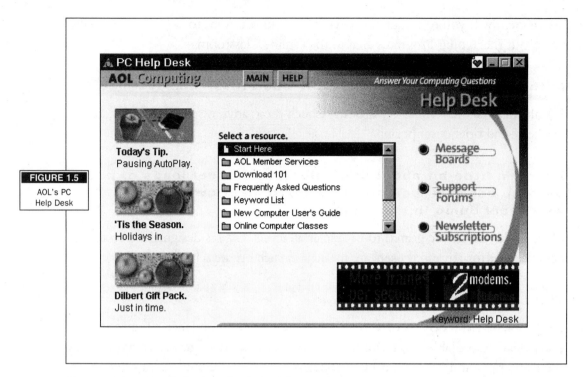

16

FIGURE 1.5
AOL's PC
Help Desk

Here's what you'll find at the PC Help Desk:

• The Help Desk (keyword: **Help Desk**) will direct you to message boards where other AOL members can answer your topic-specific questions.

• If you're having a problem, chances are that others have had the same one. Solutions to the most common ones can be found in the FAQs area.

• A picture is worth a thousand words. Go to the Visual Help area to find hints and tips on AOL topics presented in a pictorial format. Just select a featured topic from the Visual Help menu, and get step-by-step instructions accompanied by images of how your screen will look.

• To simply learn something interesting about computing, you can choose Today's Tip. That will take you to the Computing Tips area (keyword: **Computing Tips**), where you can read the featured tip of the day.

If you're dedicated to increasing your knowledge about computing, you'll probably want to subscribe to *The Weekly Byte*. This free AOL newsletter, sent via e-mail, will give you ongoing advice about computing issues and direct you to the best AOL areas for answers to computing questions. You can even get back issues.

I'm a night owl. But my computer manufacturer's technical support staff isn't available late at night or on the weekend, when I need them. Can I get technical support on America Online during off-hours?

You can get *live* help at the PC Help Desk (keyword: **Help Desk**) between 9 and 11 a.m. At other times, your best bet is to tap into message boards and support forums.

Among their other uses, message boards are places where you can post a question so others can read it and post an answer. Sometimes you'll get a response right away, though you can't count on it. Just choose the Message Boards option at the Help Desk, and you're on your way.

Support forums are a surer way to get a speedy reply to your technical question at any time of day or night. Go to the PC Help Desk and choose the Support Forum for the topic that's bewildering you. Chances are high that another AOL user will be online with the information you need.

The Companies area (keyword: **Companies**) on the AOL Computing channel is a great place to find technical support from hardware and software companies.

Where do I turn for help fixing my computer?

There are a few great places to get advice. From the Help Desk, check out FAQs, the Support Forums, and the Message Boards. These three sources will offer so many fixes for your computer that your real challenge might be in selecting one method.

Where can I go on AOL to learn how to download software?

From the PC Help Desk list, choose Downloading Files. All the instructions you need are there, and you actually download real software files while you learn.

What are keywords?

With keywords you can jump around quickly on the AOL service. All keywords are associated with areas of interest; for example, keyword **Computing** will bring you to the Computing channel.

Use can access areas of the AOL service using keywords in several ways:

• Type a keyword in the Keyword box at the top of the AOL window and press Enter or click on Go.

- Click on the Favorites button on the toolbar and choose Go To Keyword. When the Keyword dialog box appears, type the keyword for the location you want and click on Go.

- Press Ctrl + K to open the Keyword dialog box. Follow the same procedure as above.

For a list of all the AOL keywords, go to the Keyword List (keyword: **Keyword**). You can print a copy of these keywords, which will open any door in the AOL service.

Another way to get around AOL is to use the Find command. Click Find on the AOL toolbar and choose Find it on AOL. In the Find Central window, select the area of your choice to get to where you want.

I hear people discussing computer viruses with real concern. How can I protect my computer from infection?

Well, the best course is to install a current version of a good anti-virus program on your computer. However, if your machine gets infected—and it does happen, even with precautions—it's not the end of the world, or of your data.

To arm yourself with information, go to the AOL PC Virus Information Center shown in figure 1.6. Get there either from the PC Help Desk (keyword: **Help Desk**) or by entering the keyword **Virus**. You'll find numerous options there to choose from:

- Get a list of virus companies.

- Post questions on the Virus Message Board.

- Visit the Download Software area for a virus program.

- Learn about the viruses in the Essential Virus area.

- Get advice about safeguarding your computer at Protection Tips.

- Find out about the Word macro virus.

- Take a gander at McAfee VirusScan software.

- Get the lowdown about virus hoaxes at Internet Hoax Information.

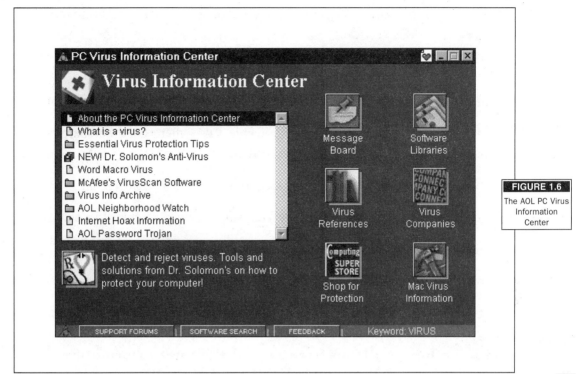

FIGURE 1.6

The AOL PC Virus Information Center

There's even a free trial of Dr. Solomon's anti-virus software.

Can I purchase virus protection software online?

Sure. At the AOL Store's Software Shop (keyword: **Software Shop**) you can browse through virus detection and removal programs and buy the one that's right for your computer.

My children would like plain-English definitions of tricky computing terms such as MB, CPU, and VRAM. Is there a kid-friendly place that explains the basics?

Your kids should head straight to Youth Tech (keyword: **YT**), one of the coolest places for children on AOL. The Tech Stuff area has a list of computing terms with plain-English definitions.

Another place for basic definitions and a Top 10 list of computing terms is AOL Computing's Webopedia (keyword: **Webopedia**). Just click on a term and Webopedia will show you the definition. To look up terms other than the ones on the short list, click on the New Terms button.

The Glossary at the back of this book also gives definitions of computing terms.

What other resources for kids are available online? Is there a place where they can get technical help?

It's all happening at Youth Tech (keyword: **YT**). This is some of what's possible:

- For help with computing, pop into Techie Pals, where children share their interests and knowledge about technical stuff.

- There's the Chat Shack, a place for kids to hang out and chat online.

- Net Surf displays a list of acceptable Web sites for youth techies to visit.

- Virtual Fun is jammed with games, clubs, and an art shop.

- Kids can subscribe to the YT Newsletter.

- At the Software Exchange, they can swap software with other kids.

I've been hearing from friends that they get information from Meg, the AOL Insider. What kind if information is available there?

Meg, the AOL Insider (keyword: **AOL Tips**), is like a well-connected, savvy online buddy. She gives you the real-deal information on how to get the most from your AOL experience: general tips, AOL navigational shortcuts, online time-savers, tips on how to get connected, and answers to FAQs.

PC Applications Forums

Since all computers need applications in order to be useful, you'll want to check out the PC Applications Forums (keyword: **APPS**), shown in figure 1.7. This is where to go for advice on choosing general applications and specific software programs. Among other things, you'll find:

- Software to download

- Chat rooms abuzz with all sorts of topic discussions

- Computer Classes, to learn about PC applications

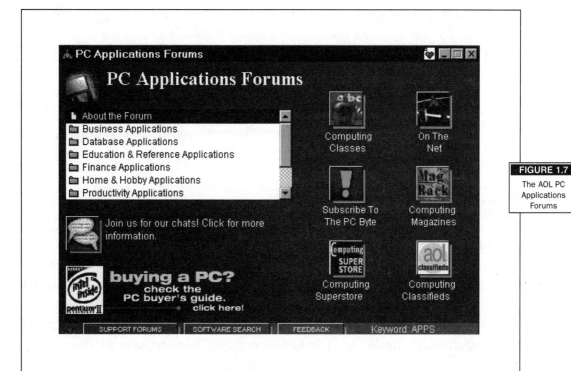

FIGURE 1.7

The AOL PC
Applications
Forums

- On The Net, for links to PC applications Web sites

- *The Weekly Byte*, a hardware and software newsletter available by subscription

- Computing Classifieds

I'm still new to computing, but I want to get the most from my PC. I know a little about word processors, spreadsheets, and financial management packages, but I want to learn more. Where do I start?

Within the PC Applications Forums you'll find scads of information about spreadsheets (such as the Microsoft Excel Resource Center and Spreadsheet templates), finance applications, word processors, and dozens of other types of useful software. Just click on one of the alphabetized topic categories, listed below, to get started:

- Business Applications

- Database Applications

- Education & Reference Applications

- Finance Applications

- Home & Hobby Applications

- Productivity Applications

- Spreadsheet Applications

- Word Processing Applications

Download Software

Software is what makes your computer an incredible tool, rather than an enormous paperweight. And each week new types of packages, or better versions of older ones, become available. Thanks to online services, it's easier than ever to download, try out, upgrade, and replace software programs, and AOL makes the process even more straightforward and reliable. For the best overall computing experience and the most advanced capabilities, you should visit AOL's online software libraries.

Start with the Download Software area (keyword: **Download Software**) shown in figure 1.8. There are literally thousands of programs here, with more added daily—utilities, applications, freeware, shareware, you name it—and each is a simple download away. Since AOL carefully screens all shareware and freeware for viruses before posting it, you can download without fear.

You'll find a complete list of downloadable files categorized by the type of software, so you don't have to wander the aisles randomly.

What's the difference between shareware, freeware, and retail software?

The main difference between these types of computer programs is the payment system. Shareware is offered on a try-before-you-buy basis, and it's based on the honor system. If you decide to keep and use the program after a trial period (usually 10 to 30 days), you're expected to pay a fee to the author.

Freeware is a program that is made available to the public free of charge. (As you can tell, greed is not necessarily the motivating force for programmers.)

Retail software is akin to the shrink-wrapped software you buy in a store, but online you get it immediately. You choose your retail software from a list, pay the retail price shown, then download the files.

I still have some questions about the details. Where can I go to learn more about downloading software?

Click on Software Help in the Download Software area (keyword: **Download Software**), and you'll find an extensive primer on downloadable software. You can also get help by choosing Download Help in the Service & Support list.

Is Download Software the only place on AOL where I can acquire a program?

Actually, there's a second way to do it: Go to the Computing Superstore (keyword: **CSS**) and click on the Download Now button to see what software is available. You'll find a vast selection of programs here to choose from, including the Top 10 featured software packages, new software, featured specials, and rebate offers.

Can I play games online?

But of course! The gaming center is located at WorldPlay (keyword: **Worldplay**). That's where you'll find every conceivable variety of diversion, all of which are avail-

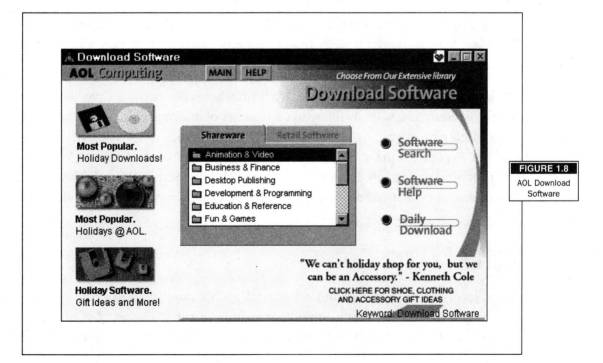

FIGURE 1.8
AOL Download Software

able to you around the clock. First select a game category—such as Adventure, Strategy & Action, Classic Card, or Puzzle & Board—and AOL will alphabetically list the games of that type. Choose one, and you're in. And when that one starts getting old, just choose another.

Where can I go to download games?

Like other programs, these goodies are available at the Download Software area (keyword: **Download Software**). You'll find the latest games here, as well as all the classics. Just make sure you have enough free megabytes on your hard drive—and free time in your life.

Where do I find out about new software releases?

Click on New Files in the Download Software area. All the new packages show up as they come out, so the list changes all the time.

Another excellent place to look for new software releases is the Buyer's Guide (keyword: **Buyer's Guide**). In addition to a list of new packages, here you'll find reviews and advice about the software.

How do I find a particular piece of software?

Just click on Software Search (keyword: **Filesearch**) in the Download Software area. Then you have a choice between Brand Name or Shareware. If you select Brand Name, AOL will taxi you over to software.net.

If you choose Shareware, up pops a search form where you specify the type of shareware or freeware you want by filling in a few pieces of information: Timeframe–such as all dates, past month, or past week–and Category—such as file compression, to find, for example, WinZip. If you don't know the exact name of the file, you can enter keywords to narrow the search. After you click on Search, AOL displays a list of files that fit your specifications. Choose the software you want and download it.

The PC A & V Forum

It's no surprise that animation and video (A&V) is hot now. Just add sound and you have full multimedia: videos, computer animation features, movies. Technological advances are making these grand possibilities accessible to a lot more people than in the past. The PC Animation & Video Forum (keyword: **A&V Forum**) shown in figure 1.9, is where amateurs and professionals alike share their knowledge about and experiences with multimedia.

For starters, this is the area where you'll find the latest product data, such as:

- The PCs that are best for multimedia applications

- The special tools that are multimedia must-haves, such as a plug-in (a hardware or software component that adds a specific feature or service to a larger system, such as audio or video messages in the AOL browser)

- The CD-ROMs, video capture expansion cards, and digital imaging cameras that are the most advanced or useful for your purposes

Don't let these technical terms keep you from exploring the A&V Forum. Just check this book's Glossary for the definitions, then dive right in.

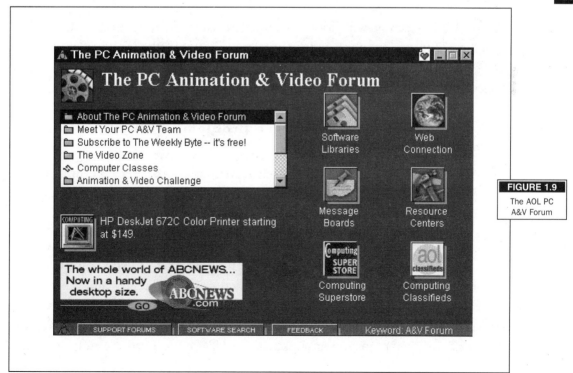

FIGURE 1.9

The AOL PC
A&V Forum

Can I get to multimedia-related Web sites from AOL?

Definitely. In fact, a primary purpose of a forum such as this is to offer one-stop jump-off points to all the interesting sites. Choose Web Connection in the A&V Forum and you'll find an exhaustive list of Web sites that focus on animation and video products, publications, and manufacturers. The sites are categorized as follows:

- CD-ROM Drive Manufacturers

- Computer Manufacturers

- Cool Multimedia Sites

- Modem Manufacturers

- Multimedia Magazines

- Multimedia Software Manufacturers

- Sound Card Manufacturers

- Video Card Manufacturers

- Miscellaneous Manufacturers

The Web Connection will hook you up with the best multimedia-related sites, including Duplexx Software (video software), Creative Labs (Sound Blaster products), and Microsoft. If you can't find a particular site, go to the Web from the Welcome screen, and use AOL NetFind to search for a site on the Web.

How can I get help when I have problems with my multimedia hardware and software?

One straightforward way is to post your questions on the A&V Forum message boards. Other AOL members will post answers to help you work through any particular problem.

Another excellent place for help and insights is an online live multimedia conference. These gatherings are happening all the time on AOL, so you're likely to find just what you need. It's easy to access the schedule of conferences and times. From the PC A&V forum (keyword: **A&V Forum**), go to Support Forums (keyword: **Help Desk**) and choose Live Events or you can get there with the keyword **Computing Live**. To see events for the upcoming week, choose Upcoming Events. You'll also find a similar list of conferences with dates and times in the Computers & Software area.

Where can I get video files and animation software?

For video and animation, there are two primary places:

At the Video Zone in the A&V Forum, you'll find a comprehensive list of AOL areas and Web sites that provide information about video files, organized as follows:

- What is this area?

- Video Message Boards

- Tips & Tricks

- Viewer Resource Center

- Video Companies on the Web!

- Animation & Video Challenge

- Animation & Video Files

- Video Applications

- Video Utilities

The Video Zone also gives you access to videoplayer software and videoplayer drivers, called QuickTime Players.

And the A&V Resource Centers (keyword: **A&V Forum**) and Download Software area (keyword: **Download Software**) offer animation shareware, retail software, and CD-ROM video files. The list of categories from the Resource Center should give you an idea of the scope:

- 3-D Rendering Resource Center

- Corel Resource Center

- Desktop & Web Publishing

- Picture Web Resource Center

- Searching the Internet!

- The Video Zone

- Tips & Tricks

- Viewer Resource Center

- Virtual Reality Resource Center

- VRML Resource Center

- Web Art Resource Center

- Youth Tech Center

I'm a Webmaster. Where can I find video multimedia tools to add to my computer?

The best place to find new multimedia tools are the AOL Store Software, Hardware, and Digital Shops (keywords: **Software Shop**, **Hardware Center**, and **Digital Shop**). But, if you don't mind buying tools secondhand, then look in the Computing Classifieds (keyword: **Classifieds**) in the PC A&V Forum.

Are there online classes on multimedia topics?

Plenty. And this is another way the A&V Forum helps, because when you click on Computer Classes you'll be led specifically to multimedia classes (keyword: **Online Classroom**). Here's a sampling of these courses (but new ones are added continually, so check the area often):

- Digital Cameras

- Digital Imaging

- Mac Music Studio

- Midi—Advanced

- Midi—Beginners

- Scanning Tips & Techniques

- Video Capture and Editing

I just bought a digital camera, so now I need digital imaging

software to go along with it. Where do I look?

One place to go is the Software Libraries in the PC A&V Forum (keyword: **A&V Forum**).

Also, the AOL Store's Digital Shop (keyword: **Digital Shop**) offers digital imaging software in the Software and Download areas. To purchase digital imaging programs such as Adobe PhotoDeluxe and PhotoFinish 4, choose Software. Or choose Download if you want to access the Shareware category list in the Download Software area. Under the Animation & Video category, you'll find files such as KanImage GA Digital Camera, PhotoQ: V1.0 Modem Print Services, and PhotoQ: V1.01 Online Photoprinter.

If you don't know which program to buy, you can get help by reading the Buyer's Guide (keyword: **Buyer's Guide**), which gives advice and reviews on the latest digital imaging software.

PC Music & Sound Forum

Many people have a passion for music, so it's hardly surprising that this forum is hopping. The PC Music & Sound Forum (keyword: **PC Music**) shown in figure 1.10, is for music buffs, players, recording artists, and anyone else who wants to make beautiful sounds. Here's where you can find advice and tips about using add-ons to turn your computer into a miniature multitrack recording studio and produce digital-quality audio. Or learn how to create professional-sounding music presentations. Explore musical tools, such as MIDI. Or take a class at Computing Classes (keyword: **Online Classroom**) to learn more about audio. If

29

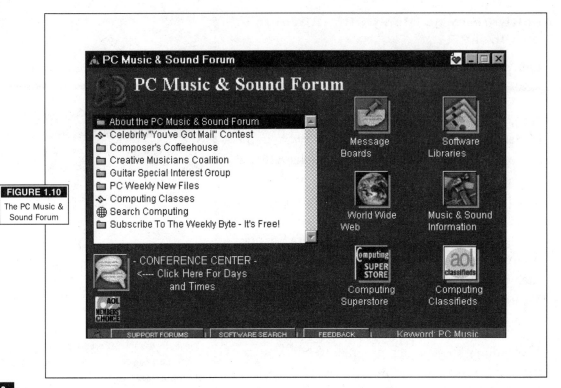

FIGURE 1.10

The PC Music &
Sound Forum

you're into music, you're likely to find some incredible information and resources here.

Where can I get the latest news on hardware and software for music and sound?

At the PC Music & Sound Forum (keyword: **PC Music**), you can subscribe to *The Weekly Byte* newsletter to get the scoop on hardware and software for music and sound, plus a broad range of other computing topics.

I bought a multimedia PC. How can I get the most out of it, soundwise?

There are several ways to learn more about your computer's multimedia capabilities. One is to check in at the PC Music & Sound Forum Conference Center (keyword: **PC Music**). Attend a conference where you can speak with experienced multimedia mavens. Or go to the Software Libraries to download free audio files (keyword: **Download Software**). Finally, use the World Wide Web option to visit Web sites dedicated to music and sound.

Where can I buy audio, music, and sound add-ons for my computer?

There are a couple of ways to purchase sound-related equipment on AOL. From the PC Music & Sound Forum (keyword: **PC Music**), go to the Computing Classifieds (keyword: **Classifieds**) to find good deals on both new and used goods. Or you can go to the AOL Store Software Shop (keyword: **Software Shop**) and Hardware Shop (keyword: **Hardware Center**) to purchase new audio, music, and sound add-ons.

As an amateur musician and composer, I'm looking for collaborators and peers. How can I meet others like myself on AOL?

The Music & Sound Forum is definitely the right venue in which to meet other musicians. Try the Creative Musicians Coalition to find players interested in jamming online. If you're a guitarist, take a look at the Guitar Special Interest Group.

What does the PC Weekly New Files offer?

The PC Weekly New Files at the PC Music & Sound Forum (keyword: **PC Music**) offers all kinds of software files, including audio files that you can download and play on your PC. The categories include:

- Animation & Video

- Business & Finance

- Desktop Publishing

- Development & Programming

- Education & Reference

- Fun & Games

- Graphics

- Home & Hobby

- Internet

- Music & Sound

- Networking & Telecom

31

- Pers Digital Assts (Personal Digital Assistants)

- Utilities & Tools

PC Telecom & Networking Forum

The days of a single national phone service have never seemed so distant. More technological change is coming along in the telecommunications and networking areas than in any other digital technology area. And much of it can be confusing, especially as the hype and spin factors distort the facts.

The PC Telecom & Networking Forum (keyword: **PTC**) shown in figure 1.11, is where to dial in when, for example, you're looking to buy a new modem or figuring out the best way to network your computer with a printer or another computer. And if you're dealing with more complex network tangles, this is where you'll find the most knowledgeable AOL users. And, as with other AOL forums, you have access to forum-specific message boards, software libraries, the Virus Info Center, the Resource Center, the Computing Superstore, and Computing Classes.

Where can I find out how to network my computers?

At the PC Telecom & Networking Forum, visit an area called Join the Telecom & Networking Team. Here you'll gain access to the telecom and networking Web sites that offer information about how to network computers. If you have a Mac, check out the Mac Communications & Networking Forum (keyword: **MCM**).

I want to build a Web site for my business. Where do I begin?

From the PC Telecom & Networking Forum (keyword: **PTC**), click on the Put Your Business on the Web with Primehost area (keyword: **PRIMEHOST**). This is where you'll learn all about small-business Web sites: why people want them, how much they cost, what you can put on the site, and what exposure your site will have on the AOL service and the World Wide Web.

How do I build a personal Web site?

AOL makes it incredibly easy to build a personal web site. Check out the fill-in-the-blank templates in the Personal Publisher area (keyword: **Personal Publisher**). You

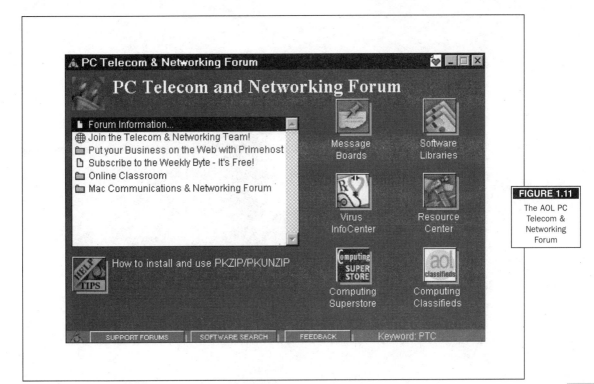

FIGURE 1.11

The AOL PC
Telecom &
Networking
Forum

don't have to know anything about HTML (hypertext markup language—the language used to write Web pages). The program will step you through with simple questions about text, layout, and any multimedia elements you want to add, such as sound, graphics, or animation. Answer the questions in plain English and this program does all the work for you. It even publishes your page on the Web when you're finished.

PC Windows Forum

Now that Microsoft Windows is the near-universal platform for personal computing, it's a good idea to know how to use it well. Most people settle for the minimum, and so they're using only a fraction of its capabilities. But your computing life will be much more efficient and satisfying when you really know your way around Windows 3.x, Windows 95, or Windows 98.

AOL's PC Windows Forum (keyword: **WIN**) shown in figure 1.12, is the place to go for advice on using Microsoft Windows. Here you can access software from an extensive library of public domain files (released to the public with no restrictions

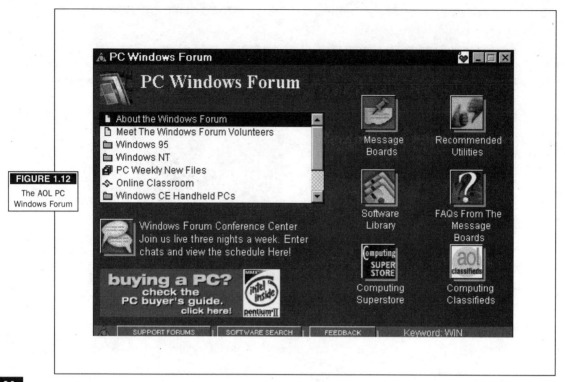

34

on copyright or use) and shareware files, participate in an active message board, and attend live online conferences three nights a week. Whether you're a user of Windows 3.x, 95, NT, or 98, you'll find interacting with other AOL members and experts a great learning experience.

I'm having problems uninstalling software from my Windows-based computer; I can't seem to get all the unwanted program files off my hard disk. Where can I find out about software that will purge programs from my computer?

The kind of software you want is a utilities program. The place to find out about the very best utilities software for Windows is at Recommended Utilities in the Windows Forum (keyword: **WIN**). You'll find suggestions on how to use utilities to uninstall software, protect against computer viruses, use encryption, back up your files, and run diagnostics. When you've decided which utilities you need, you can buy them at the AOL Store's Software Shop (keyword: **Software Shop**).

I'd like some tips on how to make Windows 95 run more efficiently. Where can I get them?

Go to the Windows 95 and Windows NT areas at the Windows Forum (keyword: **WIN**).

Where can I get the latest information from Microsoft about Windows?

At the Windows Forum, click on the Surf to the Windows Home Page option and you'll be whisked to Microsoft's Web site.

Mac Support Forums

Mac users are a breed apart, and proud of it. Even many Windows users agree that Apple's technology is the most elegant going. And Mac people tend to enjoy speaking with others about the wonders and finer points of their chosen platform. You'll find a very active digital subculture in the Macintosh support forums (keyword: **Computing**) available on AOL (see figure 1.13). Some of the Macintosh topic-specific forums are:

• Mac Applications Forum (keyword: **MAC APPS**)

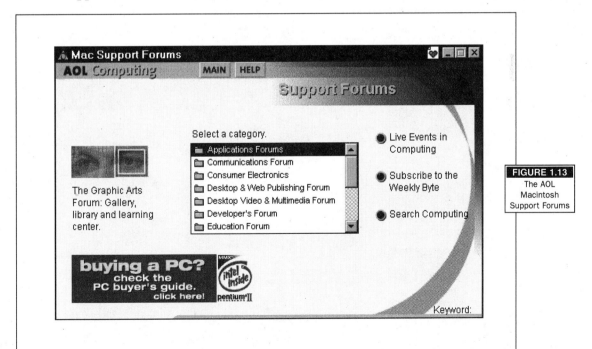

FIGURE 1.13
The AOL Macintosh Support Forums

- Mac Communications & Networking Forum (keyword: **MCM**)

- Desktop & Web Publishing Forum (keyword: **DTP**)

- Mac Animation & Video Forum (keyword: **MMM**)

- Macintosh Developers Forum (keyword: **MDV**)

- Macintosh Games (keyword: **MG**)

- Mac Graphic Arts Forum (keyword: **MGR**)

- Mac Hardware/OS Forum (keyword: **MHW**)

- Macintosh Music & Sound Forum (keyword: **MMS**)

- Macintosh OS Resource Center (keyword: **MOS**)

- Mac Utilities Forum (keyword: **MUT**)

What do the Mac Support forums offer?

Basically, everything that all the other forums do: message boards, newsletter subscriptions, software libraries, special interest groups, online classes, a chat schedule,

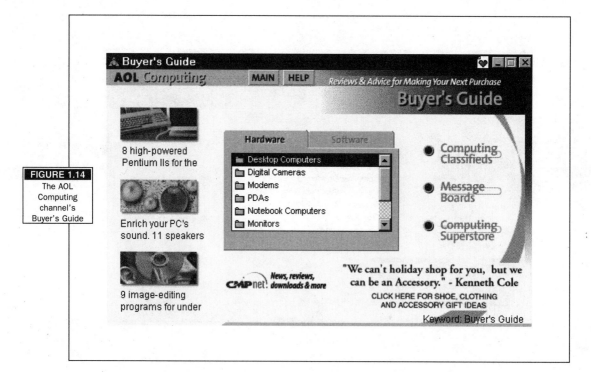

FIGURE 1.14
The AOL Computing channel's Buyer's Guide

and so on. (You might find that these forums also offer a more intense spirit of camaraderie than most technology groups.)

Buyer's Guide

We all know that last year's top of the line is this year's middle of the road. And that it's still incredible technology, only now it's much less costly. But there's still plenty of anxiety associated with buying a new computer or other hardware: What if it's obsolete in 18 months? (It probably won't be.) But when you're in the market for a new computer, reading some advice and well-organized reviews can be very valuable and reassuring. Just visit the AOL Buyer's Guide (keyword: **Buyer's Guide**), shown in figure 1.14.

When I bought my last computer I found good advice and reviews in *Home PC* magazine. Can I get the same information online?

You're in luck! You'll find that magazine's extensive product reviews on computers, monitors, printers, modems, and software at its AOL location, *Home PC* (keyword: **Home PC**).

I'd like to compare a computer from Dell with one from Gateway. Where can I get comparative product information?

You'll find this essential info at ZDNet PC Reviews (www.zdnet.com).

I already have a desktop computer, but now I'd like to buy a laptop to maximize my flexibility. Where can I get the lowdown on which ones are best?

For laptops, desktops, software, and accessories, you'll find loads of accurate data and thoughtful assessments at TechWeb Buyer's Guide (keyword: **TechWeb**).

Company Connection

If you've ever had to wait on hold interminably for technical support assistance, you'll be happy to know that the AOL Service has an alternative. Just connect to the Companies area (keyword: **Companies**) shown in figure 1.15, and look for your computer manufacturer. There are already hundreds of companies you can access

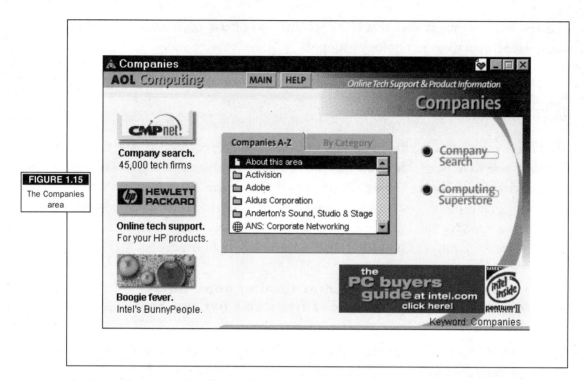

FIGURE 1.15

The Companies area

this way, from small utility software publishers to the major hardware manufacturers. The companies you need to contact are probably online now or will be soon.

The Companies area is divided into two folders: Companies A–Z, where you can select a particular business from an alphabetized list; and By Category, which lets you search for the company.

In the Companies area, you can easily gather product information on hardware and software, including prices. But more important, many of the major manufacturers have technical support staff on call to answer your technical questions on their products for free. They'll even give you advice on how to use a product more effectively.

How do I find a specific computer manufacturer on the AOL service?

In the Companies area, choose Company Search, and enter the company name.

AOL Store

It's nearly inevitable: As you continue to learn about your computer and its potential uses, there will be some toys you covet. Some will be absolutely essential (such as a good anti-virus program) and others optional (extra memory). But regardless of the product, you'll enjoy the convenience of online shopping, ordering, and shipping. Any time, around the clock, you can order computing goods at the AOL Store (keyword: **AOL Store**) shown in figure 1.16, and have them shipped directly to you.

This megamall of digital wares is composed of the following shops:

- Hardware (keyword: **Hardware Center**)

- Software (keyword: **Software Shop**)

- Modem (keyword: **Modem Shop**)

- Book (keyword: **Book Shop**)

- Logo (keyword: **Logo Shop**)

Each shop offers feature items, rebates and promos, help and tips, news, upgrade information, and just-for-fun stuff.

What is a feature item?

A feature item is a new product a shop is introducing. An item will be chosen to be featured because it's new, low priced, easy to use, feature rich, or timesaving.

What kind of computing equipment does the AOL Store carry?

The Hardware Shop (keyword: **Hardware Center**) car-

SOLVE A HARDWARE PROBLEM TODAY

Go to these support companies' areas to solve a problem with a specific product:

- Apple on AOL
  (keyword: **Apple**)

- Compaq on AOL
  (keyword: **Compaq**)

- Dell (keyword: **Dell**)

- Gateway
  (keyword: **Gateway**)

- Hewlett-Packard on AOL
  (keyword: **HP**)

- IBM (keyword: **IBM**)

- Intel/PC Dads Main Page
  (keyword: **Intel**)

- Iomega (keyword: **Iomega**)

- Micron Electronics
  (keyword: **Micron**)

- NEC Online
  (keyword: **NecTech**)

- Packard Bell
  (www.PackardBell.com)

- Toshiba (www.toshiba.com)

39

40

ries PCs, printers, PDAs (personal digital assistants), and any other type of hardware on the market today.

The Software Shop (keyword: **Software Shop**) offers all types of software programs, games, clip art, and utilities.

At the Modem Shop (keyword: **Modem Shop**), you'll find a feature item, rebates and promos, modem help, modem news, and upgrade information. You can purchase modems of all stripes, including such major brand contenders as:

- Cardinal

- Global Village

- MAXTECH

- Megahertz

- 3COM/US Robotics

- Zoom

In addition to selling many of the top computer books, the Book Shop (keyword:

Book Shop) also offers several areas that provide all kinds of information such as an A–Z Listing, the Book Bargains area, and the Best Sellers area. The main section is the BookShelf area, where you can browse through books organized by the following categories:

- AOL Guides

- Internet

- Graphics & Multimedia

- Computing

- Business & Productivity

- Game Guides

- General Interest

The Computing Superstore

You can find hardware, software, digital imaging equipment, and any other computing equipment you can imagine at the AOL Computing Superstore (keyword: **CSS**) shown in figure 1.17. This store also leads you to the other sales areas, such as the Cyberian Outpost (keyword: **Cyberian Outpost**) and the AOL Store shops (keyword: **AOL Store**). The Computing Superstore is always open.

Does the Computing Superstore carry virus protection software?

Yes. Choose the Virus Protection aisle at the Computing Superstore (keyword: **CSS**) to browse through virus detection and removal software and buy the program that's right for your computer.

I would like to shop online for digital imaging equipment and compare the online prices to those at my local computer superstore. Where do I go?

The Digital Imaging aisle at the Computing Superstore carries digital imaging cameras, scanners, and any accessories that go with digital imaging equipment.

FIGURE 1.17

The Computing
Superstore

42 **How do I find specific products in the Computing Superstore?**

Click on Search for Products and enter the requested information.

Are there any hot deals at the Computing Superstore?

As soon as you enter the Computing Superstore, you'll see all the good deals. Click on any of the bargain images to find out about them.

Can I hire a personal shopper at the Computing Superstore?

If you have too much on your plate and you want a helping hand, choose the Personal Shopper at the Computing Superstore and you'll go to the Buyer's Guide (keyword: **Buyer's Guide**). Just enter your computer specifications and the Buyer's Guide will tell you what products meet your needs.

Does the AOL service have online auctions?

Just point, click, and bid to save at Onsales Live Auctions (keyword: **Online Auctions**)

Online Publications

Information glut is a big problem in the computer field. Hundreds of magazines on computer subjects are published each month. Through AOL, you can read many of them online. You can easily bounce around reading only the information you need and want, 24 hours a day, with frequent updates to stay current. In fact, you may never pay for a paper magazine subscription again.

Where can I go online to read the computing magazines I rely on, such as *Home PC, Windows,* and *Wired?*

Stop by the Computing Newsstand (keyword: **Computing Newsstand**) shown in figure 1.18, for all the online computer magazines you can manage.

I'm in the market for a CD-ROM drive and several other pieces

HomePC (keyword: **Home PC**) is for users of either IBM PCs and compatibles or Apple Macintosh computers. Since the emphasis here is on home rather than business users, the tone and approach are more personal than in many other computing publications. Novell's WordPerfect is among the most popular cross-platform word processing programs. Whether you run the program on a PC or a Mac, the WordPerfect area on AOL (keyword: **WordPerfect**) gives you great advice and information about how to best use the software. The magazine comes in a regular version and a special Windows edition.

43

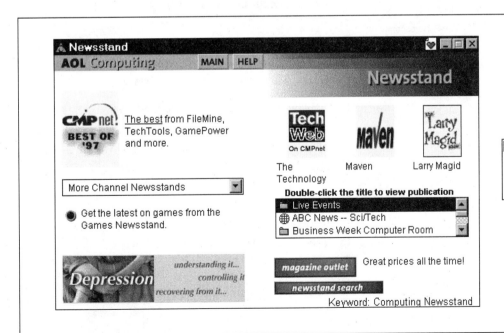

FIGURE 1.18

The AOL Computing channel's Newsstand

If you're a home worker, take a look at Home Office Computing (keyword: **Home Office**). This online magazine caters to small-business owners, and its advice on buying new hardware/software and tips on making your office more productive are invaluable. It's an excellent resource.

Some of the features Home Office Computing offers are:

- HOC's Daily Dispatch—Provides new absorbing, arresting, and amusing stories from the business and technological worlds every day.

- HOC Recommends—HOC picks the best hardware and software for home computing.

- Weekly Business Horoscopes

- Back Issues of HOC

- Home Office Computing Message Boards

of hardware. Where can I get information on the best goods?

One of the best sources if you're interested in computers is *Maven* (keyword: **Computing Newsstand**). This publication, which is *Business Week's* computer buying guide, reviews the latest products and offers computing tips and hints.

Which online publications cater to Net surfers? And are there any computer newsletters I can subscribe to?

Among the best Internet magazines at the Computing Newsstand are *Net Insider Magazine* and *Wired*.

As mentioned previously, another key publication is *The Weekly Byte,* a computer newsletter distributed by e-mail every week that provides information on where to go on the AOL service to find hardware, software, or anything else related to computing. For a subscription, go to the Computing channel (keyword: **Computing**) and sign up.

I'm not sure which computer magazine I want to subscribe to. Can AOL help me decide?

At the Computing Newsstand, you can preview magazines before you buy them. Click on the magazine you want to preview and browse through the current issue.

If I needed to find an article from a back issue of, say, *Home PC* magazine, could I find it online?

Yes. You can easily search through back issues of a computer magazine for a specific article.

Are there any discounts on magazines at the AOL Computing Newsstand?

The Magazine Outlet in the AOL Computing Newsstand offers dozens of publications at deep discounts.

THE MOBILE OFFICE

Do you fax and print documents while traveling? If you're a road warrior with a laptop as your trusty companion, the area you want is the AOL WorkPlace (keyword: **Work Place**). Here's where you'll find everything from job listings to advice for the self-employed, including: business and career information, professional forums, business services, news, research, classifieds, chat rooms, message boards, and small business information.

Some features include:

- The Meeting Place—Provides networking opportunities in forums tailored to different professions.

- Your Career—Offers resources for finding a job, as well as online courses and career message boards.

- Your Business—Features Business Talk with live, expert advice and the Small Business Site Index.

2
UNDERSTANDING WHAT YOU'VE GOT

To take advantage of all your computer can do, you have to understand its basic capabilities. And to troubleshoot, talk intelligently with a technical support person, or install new software with confidence, it's useful to know a bit about your computer's components and how they work together. This chapter provides some computing basics.

47

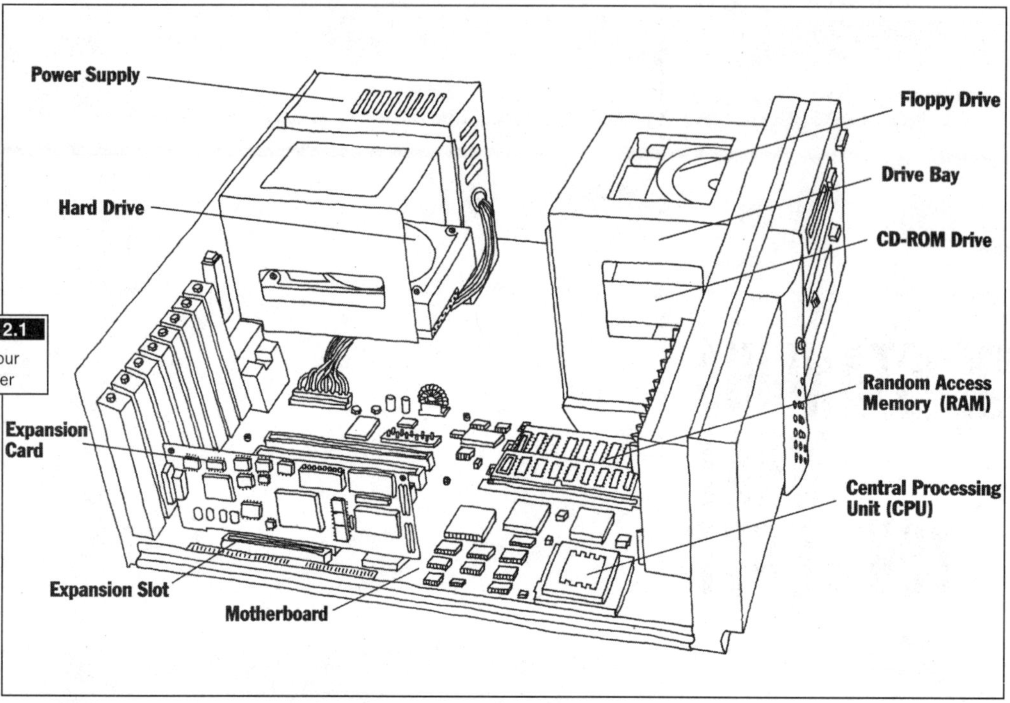

FIGURE 2.1

Inside Your Computer

Labels: Power Supply, Hard Drive, Expansion Card, Expansion Slot, Motherboard, Floppy Drive, Drive Bay, CD-ROM Drive, Random Access Memory (RAM), Central Processing Unit (CPU)

Your Computer Is the Sum of Its Parts

You don't actually need to know how your computer works, any more than you need to understand the details of fuel injection to drive your car. But it's useful to know the basics. After all, it's inconvenient to transport a broken desktop computer to the shop, and gratifying to be able to describe your problem to an expert without sounding like a rank beginner. So we'll give you a detailed rundown of what's inside your computer and what it does, along with answers to some basic questions. If any of the terms are head-scratching, you'll find their definitions in this book's Glossary.

You might also want to refer to the AOL Glossary (keyword: **Glossary**), shown in figure 2.2, to find definitions of other common computing terms.

Today's personal computers have at least one of each of these components, shown in figure 2.3:

- Case—holds the power supply, the hard and floppy drives, the mother-board, and the CD-ROM drive. It can either be a full tower, medium tower, or mini-tower (which stand vertically somewhere in the vicinity

FIGURE 2.2

The AOL Glossary

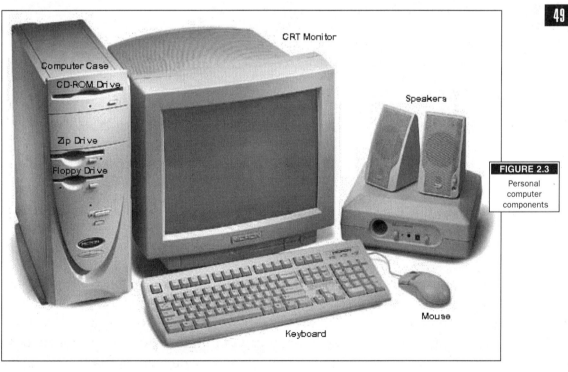

FIGURE 2.3

Personal computer components

of your workspace), or a desktop (which sits horizontally, often with the monitor on top).

- Motherboard—the large internal circuit board that contains the CPU, RAM, cache, and slots for additional circuit cards

- Power supply—converts the power from your wall outlet to the correct voltage for your delicate machine

- Floppy drive—accepts 3.5-inch floppy disks for storing data

- Hard drive—holds massive quantities of data in storage

- CD-ROM drive—plays your CD-ROM disks

- Video card or circuits—provides video signals to your monitor

- Sound card or circuits—records audio input and provides audio output to your speakers

- Speakers—play audio signals

- Microphone—records spoken input

- Modem—connects to your telephone line and communicates with AOL and other Internet or dial-up services

- Monitor—lets you see what's happening on your computer

- Keyboard—An input device with letters, numbers, special characters, and function keys

- Mouse, trackball, or pointing pad—an input device that positions the cursor on the screen and has buttons you can push to make selections

- Software—the BIOS, operating system, applications programs, and other programs

An ordinary desktop computer has a case containing the computer's "brains" (also known as the central processing unit, or CPU), plus at least a couple of storage devices for software and data, a power supply, and a fan to keep it all cool, and perhaps other odds and ends (modem, sound card, video card). There's a monitor so you can see your work. There's a keyboard and a mouse or trackball for letting the computer know what you want it to do. If you want to get fancy, or if you have a

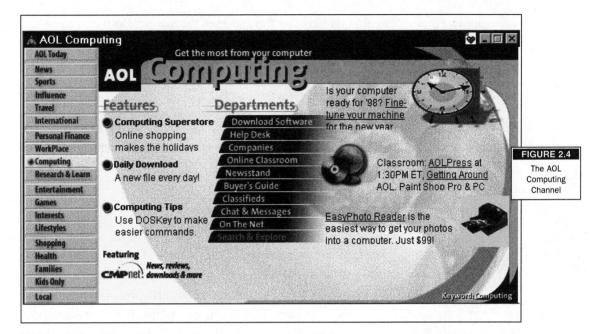

FIGURE 2.4

The AOL Computing Channel

disability that prevents you from using a keyboard or a mouse, you can equip your computer with a microphone so you can give voice commands.

Some hardware and software items are common to all personal computers; others are special-function accessories. In the rest of this chapter, we'll explain how the must-haves function, individually and together. You'll also find out about the nice-to-have or specialized components. And we'll point you to resources on AOL, especially the Computing channel (keyword: **Computing**), shown in figure 2.4, that can give you all sorts of advice and help about hardware, software, and other computer-related topics.

Types of Computers

Computers permeate your life, whether you realize it or not: in your car, your coffeemaker, your CD player, your thermostat. If you have to program it, there's a computer chip involved somewhere.

Computers come in several categories, distinguished mostly by size and the type of operating system they use.

Desktop personal computers are available as "PCs"—which run on Intel Corp. microprocessors and use various operating systems made by Microsoft Corp.—or as Macintosh computers, which are made by Apple Computer and use the MacOS, also made by Apple. PCs currently have the lion's share of the market. Both PCs and Macs have price ranges in the low four figures, with low-end PCs costing even less than that.

Laptop computers come in the same varieties as desktop machines. They're smaller and more expensive but designed to lug around.

Personal Digital Assistants, or PDAs, are smaller than laptops and cost only a few hundred dollars. They're useful mainly for jotting notes and keeping track of appointments and contacts. (More about these below.)

What is the difference between a computer that sits on your desk and a laptop computer?

In terms of raw computing power, not much. Laptops (also called notebook computers) used to be primitive cousins of desktop PCs, with dim screens and minimal if any, hard disk space. These days, if you're willing to pay the price (up to twice as much as a comparable desktop computer), you can get a laptop with all the processing power and storage space of your desktop machine. But the difference in size means you have a different type of display (and one that's still probably not up to the standard of a good-quality desktop monitor), probably a more limited keyboard layout, and a different way of moving the screen's pointer around. Laptops are also more rugged, having been designed to take a few bumps.

Laptops can work without being plugged in, but most have a limited battery life—four hours, tops. This can go by quickly if you're trying to get work done during a flight delay.

For good advice and reviews on desktop and laptop computers, read the Buyer's Guide (keyword: **Buyer's Guide**).

The PC Hardware Forum (keyword: **PC Hardware** or **PHW**) is a great AOL resource that will give you information on what computers other AOL members are buying and what they think of desktops and laptops.

A friend of mine is a dedicated Macintosh user who is always poking fun at my PC. Is one platform superior to the other, or is this just a matter of preference?

This is a dangerous question to answer, since the PC vs. Macintosh debate is one of the longest-running "holy wars" in computerdom. If you pose it at a dinner party attended by members of both camps, be prepared for a long and heated argument.

The Macintosh marked the first mass-market appearance of the graphical user interface (GUI). The GUI made it possible for just about anyone to understand how to operate a computer because instead of having to type in commands to access information, one need only click on familiar-looking icons, such as a desktop, file folders, pull-down menus, and a trash/recycle bin. Sound familiar? That's because the GUI is now emulated by Windows 95.

PCs have advantages, primarily stemming from their sheer numbers. PCs dominate the personal computing market. As things stand now, there's a great deal more software developed for the Wintel platform (as when a Windows operating system runs on an Intel microprocessor) than for the Mac, and many more manufacturers make Wintel cases, which keeps prices low.

For more information, review the AOL Computing Buyer's Guide (keyword: **Buyer's Guide**) to get helpful advice and the latest reviews on PCs. The Macintosh Support Forums area on AOL (keyword: **Computing**) is a good place to search for Macintosh information.

My daughter is away at college and just bought a Mac PowerBook. Does this mean she won't be able to read the files I send her because they were created on my PC?

Macs have a built-in ability to read PC diskettes, and software made for Macs can easily translate files created using most types of PC software, so you shouldn't have any problems. She can also format any files she sends to you so that your PC can read them.

What is WebTV?

WebTV is the brand name for one type of set-top case that lets you connect to the Internet from your TV. There are several other brands as well, such as NetChannel, a company that is now part of AOL. They're very inexpensive (as low as $100), but there are usually some limitations. They generally don't come equipped with a hard drive, meaning you can surf but not save. The controller, similar to a TV remote control, has a few basic functions, but you may have to pay extra to get a keyboard (which you'll probably want in order to send e-mail.) You must pay a $20 monthly fee to an Internet service provider in order to actually connect to the Web, and only a few providers work with WebTV and the other set-top case makers. Currently the boxes are not very expandable either, but that is changing.

Unlike PCs, these machines are dedicated to one thing: Internet access. They gener-

PDAS AND HPCS: THE SMALLER THE BETTER?

Palmtop computers and personal digital assistants (PDAs) are lighter and easier to carry than laptops and notebooks. But you usually get less functionality, and less flexibility, because you can't run your familiar software on them. It's the rare user who will be able to forgo a desktop machine, or even a full-function notebook, for a PDA. But for specific applications they may be just the thing.

PDAs, of which the most successful currently is 3Com's Palm Pilot, resemble electronic scratch pads. They can fit in a shirt pocket, and run on lithium ion batteries. Currently, prices start at under $400, though extra batteries, carrying cases, connecting cables, modems, and other frills can add $50 to $100 to the cost. Other PDAs are made by Hewlett Packard, Sharp, Casio, and Texas Instruments.

PDAs have software built in, though there are add-on programs available for popular models. Palm Pilots, for example, come preloaded with software that includes an address book, a calendar, a to-do list, an expense tracker that can download to a desktop spreadsheet program, a calculator, a memo pad that records notes jotted with a stylus using a special set of simplified letters, and the ability to connect to e-mail.

Most people use PDAs the same way they use hard-copy Day-Timers or Filofaxes—as a way to keep track of their appointments and contacts. The usefulness of PDAs is directly proportional to the quality of the data they carry. If you're the kind of person who can keep a paper appointment book up-to-date, you might be a successful PDA user. If that kind of order eludes you, a PDA will not make you more organized.

If you're inclined to computerize your address book and calendar, you'll likely want to have it on your desktop PC as well as in your PDA, and keeping both in sync can be a challenge. Most PDAs have a method of interfacing with programs on your desktop PC. Make sure the model you're considering can talk easily with whatever desktop software you're using. You may have to pay $75 to $100 extra for desktop connectivity, depending on which model you purchase.

Palmtop computers, also called handheld personal computers or HPCs, differ from PDAs in that they are built to look like very small notebooks, with teeny keyboards rather than a scratch pad with buttons. Some HPCs have color screens, 8 or 16MB of RAM, built-in fax modems, and speakers and microphones. And they usually accept expansion cards, which can give them more capabilities. Their prices now range between $500 and $1,000, though the cost of accompanying gadgets can run this up considerably. Good HPCs are made by Casio, Sharp, Philips, Hewlett Packard, and NEC.

HPCs run a special version of the Windows operating system called Windows CE (for Compact Edition), and many run on regular AA batteries. Files created by Windows CE can be read by the Windows operating system on your desktop PC. Because the batteries are both easily obtainable and extremely portable (unlike the expensive and bulky battery packs that power most laptops), you can operate an HPC without becoming obsessed with battery life. Whether you can work for long periods on an HPC is a matter of ergonomic limitations rather than technical ones, and you'll still want a way to synchronize it with your desktop machine.

Check out the handheld computers at the AOL Store's Hardware Shop (keyword: **Hardware Center**) and at the Computing Superstore on AOL (keyword: **CSS**).

ally should not be taken apart or even opened, and usually they cannot be upgraded.

PCs, on the other hand, are like stereo systems, in that you can buy all the separate parts and assemble them yourself if you like (and some people do). You can also upgrade components relatively easily (if you know a few of the secrets we reveal in this book).

Oddly enough, most early WebTV buyers already owned a computer, confounding the manufacturers' expectation that WebTV would appeal to people who think computers are too expensive and/or difficult to use.

The PC Hardware Forum on AOL (keyword: **PC Hardware**), shown in figure 2.5, is a great place to learn about computer hardware.

Operating Systems

Without software your computer setup is just a useless hunk of metal, plastic, and glass. Some of the software is permanently (or semipermanently) encoded onto the chips and is called firmware. The rest is in mass storage on your hard drive, or on a floppy disk or CD-ROM, and it becomes active when you turn on your computer.

Think of the software as layers of instructions, from simple to complex, each layer preparing a foundation for the next higher level to work on. Turning on your computer starts a chain of events where each layer is activated one by one.

What exactly does the operating system on my computer do? Is it self-sufficient, or do I need to do something to keep it running smoothly?

The operating system runs your computer. It determines how all the components talk to each other, how data is stored on your hard disk and floppies, how the information you enter is interpreted. It also determines how applications software, such as word processing programs, spreadsheets, Web browsers, and appointment calendars, is written. Software written for one operating system can't, in most cases, be used on another.

There are several operating systems commonly used. The one talked about most in this book is Windows 95, but Windows 98 is now the latest Microsoft Windows operating system. Others you may encounter in your computing life include Windows 3.x, the predecessor to Windows 95. DOS, the predecessor to Windows, continues to underlie Windows 95, so you may want to learn something about it at some point. OS/2, made by industry giant IBM, is a minor player in the marketplace. Windows NT is used to run computer networks rather than individual machines. The MacOS is specific to Apple Macintosh computers and a handful of Macintosh "clones" made by companies other than Apple. Unix, is used by individual machines called workstations and by computer networks. It also underlies many of the "protocols," or methods of communication, upon which the Internet is based.

We'll discuss hardware and software maintenance more fully in chapter 5. It's a good idea to upgrade your operating system when new versions become available (but not immediately—for more information see chapter 6). You'll want to install software to keep your computer free of viruses, and have a diskette or CD-ROM handy that contains certain key parts of the operating system, so you can start your computer if it crashes. It happens to everyone eventually, but it most likely won't be your fault. Before you begin working with new software, *always* read any file named "readme." This file will tip you off if there's any incompatibility between the program and others you might use, or between the program and the particular version of the operating system you're using. (This happens astonishingly often.) And always back up your data! (More later in this chapter about the best way to do this.)

The small company I work for avoids change at all costs, so we're still using an older version of Windows. Are we missing out by not upgrading our operating system?

There's no question that upgrading can be painful. Windows 95 requires at least a 486 processor to run properly—most experts strongly recommend a Pentium processor—and a machine with at least 8MB of RAM and 100 MB of hard disk space. If your company is still on an older version of the operating system, chances are it's on older computers, too—possibly too old to be upgraded. That means laying out at least $1,300 per station for new machines, plus any costs associated with upgrading the network, if your company has one.

But not upgrading has its costs, too. Before too long, your software vendors may stop supporting the versions of their products that run on Windows 3.x. If your office works with suppliers, clients, ad agencies, or anyone else who has upgraded to Windows 95, swapping data could be a pain in the neck, or even impossible. And the day will come when you need—really need—some piece of software that's simply not available on Windows 3.x because it wasn't invented until after 1995. Whether it's a database that integrates with a Web page, a program that lets you do inexpensive videoconferences over the Internet, or a bookkeeping program with the latest versions of the federal and state tax codes built in, you'll regret you can't use it.

For more information on Windows 3.x, Windows 95, Windows 98, and Windows NT, and the latest news on the Windows operating system, visit the AOL Windows Forum (keyword: **WIN**), a total resource center for any Windows questions you may have. The Buyer's Guide (keyword: **Buyer's Guide**) offers free advice and reviews on Windows 98. If you want to purchase Windows 98, take a trip to the AOL Store's Software Shop (keyword: **Software Shop**). AOL will ship it to you right away, so that you can start working with the most current operating system.

I keep hearing about drivers. What are they, and am I responsible for purchasing them separately?

Drivers are programs that work with your operating system and your peripheral devices, such as hard drives, printers, scanners, and monitors. They translate instructions from your operating system into commands these devices understand. For instance, a dot-matrix printer from Epson may use a totally different command to create the letter A than a laser printer from Hewlett Packard, so a different driver is required for each printer.

Drivers are also specific to the operating system of the computer, so a driver created for Windows 3.x or DOS won't necessarily work with Windows 95.

The Windows 95 installation CD also includes drivers for hundreds of common peripheral devices, and the system's Plug and Play feature means that it automatically detects the hardware you have and installs the appropriate drivers. Of course, this only works if your motherboard and peripheral devices are also Plug-and-Play-compatible. Fortunately, most are. If you get a new printer or other peripheral device, Windows 95 will prompt you to insert the CD-ROM so that it can find the appropriate driver.

Some drivers are upgraded often, and new devices are constantly introduced. Therefore, the driver you need may not be on your Windows 95 CD-ROM, or at least not the most recent version. But if you purchase a device new, it should come with a floppy diskette or CD-ROM that contains both the driver and simple installation instructions. If you're inheriting it from someone, the best way to get the most recent version of the driver is to download it from the manufacturer's Web site. Type the manufacturer's name into the AOL NetFind service (keyword: **NetFind**) to find the Web site. AOL NetFind is AOL's "built-in" Web search engine. Once you're there, look for a section called Products or Support or Software Download, or if it's really your lucky day, Download Latest Drivers Here. Once you've located the download page, follow the instructions, which are usually fairly straightforward.

Drivers are free (their price is factored into the cost of the device they run).

For definitions of computing terms such as driver, peripheral, and download, refer to the AOL Glossary (keyword: **Glossary**) and this book's Glossary.

I'd like to have my word processing and my desktop publishing programs running simultaneously so I can cut and paste articles into a page layout, and be able to check my e-mail while I'm working with the other two programs. I can't do this with Windows 3.1. Can I do it in Windows 95?

This compatibility is called "multitasking"—when two or more programs are making the computer "think" at the same time. There are different ways to accomplish this (OS/2, Windows 95, Windows NT, Amiga, and UNIX), but basically your PC's brain, rather than thinking about two or three things at once, alternates between them

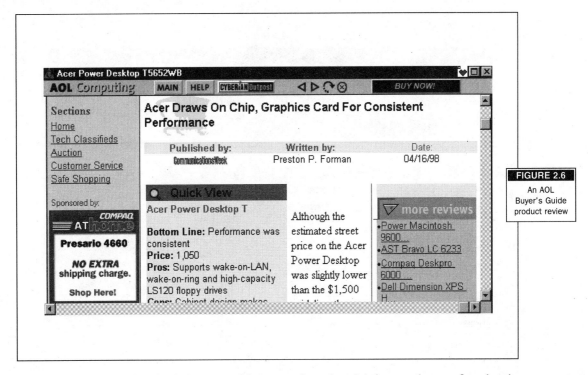

FIGURE 2.6

An AOL
Buyer's Guide
product review

very rapidly. It's still only doing one thing at a time, but it's happening so fast that it seems simultaneous to you. So you can have two or more applications open at the same time and can switch between them rapidly without overloading your computer.

The AOL Windows Forum (keyword: **WIN**) is an excellent place to find out about multitasking and other things you can do with Windows 95. On the Windows message boards at this forum, other AOL members discuss their Windows 95 experiences and provide advice. Also, the Windows News area on AOL (keyword: **WIN**) provides helpful information. Another good AOL resource is the PC Applications Forums (keyword: **APPS**), where you can get information on PC software programs.

The AOL Buyer's Guide (keyword: **Buyer's Guide**), is a great resource for getting help in determining what kind of PC to buy. We'll refer you to the Buyer's Guide resource frequently throughout this book. (One of the Buyer's Guide's product reviews is shown in Figure 2.6.)

You'll find great bargains on new and used hardware in the Computing Classifieds on AOL (keyword: **Classifieds**), shown in figure 2.7.

Go to the AOL service to find up-to-date tips using Windows 95 and Windows 98 (see figure 2.8) by using the keyword **Computing Tips**.

FIGURE 2.7
The AOL Computing Classifieds

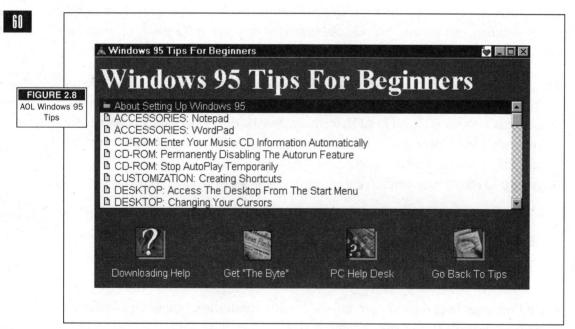

FIGURE 2.8
AOL Windows 95 Tips

Software

What are the major types of software I should have?

Your computer undoubtedly came with the two pieces of software you can't do without. One is the BIOS (basic input/output system), which is an integral part of the CPU. The other is the operating system—most likely Windows 95. The applications programs most people need are:

- A suite of business applications—word processor, spreadsheet, database, presentation creation—which are packaged to work well together

- Personal information manager, usually including a calendar and a contact manager/address book

- Internet software (included with AOL)—Web browser, e-mail, FTP (for downloading large files), dialer, Usenet newsgroup reader

- Utilities—virus checker, disk optimizer, system monitor

- And AOL, of course!

You might also want to get a money manager, development tools for Web pages, games, graphics programs, and any other software specifically designed for your line of work or your kind of fun.

If you've just bought a new computer, it's likely that at least some of the above were "bundled" with your purchase. To fill in the gaps in your software collection, visit the AOL Store's Software Shop (keyword: **Software Shop**). Browse around and you'll find all the software you'll need to get started or to add to your software collection.

**What's the difference between the BIOS and
the operating system? Or are they the same thing?**

The BIOS, or basic input/output system, is a base operating system that's built into a chip on your motherboard, so that even if the operating system that's stored on your hard drive isn't installed or working, the computer can still handle some tasks. The BIOS can do without the operating system, but the operating system can't do without the BIOS.

Even though the BIOS is encoded onto chips that don't need power to "remember" their information, the BIOS has settings you can customize. These settings must have a small but continuous supply of power (similar to an electronic watch) to remain active. That's why your computer comes equipped with a battery, usually good for at least five years. That battery also lets your computer remember the date and time even after you've turned it off.

Someone made those initial BIOS settings at the factory for you before you received your computer, but if the battery ever fails, all those settings will be lost. Losing those settings means your computer won't run until they are reset.

How can I reset the BIOS, and what information do I need?

First, replace the dead battery inside your computer. The battery usually looks like a watch battery. It is usually visible on the motherboard, but it is not always in the same place from computer to computer. Once you remove the battery, the BIOS is reset on most machines. Bring the old battery to a computer store and ask the sales-person for the same model battery with instructions on how to install it. Then restart your computer and go into the BIOS setup option when booting. In the BIOS setup, there is usually a prompt for "Set Defaults" or "Restore Defaults" that resets the BIOS to factory settings.

Different computers have different BIOS settings, but usually you can use the defaults, except for the hard drive settings. It's a good idea to get into the BIOS at start-up just after you buy a computer, then do a screenprint when you get to the settings screen. Save that piece of paper with your other documentation, so that you'll know the correct settings in case you have to reenter them.

What are utilities?

Utility programs can diagnose and fix hard disk problems, retrieve accidentally lost data, organize and straighten up your hard disk, detect and kill viruses, compress files, and manage your desktop. They are among the few programs that might start automatically when you turn on the computer, and even though you might not use them frequently, you really should have them.

If you want to buy a utility program or download one for free and take it out for a test-drive, check the Download Software section of AOL Computing (keyword: **Download Software**). Another place to purchase utility programs online is at the AOL Store's Software Shop (keyword: **Software Shop**).

Viruses

**What are computer viruses, and how would
I know if my computer has become infected?**

Viruses are software programs designed to make mischief of varying degrees of severity. They're called viruses because they attach themselves to "host" files, reproduce themselves whenever they enter a new system, and make your system "sick." Some viruses damage files, while others cause odd system behavior, make programs freeze or crash, or display a prank message.

Generally, to do their dirty work, viruses must be executable files—actual programs rather than data files, like those you create in word processing or spreadsheet programs. You can get viruses from using an unchecked floppy diskette (or any other storage medium) and from downloading software online.

They can even come as attachments to e-mail. However, your computer can't become infected if you simply open an e-mail message (without downloading an attached file) and read it. Virus hoaxes abound, and you may receive messages warning you not to open a message that has a certain subject line. (You may or may not receive the message that has the "dangerous" subject line.) Ignore these warning messages, and do not forward them to your friends. It just clutters up AOL and the Internet, and serves no purpose except to fill the perpetrators with delight.

One exception to the "executable file" rule is the "macro virus." This virus infects data files within certain applications, such as word processors and spreadsheets, that allow users to create macros, or little programs that help them use the application more efficiently. If someone sends you a document that contains a macro virus, via a floppy diskette or an e-mail attachment, and you open the document, it can then infect all the data files of the same type as the infected document, when you open them.

If you find, for example, that all of your Microsoft Word documents are being saved as templates rather than as normal documents, then your computer has undoubtedly been afflicted with the Word macro virus. If you've sent one of the "template" files to someone else without noticing the peculiar format, the recipient may well be infected, too. Go to Microsoft's Web site at www.microsoft.com and enter "macro virus" into the site's search utility. This will help you locate a page where you can download a fix. (Versions of Word released in 1998 or later have macro virus protection built in.)

I've heard about the horrors of viruses and I want to keep my computer safe. Aren't hackers creating new viruses all the time? Won't my virus detection software miss viruses that were unleashed after it was released?

Virus protection software is like a flu shot for your computer. It's been shown that having a flu shot does substantially decrease your risk of getting the flu, even though the shots are based on last year's virus. Inoculating your computer with anti-virus software is the best protection available. It's no guarantee, but it's much better than nothing. Makers of anti-virus software (the best known of which are Symantec and McAfee Associates) constantly update their products to fight new infections.

Anti-virus software works by checking for signs of known viruses. Each virus has a unique "signature" that identifies it, although the hackers who write viruses are constantly trying to develop a "mutating" code that changes its signature every time it copies itself. The virus checker contains a database of signatures, and checks for them when you start your computer, insert a floppy, or download files from the Internet. If it finds one that matches, it warns you and then deletes the offending program. If it finds damage to your files, it attempts to do a repair.

Because rogue programmers keep coming up with new viruses, the makers of the virus checkers must keep updating their databases. The better programs offer free updates for a period of time with your purchase.

The other way to protect your computer is to be careful what other computers it associates with. Don't swap floppies with anyone you don't know well, or who isn't as cautious about viruses as you are. And *never* open an e-mail attachment (click the Download Now button) from a stranger.

Download software only from sites with a good reputation. AOL screens all shareware and freeware for viruses before posting it. A safe place from which to download software is the Download Software area of AOL Computing (keyword: **Download Software**), where you'll find programs for sale and free software you can try before you buy. The Daily Download area (keyword: **Daily Download**) is another AOL site where you can safely download software.

Another precaution is to post a question in the AOL Computing forums about Web or FTP sites from which you want to download software or other files. If someone's been burned, you'll hear about it.

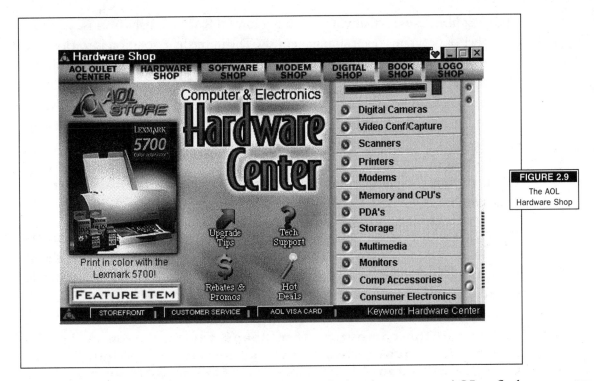

FIGURE 2.9

The AOL
Hardware Shop

The PC Virus Information Center (keyword: **Virus**) is the place to go on AOL to find out about virus detection and removal software.

Memory

RAM, or random-access memory, is where your computer stores your applications and files while it's working with them. It's measured in megabytes (MB), and physically takes the form of memory chips installed on your computer's motherboard, or sometimes on an expansion board. It should not be confused with hard disk space, which is where your applications and files are stored when they're not being used (with the exception of virtual memory—see below). These days, hard disks are generally measured in gigabytes (GB)—a thousand times larger than a megabyte. Your internal hard drive is located behind a plate at the front of your PC, and there's usually a light to tell you when it's active.

I tried to open a file recently and my computer flashed an error message saying it had insufficient memory to perform the operation. What does this mean? And what can I do about it?

The most likely cause is that you're running low on RAM, perhaps because you have a number of programs open simultaneously. The immediate solution is to close one or two of them. Longer term, you'll want to increase the amount of RAM available. If you don't want to invest in more RAM chips just now, an easy workaround is to increase the amount of virtual memory, which you can do through the System Control Panel. Virtual memory is a section of your hard disk set aside for the computer to store things temporarily to free up more RAM. One guideline is to set it for 2.5 times the amount of RAM you have installed—so if you have 16MB of RAM, set virtual memory to 40MB. Set the minimum and the maximum to the same number. If you still get "out of memory" messages, increase the number.

If you're in the market to purchase more RAM chips, there are several AOL sites that carry them: the AOL Store's Hardware Shop (keyword: **Hardware Center**) (shown in figure 2.9), the AOL Classifieds (keyword: **Classifieds**), and the Cyberian Outpost (keyword: **Cyberian Outpost**).

The guy at the computer store keeps saying, "RAM is cheap." Is he just trying to sell me something? What benefits will I see if I increase the 16MB of RAM on my Windows computer? How much should I increase it?

Well, he is trying to sell you something, but RAM *is* cheap at the moment, and is generally something you want more of rather than less. Running your operating system takes up RAM, and running each application program takes up more RAM—anywhere from a few hundred kilobytes (KB) to several megabytes. With more RAM you can run more programs simultaneously without making Windows resort to using virtual memory. Storing and retrieving data from the hard drive adds a couple of extra steps and slows things down anywhere from a little to a lot, depending on how fast your hard drive is and how frequently Windows 95 accesses it. And if you run many programs at once, you could tap out both your RAM and your virtual memory.

Ask the store how much it will cost you to add another 16MB of RAM. At this writing, it shouldn't cost more than $80 or so, but RAM pricing is unpredictable, so it's a good idea to compare prices in computer magazines at the AOL Computing Newsstand (keyword: **Computing Newsstand**), at the AOL Store's Hardware Shop (keyword: **Hardware Center**), in the Computing Classifieds (keyword: **Classifieds**), at the Cyberian Outpost (keyword: **Cyberian Outpost**), or in mail-order catalogs. RAM is one of the easiest things to upgrade, so if you can find a good deal, you might as well take it.

When I bought my first computer back in the mid-1980s, all the ads told how much ROM the system had. Now it's not mentioned, but RAM seems to be a big deal. Do computers still have ROM, or is it all RAM? And what's the difference anyway?

ROM, or read-only memory, isn't mentioned much anymore because it's become standardized and is no longer a way to differentiate one PC from another. It's still there, though. It's a permanent feature of the processor chip and has the computer's BIOS, or start-up instructions, in it.

RAM, or random-access memory, holds your software and data as they are being used by your computer's processor. RAM is a big deal because the more programs you run, the more RAM you use. And the more people use their computers, the more they want to do with them, and the more they need additional RAM. So it's become a major point of difference between various models of computers.

See the AOL Glossary (keyword: **Glossary**) and this book's Glossary for definitions of RAM, ROM, and other computing terms.

Speed

Several things determine your computer's speed, including the type of chip (486, Pentium, Pentium II), the chip's clock speed, measured in megahertz (MHz), the bus speed (how fast the components inside your computer swap information), and the access time on your hard drive, floppy drive, and CD-ROM drive.

Faster computer processors seem to hit the market every few months. Is this likely to continue? Does this mean that I'm stuck with a slow processor that's destined to soon become outmoded?

You're suffering from the effect of Moore's law, described in 1965 by Gordon Moore, a co-founder of Intel. He observed that the number of transistors per square inch on the surface of a processor chip (which determines how much data the chip can process at once) had doubled every year since processor chips were invented. Recently, the pace has slowed to every 18 months, but most experts expect the law to hold for another 20 years at that level.

Moore's law doesn't necessarily mean that chips double in power every 18 months. Often it means that chips can get smaller and cheaper and still maintain the same processing power. Either way, the short answer is yes, your processor was probably technically outmoded by the time you got your computer. But cheer up—that doesn't mean it's no longer useful. There are people today buying the same computer you have because it's a fantastic deal now.

Up to a point, having a technically outmoded computer doesn't matter, as long as it does the things you need it to do and you can still buy software and get technical support for it. And considering how many other people are in your shoes, there's likely to be a market for supporting your computer for at least several more years—no matter what you have.

If you want to upgrade your microprocessor chip in your computer, first make sure that your computer is upgradable. You could find this out in a number of ways. Go to the AOL Hardware/OS Forum (keyword: **Hardware**) and post a message on the message board to see how other AOL members have upgraded their computers. Or you could ask the service department at the store where you purchased your computer, or contact the computer manufacturer.

If you're going to upgrade the microprocessor chip in your computer, you might want to install an overdrive microprocessor chip yourself, which allows you to upgrade to a faster microprocessor chip. Intel manufactures a variety of overdrive processors. It's a good idea to comparison shop in computer magazines at the AOL Computing Newsstand (keyword: **Computing Newsstand**), at the AOL Store's Hardware Shop (keyword: **Hardware Center**), in the AOL Classifieds (keyword: **Classifieds**), and at the Cyberian Outpost (keyword: **Cyberian Outpost**). You could also check mail-order catalogs or your local computer retail store.

My new computer has a sticker saying it has MMX technology. What is this technology doing for me?

Computer chips handle a given set of instructions. The specific number and kind of instructions vary from manufacturer to manufacturer, and even between generations of the same chip.

MMX stands for "multimedia extensions" and it means the Pentium processor has an extra set of instructions built in to handle the heavy use of graphics, video, and sound. Whether it's doing much for you depends on whether you have software that's written specifically to take advantage of the new instructions. If you're buying multimedia software, look for programs optimized for MMX. Intel's Pentium Overdrive Processors for 486 or Pentium machines enable you to convert to MMX technology in minutes.

The AOL Store's Hardware Shop (keyword: **Hardware Center**), the Cyberian Outpost (keyword: **Cyberian Outpost**), and the Computing Classifieds (keyword: **Classifieds**) sell MMX chips.

Looking for a speedier computer, I traded in my old 486 computer for a 200MHz Pentium machine. But if anything, this new computer seems to be more sluggish. Could it actually be slower than my older model?

Without knowing the specifics of your software and peripherals and how you use your computer, it's hard to say. But it seems unlikely since it uses a chip that's a generation ahead of your old one and probably has almost three times the clock speed. Be sure to check the amount of RAM you have which could slow down your computer, especially if it's less than 16MB. It's probably best to pose this question, with as many details as you can, in the PC Hardware Forum (keyword: **PC Hardware** or **PHW**). The mavens there will likely have seen the phenomenon you describe and can help you diagnose your specific problem.

A friend of mine recommended investing in an accelerator board. Will this actually speed up Windows?

It depends on what you're running now. An accelerator board generally has the effect of upgrading your CPU (say, from a 386 to a Pentium). If you've already got the latest, or close to the latest, CPU, there's probably not much point. Also, if you have an older CPU, you might be able to remove it from the motherboard and plug in a later one, especially if you have something called a zero insertion force, or ZIF, socket. It's also possible that you can plug an extra processor into your motherboard. (More about this in chapter 6.)

Several factors affect your computer's speed—the CPU's speed is only one. Others are the amount of RAM and the type of bus, which is the collection of wires that sends data from one place to another inside your computer. Your computer probably has an ISA (Industry Standard Architecture) bus—also known as an AT bus—which can carry 16 bits of data at a time. It may also have a PCI (Peripheral Component Interconnect) bus, which can carry 32 bits, between some components. Some analysts believe PCI will replace ISA completely in new computers. In many cases, the bus speed, rather than the processor speed, is the bottleneck in a system.

An accelerator card won't help if your problem is insufficient RAM or an inadequate bus.

How can I make my hard drive work faster?

As you use your computer, you store data files on your hard drive. Essentially, the files are stored one after the other in the first available space. If you open an existing file and add data to it, it is now larger and won't fit into the same space. Your computer puts most of the file back where it came from, chops the tail of the file off, and then stores that tail elsewhere. Before long, all your data files are in pieces. This is called disk fragmentation.

Fragmentation slows down the performance of your hard drive, and if the files are too fragmented, parts of them can actually get lost. Running a disk defragmenter and optimizer reunites the fragmented files and frees up disk space.

Windows 95 has a disk defragmenter built in. You can access it from the Start Menu under Programs/Accessories/System. To keep your system running at its peak, defragment your hard drive regularly. Once a month is good, though you may want to do it weekly if you create a lot of files.

The PC Hardware Forum (keyword: **PC Hardware** or **PHW**) and the Windows Forum (keyword: **WIN**) are useful AOL resources for finding out what other AOL members do to make their hard drive faster.

Nowadays, disk space is vast, but transmission capabilities on the Net remain limited. Compression utilities are often used to shrink the sizes of files transmitted over the Internet or AOL, so that they take less time to download. If you download software from AOL, for example, you may notice that the file includes the extension ZIP, which means it's been compressed.

Storage

Most new computers have at least three, and sometimes four, ways to keep information that the processor isn't currently using. The one you'll use most is the hard drive—akin to your filing cabinets in the paper-based world. You probably will also have a CD-ROM drive, for loading software and resources such as encyclopedias

PUTTING YOUR FILES ON A DIET

In the beginning hard drives and disks had extremely limited capacities, and they quickly ran out of space. Compression programs were developed to handle the capacity limitations.

Compression programs decrease the size of files by stripping out repetitive characters or unneeded data. To use the files later, the program reverses the process. This is called decompression.

The AOL software will automatically decompress any file you download through AOL, as long as you've set that option in the Preferences section. (Click the My AOL icon on the toolbar and choose Preferences, then choose download.) Files are decompressed as soon as you log off.

The most popular file compression programs can either automatically compress/decompress your files every time they go to and from your hard drive, or let you handle each file individually. Either option will give you more space on your hard drive, or make it speedier to e-mail disk space hogs like software programs, book manuscripts, slide presentations, or pictures of your children.

Windows 95 has a built-in compression program called DriveSpace, which can compress all the files on drives as large as 512MB, and automatically decompress them as you need them. Several other compression programs are available that can handle larger drives. For more information, check the AOL Store's Software Shop (keyword: **Software Shop**).

For individual files, the most commonly used DOS/Windows compression utility is PKZIP, a shareware program than can make files as small as one-tenth of their original size. To decompress them, you need to run a companion program called PKUNZIP. (For Macintosh users, the corresponding programs are StuffIt and StuffIt Expander, from a company called Aladdin Systems.) Being able to "zip" files is handy whether you're sending them over the Internet or AOL, cramming them onto a 1.44MB floppy disk, or just freeing up space on your hard drive.

You can download the shareware version of PKZIP (which includes PKUNZIP) without charge from AOL's Download Software area (keyword: **Download Software**). Click on Software Search, then Shareware. Or you can purchase it from its creator, PKWare, through the AOL Store's Software Shop. Another popular compression utility, WINZIP, is also available in shareware or retail versions.

71

and dictionaries, and a floppy drive, for transferring small amounts of data or loading small software programs. You might also have a Zip drive or other type of cartridge drive, which is a handy way to back up your data. (More on cartridge drives in chapter 5.)

My hard drive is full. Do I need to buy a new computer?

No, unless you're itching to for other reasons. New computers' drives hold a minimum of 1GB (1,000MB), or as much as 10GB. If you've got a hard drive that's smaller than that, you might be feeling cramped, but you can easily expand your capacity by either replacing your hard drive or adding another one.

The decision is similar to deciding whether to buy a new house or add on to the one you have. If you have an expansion slot free, adding a drive is simpler, since you don't have to move stuff from your old drive to the new one. If there's no room to expand, or if you've been wanting to, say, upgrade your operating system, then getting a whole new drive might be easier.

To determine how much disk space you should have in all, one guideline is to estimate what you'll need, double it, and then buy the next size up. If you've filled a 500MB hard drive, it's safe to say you could easily use 2GB. If you anticipate expanding the ways you use your computer—especially if you want to get into storage-hungry multimedia applications—consider going to 4GB or even more.

Before you decide whether to replace or expand and what size disk to get, delete anything you're not using—particularly software, which is frequently the culprit when a disk is full. If you don't particularly need something but are afraid to throw it away, you can transfer it to a floppy diskette or a ZIP cartridge drive (see the sidebar "Portable Storage Media: A Brief Diskography"). Or you could compress it so it takes up less space on your hard drive (see the sidebar "Putting Your Files on a Diet"). But chances are you didn't fill up your hard drive by accident, and you need a new one.

We'll cover this in more detail in chapter 6. But if you decide to get a new hard drive or add a cartridge drive to your computer, visit the AOL Store's Hardware Shop (keyword: **Hardware Center**), the Cyberian Outpost (keyword: **Cyberian Outpost**), and the Classifieds (keyword: **Classifieds**), where you'll find good buys on hardware.

CD-ROM disks can only be read from, meaning you have to buy disks that already contain the programs and data you want. They're not for new data or backup. Audio

PORTABLE STORAGE MEDIA: A BRIEF DISKOGRAPHY

The 3.5-inch floppy diskettes in use today are not floppy at all, encased as they are in a hard plastic shell. You can toss floppies around and beat them up pretty well, and they'll still function. The size was chosen in part because it fits easily in a shirt pocket.

Occasionally you might try to store something on a diskette only to be met with the error message "Disk is write-protected." Write-protecting a disk makes it impossible to store additional data on it, so it's a good policy to write-protect disks that have files you want to keep permanently. If you buy software that's on a disk, chances are it's write-protected, and if it isn't, it should be.

It's easy to write-protect a floppy. When you look at the front, there's a notch in the top right-hand corner. On the back is a sliding plastic tab. If you can't see through the notch, you can write to the floppy. If you slide the tab up so that you can see through the notch, the floppy becomes write-protected. To make it writable again, slide the tab back so you can no longer see through the notch. Make sure you slide the tab all the way up or down until it clicks.

Current CD-ROM disks can hold 650MB of data. The first CD-ROM drives transferred data at 300Kbps (kilobits per second–a kilobit is 1,000 bits per second). Each succeeding generation of drives was named for a multiple of this data transfer speed–2X, 8X, 16X, and so on up to the current 24X.

Because CD-ROM disks hold so much data, are relatively inexpensive, and are nearly indestructible compared to magnetic media (such as floppy disks), they are the ideal medium for distributing hard copies of software. Most new computers come with CD-ROM drives, and you can also purchase them separately. You shouldn't be without one.

and computer CD-ROM disks differ only in the format of the data they contain. Most computer CD-ROM players can also play audio CD-ROM disks (but not vice versa).

Visit the PC Music & Sound Forum on AOL (keyword: **PC Music**) to get information on music and sound, as well as on CD-ROMs. Figure 2.10 shows About the PC Music & Sound Forum, which gives some background on the forum.

My computer seems to groan whenever I ask it to read something from the floppy drive. Why does this process seem to take longer than accessing the same data from my hard drive?

It does take longer—a lot longer. Floppy drives are the slowest form of storage on your computer, and substantially slower than hard drives. It takes perhaps ten times

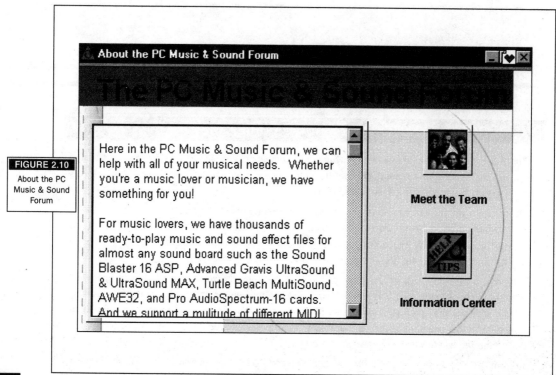

FIGURE 2.10

About the PC Music & Sound Forum

About the PC Music & Sound Forum

The PC Music & Sound Forum

Here in the PC Music & Sound Forum, we can help with all of your musical needs. Whether you're a music lover or musician, we have something for you!

For music lovers, we have thousands of ready-to-play music and sound effect files for almost any sound board such as the Sound Blaster 16 ASP, Advanced Gravis UltraSound & UltraSound MAX, Turtle Beach MultiSound, AWE32, and Pro AudioSpectrum-16 cards. And we support a multitude of different MIDI

Meet the Team

Information Center

longer for the computer to find data on them (called the access time), and perhaps twenty times longer to load the data into RAM (called the data transfer rate), where the computer can work with it. While all these times are measured in seconds and milliseconds, it still adds up if you're using floppies a lot.

CD-ROM drives are slower than your hard drive too, generally, but the difference isn't as marked.

By the way, if your computer is literally groaning—if the floppy drive is emitting more than a steady whirring sound—you may be using a damaged diskette, and it could hurt the drive eventually. Transfer any data you really need to your hard drive, and then chuck the diskette—at about $1 apiece, floppies aren't worth taking any risks over. The same is true if your computer ever tells you that a floppy has bad sectors, which means that data stored on it will be damaged or lost.

Recently a friend of mine lost just about all of the data on her hard disk when an electrical storm zapped her computer. She had backed up her system—but it was so long ago that the data she had saved was of little use. How often should I back up my system, and what's the easiest way to back up?

Dental hygienists have a saying, "Only floss the teeth you want to keep." A similar principle applies to disk backup, "Only back up the data you don't want to lose." But like flossing, data backup is easy to forget. Many people back up only after they've had a disaster or heard about a friend who had one. They back up if they're working on a project whose loss would cause them particular agony, or if their hard drive starts making funny grinding sounds. The rest of the time, people who own generally reliable computers are lulled into a complacency that could be shattered at any time.

Technically, you should back up as often as you generate new work or revise old work. Daily is great, and even hourly isn't too often for a big project that you're doing on a deadline. For most people, weekly is more realistic, as long as you realize that you could get skunked at the wrong time and lose several days' work. If you use your computer mostly for playing games, wandering around AOL, or surfing the Web, you might not ever need to back up, as long as you have copies of all your software stored in a safe place.

We'll discuss this subject at more length in chapter 5, but the most convenient back-up device now on the market is the cartridge drive. The best-known ones are made by Iomega (keyword: **Iomega**) and Syquest, and are called Zip drives. A Zip drive holds 100MB in a small removable cartridge, and the Jaz drive, which holds 1GB in a similar sized cartridge. Imation's Super Disk Parallel Port drive provides 120MB of storage at a reasonable price. You can copy files to these cartridges just as you do to a floppy, but one cartridge will likely hold everything that you need to back up. Zip drives are frequently offered as an option on new computers, and both kinds can be easily added later, either externally or internally.

To check the competitive prices on cartridge drives, you can go directly to the Iomega Web site (keyword: **Iomega**). Or do your comparison shopping at the AOL Store's Hardware Shop (keyword: **Hardware Center**).

Monitors, Keyboards, and Mice

I'd like to move up from a 15-inch to a 17-inch monitor. Are there any compatibility issues, or will just about any monitor work with my computer?

There's a huge selection of monitors that work with Wintel computers, but your best bet is to look for one that has Plug-and-Play compatibility. That means it is designed to work well with Windows 95, and the computer should be able to find and install the correct driver with no help from you. You should also know what type of video card you have, if any. Some computers don't have a separate video card, and the video functions are handled on the motherboard. And make sure the monitor you buy can support all of your video card's abilities.

The booklet that came with my monitor claims that it's capable of delivering a resolution of 1280 x 1024, but I can only get it to work at 800 x 600. What am I doing wrong?

It could be that you've selected the wrong display adapter or monitor in the Windows Device Manager, particularly if your monitor is not Plug-and-Play compatible and you've handled the installation by hand instead of Windows installing it automatically. It could also be that Windows 95 didn't have the correct drivers on hand for your monitor or video card, or both. Or perhaps you're using a video card that conflicts with your monitor, since your video card is the element that ultimately controls resolution.

Double-check the settings in the Device Manager (accessible through Settings/Control Panel/System), and if there's nothing obvious to change, check with your monitor's manufacturer. The Companies area (keyword: **Companies**) is where you can find your manufacturer. Be sure to have the information about your video card on hand. (You should have received documentation on it when you bought your computer.) If your new monitor was purchased after you bought your computer, be prepared to invest anywhere from $75 to $300 in a new video card, depending on what the manufacturer recommends. If it was purchased at the same time, you have the right to raise a ruckus with your computer dealer for selling you a video card that wasn't the right one for your monitor. Any dealer who values his reputation will replace it.

You can explore other possibilities with the experts who hang out at the AOL Hardware/OS Forum (keyword: **Hardware**).

Does the keyboard key with the Windows logo do anything special, or is it just a handy place for a logo?

The Windows key is used for keyboard shortcuts, just like the Control, Alt, and Shift keys. The Windows key shortcuts are specific to desktop functions, and include:

Windows-R	Display the Run dialog box
Windows-M	Minimize all
Windows-Shift-M	Undo Minimize all
Windows-F1	Open Help
Windows-E	Open Windows Explorer
Windows-F	Find files or folders
Windows-Ctrl-F	Find computer
Windows-Tab	Cycle through taskbar buttons
Windows-Break	Display System Properties dialog box

You can get other Windows tips at the AOL Computing Tips area (keyword: **Computing Tips**) and from experts at the PC Windows Forum (keyword: **WIN**).

Lately I've had trouble getting my mouse to respond to my hand movements. Does this mean it's time to buy a new mouse?

Probably not, but it could well be time to give it a good cleaning. (More on this in chapter 5.) The surface of the little ball under your mouse, which controls the cursor's movement, can accumulate crud to the point where it sticks. It may then move erratically or not at all when you roll it around the mousepad. To help prevent buildup, clean your mousepad occasionally to keep it free of dust and grime as explained in chapter 5. Some experts recommend a monthly cleaning of the mouse itself.

I recently bought one of those new ergonomic keyboards. It works fine, but now I don't have enough space in my keyboard tray for my mouse. Any ideas for alternatives to a mouse that might work in a tight spot?

Try a trackball. Trackballs operate using the same technology as mice, but there are differences. The ball, usually much bigger than the one in your mouse rests in a fixed base. You move the ball itself, using your hand or a finger, rather than the whole unit, as you do with a mouse. As a result, trackballs require an area only as large as their base. Some people prefer them to mice, though they take some getting used to if you've been using a mouse.

The AOL Store's Hardware Shop (keyword: **Hardware Center**), the Cyberian Outpost (keyword: **Cyberian Outpost**), and the AOL Classifieds (keyword: **Classifieds**) carry trackballs.

Ports

I understand that I need a "port" in my computer in order to connect my modem. But why do I need more than one port? And what's the difference between a serial and a parallel port?

Ports are data communications pathways that your CPU uses to work with things like modems, printers, joysticks, and the like. Windows computers use COM ports 1, 2, 3, and 4 (serial ports) and LPT ports 1 and 2 (parallel ports). You need a port for each device you want to connect: a printer, a modem, an extra drive, and so forth.

Serial ports transmit 1 bit at a time, in a series. Parallel ports communicate multiple bits at once, in parallel. Printers have traditionally been connected to parallel ports (hence the name LPT, or line printer) and modems to serial ports (hence the name COM, or communications). However, both types have continually been upgraded in speed and capability and can now accept many of the same kinds of devices. But a device designed for a parallel port won't work with a serial port and vice versa. So as you shop for peripherals, consider how many of your ports are currently free, and which kind they are.

One thing to watch out for if you have an older computer is the speed of the serial ports, which you can determine by checking the Universal Asynchronous Receiver/Transmitter (UART) chip. An 8250 UART was standard in older PC systems and supported speeds up to 9600 bps (bits per second). A 16550 UART is now standard in most PCs, and supports speeds up to 57,600 bps and beyond. A 16550 UART is essential for using a high-speed modem. If you have a computer running Windows 95, you almost certainly have this type of UART. If you're running an older machine, there should be a way to check which one you have by running a diagnostic program in DOS that shows your system configuration. Check your owner's manual for specifics.

My friend says he'll give me an extra hard drive that he has, but it needs a "scuzzy" port. I assume

that doesn't mean a port that's dirty, but what does it mean? How do I tell if my computer has one?

Scuzzy is the computer world's best effort to pronounce the acronym SCSI, which stands for "small computer system interface." It's simply an interface standard for attaching peripheral devices to a computer. All Macintoshes come with a SCSI port built in, as do some PCs. If your PC doesn't have one (and your documentation should tell you), you can add a controller card for less than $100 that will give you a SCSI port.

One virtue of SCSI devices is that many can be linked off one controller. This depends on the particular controller—the number of devices ranges from 7 to 28.

This means that you can run many more devices than the number of ports in your computer might suggest. SCSI interfaces also transmit data faster than standard serial and parallel ports.

The drawback is that although SCSI is a "standard," there are about nine different versions of it, and two SCSI interfaces may not be compatible. For example, different SCSI interfaces support different types of connectors. You can sometimes lick this problem by using adapters designed to connect two different connectors. But it's best if your controller accepts the particular variety of SCSI used by your friend's hard drive.

Printers

I've always used a laser printer to print memos and standard business correspondence. Now it's time to replace the old printer. Should I switch to the less expensive ink-jet technology or will I regret the move?

It depends on how much you print, and on whether you think you'll ever need or want to print in color. Inkjet printers work by squirting tiny drops of ink onto the paper whereas laser printers use a laser to form an image on a rolling drum that transfers it to paper, much like a photocopier. Both printers produce high-quality black-and-white images. And the price of printers has probably dropped dramatically since the last time you bought one. So even if ink-jet printers are half the price of laser printers, neither is likely to break your bank. Leading manufacturers of ink-jet printers include Lexmark, while Hewlett-Packard is the leading name in laser printers.

Laser printers cost more to buy, but less per page to run, than ink-jet printers, primarily because you need to replace the ink-jet print heads relatively often, and they can run you $30 to $40 each.

Get prices on two printers that will fit your needs, one of each kind. Figure your costs at 2 to 3 cents per page for a laser printer, and 4 to 5 cents per page for an ink-jet printer. Estimate how many pages you print per day (or week, or month), and how long you expect to use your new printer, and you should be able to determine fairly easily at what point the higher operating cost of the ink-jet printer cancels out the lower purchase price.

If you want color, though, inkjet is the way to go. Color laser printers still cost several thousand dollars, whereas you can find color ink-jets for as little as $150 for personal use, and well under $1,000 for models that can stand up to office use.

You'll find some good buys on printers at the AOL Store's Hardware Shop (keyword: **Hardware Center**) and the AOL Classifieds (keyword: **Classifieds**).

My new computer doesn't seem to recognize my old printer. What do I do?

It depends on how old your printer is. The older it is, the less likely it is to be in the Windows 95 device database. You can check whether it's there by following the process described below for installing an old Sound Blaster card, and checking the list of manufacturers and models for printers. If you don't spot your particular device, see if you can get a Windows 95 version of your printer driver. As noted elsewhere, drivers are frequently available from the manufacturer's Web site. If you strike out there, call the company's tech support number. Ask if your printer has been used successfully with Windows 95, and get details on how it was done.

With the driver in hand (or rather, on a floppy ready to pop in), go to the Add New Hardware Wizard. When presented with the list of manufacturers and models, click on the Have Disk box instead of choosing a make and model. Follow the prompts.

If all that doesn't work, it might be time to throw in the towel and get a new printer.

The experts at the AOL Hardware/OS Forum (keyword: **Hardware**) and the AOL PC Help Desk (keyword: **Help Desk**) can help you out with printer problems. If you're ready to purchase a new printer, check the prices at the AOL Store's Hardware Shop (keyword: **Hardware Center**), the AOL Classifieds (keyword: **Classifieds**), and your local retail computer store.

81

My laser printer has worked well for a while, but now whenever I try to print my computer tells me that the printer is not available. I recently installed a fax modem. How can I get my printer back online?

It's possible that when you installed your fax modem, you inadvertently made it your default printer. Open the Control Panel window and then open the Printers folder. Select your laser printer from the list by clicking the right-hand button on your mouse, and then choose Set as Default. For extra insurance, reboot your computer after you do this.

You can still send faxes by choosing the fax modem as your printer after you've selected Print from the File menu.

If resetting the default printer doesn't do the job, refer to the Print Troubleshooter in the Windows Online Help.

Two good resources for getting your printer questions answered are the PC Hardware Forum (keyword: **Hardware**) and the AOL PC Help Desk (keyword: **Help Desk**).

The other day I was checking out the selection of fonts at the computer store, and I was amazed at how expensive they were. I could spend a bundle on a handful of fonts. Is there somewhere to get fonts that don't cost a fortune?

Look into shareware, which is software that you can download without charge from AOL (keyword: **Download Software**) or the Internet. If you find it useful, simply send the author a check and become a registered user. Most shareware works on the honor system and will continue to function even if you don't pay for it. Some programs have a built-in usage limit, after which you must enter a password provided by the author in order to continue using it. It's always a good idea to pay for any shareware program that is useful to you.

On AOL, go to the Download Software area (keyword: **Download Software**), and choose Software Search, choose Shareware, select a timeframe, a category, and type "fonts" in the Search definition box to narrow the search. You should get several thousand possible files to download. You can get more information about them by clicking on the Read About It box. Check the information and your system's documentation to be sure the fonts will work with your computer and your printer, and download away.

Enhancements

If you recently bought a PC, you probably got all the components we've discussed so far. There are a slew of other devices you can connect to your computer as well. Some are on the verge of becoming must-haves, and others are only for serious hobbyists or unique applications. Together, they are lumped into the category of peripheral devices, meaning any gear that can be connected to, and communicate with your computer.

After years of working as a court reporter, my husband

recently went on disability to recover from work-related wrist problems. He'd like to continue to use a computer without having to bang on a keyboard. Any suggestions?

Journalists and others in keyboard-intensive professions have successfully used voice-recognition (VR) technology to carry on after being struck by repetitive stress injury. It involves installing special software (which can be had for less than $150), and using your computer's microphone to speak commands and enter text. Some well-known companies in VR software include Dragon Systems, Voice Pilot Technologies, and IBM.

Using VR software takes practice, and it also is memory-intensive, so you should equip your computer with a minimum of 32MB of RAM if you decide to go this route.

For more information, check the AOL Computing's Webopedia (keyword: **Webopedia**), using the search term "voice recognition." If you want to buy VR software, check the AOL Store's Software Shop (keyword: **Software Shop**).

One of my workmates bought a hot new sound card, so he gave me his old SoundBlaster. I can't get my new toy up and running. Shouldn't I be able to just plug it in to my computer?

Wags in the computer professions frequently refer to Windows' Plug-and-Play feature as "Plug and Pray." In other words, it's not infallible. As previously mentioned, you need not only the device, but the device driver, to make things work properly. If the card is old enough, it's not a Plug-and-Play device. And Windows 95 won't recognize it right away, or won't have the driver handy, so you may have to help things along a bit.

First, close all your open programs, because you'll most likely have to restart your computer at some point in the following process.

You have to inform Windows 95 that you're adding this new piece of equipment. Do this using the Add New Hardware Wizard, accessible through the Control Panel. Click on Next and then Yes when it asks if you want Windows 95 to search for your new hardware. Click on Next again. If Windows automatically detects the card and installs the driver, you should be in business.

If not, it will ask you to manually select the manufacturer and model of the card, which you'll find under Sound, Video, and Game Controllers. Then it will show you a group of possible settings, which you should compare to the settings on the card itself. To do this, you'll have to print out the suggested settings, then shut down your computer and unplug it. Open up your computer, and take a look at the card. If the settings on the card and printout don't match, either change the settings on the card (by adjusting the jumpers or switches) or open the Device Manager in the System Control Panel and change the settings there.

If your card still doesn't work, consult the Hardware Conflict Troubleshooter in Windows Help. Also, you can get help from the experts at the PC Hardware Forum (keyword: **PC Hardware** or **PHW**), PC Music and Sound Forum (keyword: **PC Music**), and the AOL PC Help Desk (keyword: **Help Desk**).

What is a tape backup unit, and do I need one?

Tape backup units are designed expressly for backing up your hard drive. The theory is that when your hard drive fails (due to age or accident) you will be able to replace it, reload all your programs, and then reload all your data from the tape, and be none the worse for wear.

Tape backup units store data on a cassette cartridge much like the ones you may have in an older style tape player. Some models today use a DAT (Digital Audio Tape) storage format to allow very high data density (high capacity). Their primary drawbacks are slow speed, compared to other media, and poor software for finding specific files. If it takes forever to do a complete backup, and then you can't find the files you want when you need them, how useful is it?

Tape backup units are used extensively in large companies because backup is essential for them. For home use, a cartridge drive is a bit simpler and more versatile. For doing the regular backups that you should be doing, though, you will need one or the other.

For good advice and help from tape backup experts, visit the AOL Hardware/OS Forum (keyword: **PC Hardware**).

What are the advantages of DVD drives?

DVD stands for Digital Versatile Disc or Digital Video Disc, and it works like a CD-ROM player but at a much higher data capacity and speed. Where CD-ROM disks hold roughly 650MB, the DVD disk holds 4.7GB—more than seven times the amount of data! Plans are in the works for 9.4GB and 18.8GB versions. The standard data transfer rate is also 1.3MB per second, quite a bit faster than the standard

AMERICA ONLINE'S GUIDE TO PERSONAL COMPUTING

CD-ROM transfer rate of 300 kilobits per second.

DVD drives can hold 135 minutes of video compressed using the Moving Picture Experts Group standard, called MPEG2, which is good enough quality for today's TVs. They were developed specifically to store whole movies more cheaply and more durably than videotape.

The Buyer's Guide (keyword: **Buyer's Guide**) can give you advice and reviews on DVD drives. And if you're ready to buy a DVD drive and want to get a good price on one, stop by the AOL Store's Hardware Shop (keyword: **Hardware Center**) or read the AOL Classifieds (keyword: **Classifieds**). Some high-end computers now come with DVD drives.

What is a CD-ROM writer?

CD-ROM writers are CD-ROM drives that can not only read CD-ROM disks but record data on them as well. Most models will write only once, but some models can read and write many times to the same disk. These latter disks are a special model that can't be read by regular CD-ROM drives, however. Currently, CD-ROM writers are a frill for most people, though the write-once variety is handy for archiving large amounts of data in a permanent format. If you get one, it's probably best to opt for the kind that writes only once, so that your disks will be readable on any CD-ROM drive.

For advice and reviews on the latest CD-ROM writers, read the Buyer's Guide (keyword: **Buyer's Guide**). If you're ready to buy a CD-ROM writer, it's worth looking at the competitive prices at the AOL Store's Hardware Shop and AOL Classifieds.

Do I really need a surge protector?

Yes, you need one. Considering that the tiny wires inside your CPU are so small that you can't even see them, it's a wonder that they don't all burn out instantly when you turn the machine on.

Electrical noise, power surges or sags, and total blackouts can all affect your computer. Noise can invade your system when someone turns on a mixer in the kitchen (you've seen what that does to the TV, haven't you?). Sags or brownouts occur when the available power dips dramatically, while blackouts mean no power at all—and when you least expect it.

WIRELESS CONNECTIVITY

The back of a desktop computer usually looks like the display area at a wire-and-cable specialty store, with a confusing array of power cords and device connectors. And if you've ever taken a laptop on the road, you know the challenge of finding somewhere to plug it in—not just to give it power, but also to let it connect to a phone line to retrieve e-mail, send a fax, or surf the Web.

We're stuck with power cords in one form or another until someone invents an inexhaustible battery. But wireless computing is already doing away with some of those connecting cords, at least for some purposes and in some settings.

Any laptop worth its salt has an infrared port, which will allow it to share data with other devices that have the ports, such as a printer or desktop computer. Infrared ports make it easy to print without the fuss of hooking up a cable, and to keep data synchronized between your desktop machine and your laptop. Infrared ports can operate at roughly the same transmission rates as traditional parallel ports. The two devices must be within a few feet of each other and have a clear line of sight between their infrared ports.

If your desktop computer or printer doesn't have an infrared port (and odds are they don't, unless you went out of your way to seek out models with this capability), you may be able to get them as add-ons, depending on the manufacturer and model of machines you have. At this writing, adapters cost under $50.

Wireless voice communication technologies are also impacting data communications. Laptop computers can now be equipped with cellular modems that connect to the public cellular phone system, or with special modems that operate with a private wireless network. That means that in theory you could use your laptop, while riding in a car, for any of the tasks typically done by a modem-equipped desktop computer: sending e-mail, surfing AOL and the Internet, sending a fax, or using a dial-up service at your bank.

In reality, wireless networks are still so slow, expensive, and vulnerable to hackers that it's not practical to use them for all these things. Instead, companies are exploring ways to provide small amounts of time-sensitive information, such as e-mail messages, phone pages, real-time stock quotes, and the like. But look for wireless options to expand over the next few years as the service providers increase speed and tighten security, and as more corporate road warriors need nonstop connectivity to their home and office databases and other strategic information.

Power surges happen when lightning strikes, but there are also many small surges occurring all the time. In fact, if you carefully measured the power your computer is receiving, you'd be astonished how dirty and inconsistent it is.

Most of these problems have no effect on your computer, because it's built to be tough. But if a surge does cause damage, it can range from lost data on your hard drive to complete burnout of every component. Ouch!

Your first line of defense is a good surge protector. These usually come combined with power strips. Power strips are convenient because they make plugging in and controlling all your peripherals easy. They do double-duty as surge protectors and thus handle both jobs quite well. They are also very inexpensive. Get one!

What is an uninterruptible power supply?

Your second line of defense is an uninterruptible power supply (UPS). A UPS which can be purchased as a combination device with the power strip and surge protector, is the first device plugged into the wall, and other devices take their power from it. It contains a battery and sensors. Whenever the sensors detect any problem with the power supply, they automatically switch your computer to battery power. If the event continues, the sensors warn you so you'll have enough time to power down the computer properly without losing precious data. UPSs also contain circuitry that continually smoothes and cleans the power flowing to your computer. This action helps extend your computer's life.

87

You can get UPSs in a range of power ratings, from just enough for a personal computer to enough for a roomful of servers. Some will even connect to your network and notify you of a power failure via your pager. You can find more information about power protection products at www.apcc.com, the Web site of American Power Conversion (AP). Products from APC are available under Accessories in the AOL Store's Hardware Shop (keyword: **Hardware Center**).

3

LINKING UP AND COMMUNICATING

One of the great advantages of having a computer these days is the ability to link up to America Online and the Internet and communicate with people all over the world. And going online is not only fun; in the business world it's a necessity. But how do you link up, and what can you do once you're there? This chapter tells you how to make the most of your online experience, whether it's for business, for household tasks, or just for fun. You'll find out what kind of equipment you need; how to use each of the tools on America Online, such as e-mail, chat, and Instant Messages; and how to take advantage of the features offered by the AOL Member Services area. Appendix I at the back of this book also answers the questions most frequently asked of AOL Member Services. And if any of the terms are unfamiliar, you can find their definitions in this book's Glossary.

Getting Connected to AOL

Aside from your computer, to go online you need (1) a software program to browse the Internet, which comes free with a subscription to the AOL service, and (2) a modem. You also need a telephone line to connect your modem to AOL and the Internet.

Buy the fastest modem you can afford, because the speed of your modem determines how quickly you can move around online.

Chapter 2 discussed the different ways you can get a faster connection to the Internet and AOL. Later on, you may want to check out the section in chapter 6 that describes in more detail about upgrading your modem and the practical alternatives.

The AOL Store (keyword: **AOL Store**) is a great place to buy any of the hardware or software you may see mentioned here. Take a look around the AOL Store's Modem Shop (keyword: **Modem Shop**) and check out Why Upgrade (shown in figure 3.1)

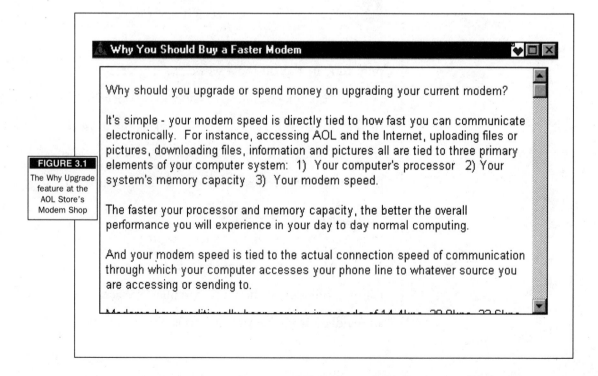

FIGURE 3.1
The Why Upgrade feature at the AOL Store's Modem Shop

for information on the latest modem technology.

Is AOL the same as the Internet?

No. America Online is a publicly owned company that provides software and an online service—a way for your computer to connect to other computers and exchange information. With America Online you can shop online, read daily newspapers, magazines, and reference books, get the latest weather reports, and meet other AOL users, all within the AOL Channels. There are areas where you can buy hardware and software, or download shareware. From the AOL service you can also go out onto the Internet and the World Wide Web to visit Web sites and newsgroups. You can e-mail anyone in the world who has an Internet address, whether they're AOL users or not. This is all done by means of ordinary telephone lines and your computer modem.

The Internet consists of many computer networks linked together all over the world that allow people to connect to research facilities, businesses, educational institutions, government offices, and anyone who creates a Web site. The World Wide Web (WWW) is a graphical way of exploring the Internet. A World Wide Web browser enables you to view, download, and execute files coded for the WWW.

Once you're on the Internet, you can send and receive e-mail, have discussions with people on newsgroup message boards, join mailing lists to receive information, and search through databases stored on remote computers for files and information. The Internet was designed for the most computer-literate, but AOL makes all that the Internet offers accessible and easy to use.

How do I get AOL version 4.0?

If you have a previous version of the AOL software, you can download version 4.0 when you're online (keyword: **Upgrade**). If you are not already an AOL user, AOL will send you a copy of the software on CD via U.S. mail. Just call 1-888-265-8002.

How do I install AOL on a second computer?

If you are already an AOL user and want to put the AOL software on your second computer from a CD, the install directions will give you options to choose from.

What is a modem, and how to I choose one?

A modem is the device that enables you to connect your computer to the AOL service and the Internet via ordinary phone lines. Phone lines are analog, not digital, so there are significant limitations on how much digital data they can carry. However, faster modems hit the market with startling frequency, so the days of slow Internet connections using 14.4K modems (a data transfer rate of 14,400 bits per second) are over. The latest improvement is the 56K modem—which moves data almost four times as fast as the 14.4K version and is competitively priced. (See the sidebar "What Is Bandwidth?" for an explanation of data transfer rate.)

Choose a modem with the highest possible speed you can afford. At a minimum, go with a 33.6K modem.

High-speed modems transfer information more quickly and will save you time and thereby reduce your online service charges if you use a per-minute payment plan. However, if you have the AOL Unlimited Use plan, at $21.95 per month for unlimited time online, and if you're also using a local access phone number, you are already keeping online costs down to a minimum.

What is the highest-speed connection to AOL?

There are three high-speed connections through standard phone lines—56K, x2, and V.90. Before February 1998, there were two 56K modem protocols that were not compatible with each other: K56Flex and x2. When one of these modems was connected to the other, speeds greater than 28.8K could not be achieved. V.90 is the new standard modem protocol for 56K modem technology. U.S. Robotics and Rockwell are developing V.90 software, which will allow a 56K modem that connects to another 56K modem to achieve speeds above 28.8K. Robotics makes 56K modems with the x2 high-speed protocol. Rockwell and Lucent make chips with a K56Flex protocol, similar to the x2 technology. Other modem manufacturers offer new modems with the Rockwell and Lucent chips. For more information on new modem technology, go to keyword: **High Speed**.

If you have a 56K modem and choose a 56K AOL access number, you can connect at a speed up to 56K. This connection is twice as fast as the previous generation of 28.8K modems. A 56K connection can reduce the time you must wait for a response from AOL and the Internet. Downloading a file will be faster, too. However, when you upload a file, the speed will not increase.

If you purchase a 56K modem with an x2 protocol, and use an x2 AOL access number, you can achieve a high-speed connection, only if you're connecting to another

WHAT IS BANDWIDTH?

Whether you're getting Internet access, renting space for a Web site, buying a modem, or buying a network card, you should be concerned about bandwidth limitations. Bandwidth is the amount of information a piece of hardware (e.g., a modem) can transfer during a given time period. For example, the data-carrying capacity of your connection to the Internet is measured by the number of bits per second (bps) that can be carried. You've probably heard people speak of a "56K" modem. This means that the modem has a data-carrying capacity of 56,000 bps (56K bps)

Sometimes companies use different names for bandwidth, such as traffic or data transfer rate, but it all refers to the number of bits per second that can be transmitted by a modem, through a cable, or over the air.

Normal dial-up service (to AOL, for example) is either 14.4K, 28.8K, 33.6K, or 56K. Integrated Services Digital Network (ISDN) dial-up service is either 64K or 128K. Direct connection service ranges from 64K, for single-channel ISDN direct service, to a T1 line which transfers 1.54 megabits per second (Mbps)—a megabit is 1 million bits, or a T3 line at 44.75M.

Suppose you have a 1 megabyte (MB) file that is transmitted in 1 second by a particular technology. If that file alone takes up 1MB and is transmitted in 1 second, the bandwidth is 1MB per second. In reality however, the data might make up only a small part of the transmission. Because data is usually broken into small chunks called packets, each with its own error correction and addressing data, it could take many more bits to execute a successful transmission of a 1MB file.

x2 modem. Check out the 56K modems with x2 technology at the Modem Shop in the AOL Store (keyword: **Modem Shop**).

Your modem and the modem to which you're connecting must be running the same protocol (or speak the same language) in order to achieve the 56K speed. For example, if you have a 56K modem, it will only connect at a high speed if it's connecting to another 56K modem. The same goes for the x2 technology. The high speed may vary from 36K to 53K. If the modem to which you're connecting runs at a lower speed than your modem, the connection rate will decrease to about 28.8K or 33.6K. The same thing happens with K56Flex modems–there has to be a K56Flex modem at the other end of the connection to attain the higher connection speeds.

The 56K modem technology is still being developed. AOL is conducting field trials with the x2 and K56Flex technologies. If you have a 56K modem, take a look at the AOL field trial area that applies to your modem's protocol. If your 56K modem uses the x2 protocol, go to keyword: **x2**. If it uses the K56Flex protocol, you can get information at keyword: **K56Flex**.

Is there anything that can affect the speed of my modem?

Yes. The speed at which information transfers depends on the phone line quality. For instance, a 56K modem may not reach that speed if the quality of the phone line is poor. Modem speed also depends on whether you are using your modem for online purposes or faxing. Information that you access online can also max out at 53K, even with a high-speed modem operating over a top-quality line. And faxing documents is always much slower than 56K. A fast modem can talk to a slower modem, but they will communicate at the slower speed. Select the highest speed your modem supports when setting up AOL. That way, you're sure to get online and access information at the fastest speed possible.

How do I connect the modem to my computer?

Your modem can be either an external device connected to one of your ports at the back of your computer, or a circuit card that plugs into the motherboard like a video card or sound card. If you are using an external modem, plug the phone line into the back of the modem. If your computer has a circuit card modem, plug the phone line into the back of your computer.

Do I need a separate phone line to use a modem?

You don't need a separate phone line, but it's a good idea to have one. Although the same phone line will work for both telephone and modem calls, you cannot use them simultaneously on a single line. (Unless you have a special ISDN line. These are covered later in this chapter). If you are online you cannot make or receive phone calls, and if you are talking on the phone you cannot go online.

Another potential problem to be aware of if your telephone and modem share the same phone line is the call waiting feature of your phone service. The call waiting beep will disconnect your modem connection. To avoid this, insert the code *70 into the dialing instructions in the Setup screen of your AOL software before you go online. This will turn off call waiting while you are online, and automatically restore it after your modem hangs up.

Sometimes I hear static when I use my modem. Is there any way to improve phone line quality?

Yes. Static can be caused by bad wiring (in your phone or in the one you're calling), phone wiring that is not up to speed. There are several things you can do to isolate the origin of static or phone line noise. First, disconnect your cordless phones and all other phone extensions. Leave them unplugged for about 10 minutes. Then plug the phones back in. If the phone line noise doesn't clear up, ask your neighbors whether they hear any static when they're talking on the phone. If they do, then it is likely your whole neighborhood has phone wiring problems.

In that case, call your phone company. While you're talking to the phone representative with the static on the line, someone else at the phone company can check the wiring that runs to your house. They can also check the lines at the main substation or in the connection box outside your home. Static on the line indicates that there is a problem with the phone wiring from your house to the telephone pole or beyond.

When you talk to a representative at the phone company, mention that you are using a modem. In some areas, the wiring is not up to speed for use by a modem. If that's the case, most phone companies can install a data line. This may cost a little more than your standard phone line, but you'll get a noise-free line into the telephone's network.

95

What is AOLnet?

AOLnet is America Online's high-speed access network. It provides special phone numbers for modems to call to get a faster connection to the AOL service. For more information on AOLnet, go to keyword: **Access**, shown in figure 3.2. You'll find instructions there for using it.

The AOL service constantly adds cities to its network. In the AOLnet online area, AOL provides a list of cities that will have the high-speed access numbers in the near future. These cities are not up and running yet, but will be soon. If your city is not on the list, be sure to check periodically for updates.

You can request an access number in your area by going to the Requests for Access Numbers in the AOLnet area. America Online will try to add an access number for your city in response to your request.

How do I dial up the AOL access number to get online?

Your AOL software comes with a dialer program that will automatically dial your

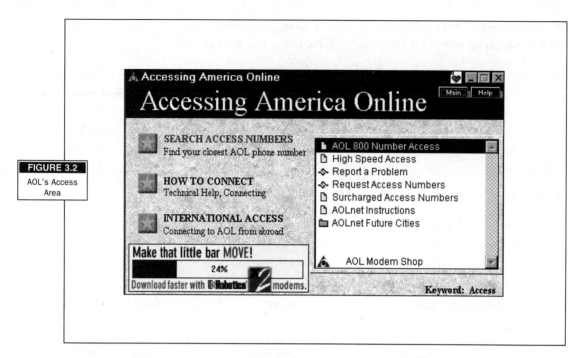

FIGURE 3.2

AOL's Access Area

selected local access number using your modem. (When you initially set up your software, you select these local numbers from a list.) Once you are set up, you don't have to enter any numbers yourself. You'll hear the dial tone and then the number tones as they are dialed. With a 28.8K modem you'll also hear electronic-sounding noise, similar to a fax machine connecting, as your modem and the modem on the other end establish a connection. The hissing noise is always present as long as there is a connection, but the software is programmed to turn off the sound after the initial connection is made. After the AOL software makes the connection to the America Online service, you are prompted to enter your password (if you have not previously elected to store your password). Once your password is accepted, you are online.

How does a fax modem work?

Most of the modems on the market today can send and receive faxes. To send a fax using a fax modem, first create a document on your computer, such as a letter with word processing software, or a sales report with spreadsheet software. Then fax the document to another computer or fax machine by using the Fax commands in Windows under Programs, Accessories. Or, when you go to print your document, choose the Fax modem as the printer type in the Print dialog box. When a computer receives a fax, the document appears on screen. The advantage of sending a computer fax is that the receiver can review, edit, and print the document. With some documents,

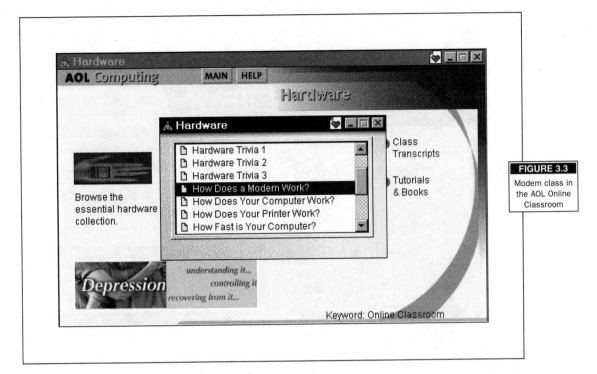

FIGURE 3.3

Modem class in the AOL Online Classroom

however, you may not be able to edit unless you have Optical Character Recognition (OCR) software.

Where can I get more information on modems?

There are many places on AOL to find out more about modems. For starters, you can attend a modem class in an AOL Online Classroom (keyword: **Online Classroom**). To do this, choose the Hardware category in the Online Classroom list, then choose Modems. From there select the How Does a Modem Work? class, shown in figure 3.3.

Another place to learn about modems on the AOL service is the Hardware/OS Forum (keyword: **Hardware**). The forum leader and other AOL members can give you the ins and outs of modem technology. While you're in the Hardware Forum, you can also attend a conference about modems.

Get up-to-date news about modems by subscribing to the C&S News channel newsletter or any of the computing magazines you'll find at the AOL Computing Newsstand (keyword: **Computing Newsstand**). These magazines offer advice, tips on connecting to AOL areas, and reviews on the latest modems.

Where do I go online to buy a modem?

You can buy a modem online at the AOL Store's Modem Shop (keyword: **Modem Shop**) (see figure 3.4), the Computing Superstore (keyword: **CSS**), the Cyberian Outpost (keyword: **Cyberian Outpost**), or through the AOL Classifieds (keyword: **Classifieds**).

I can't connect to the AOL service. What should I do?

First, make sure your modem is working properly. Try sending a fax document with your word processing software. Check your modem setup options in Windows. Then, if you still can't go online, get offline help in AOL by choosing Help in the menu bar. From there, you can get troubleshooting information and AOL technical support phone and fax numbers.

Your problem could be an invalid access number. In that case, use Setup on the sign on screen to get online, enter your local area code, and then select your access numbers from a list of telephone numbers. Be sure to pick telephone numbers you can call without incurring a long-distance charge.

What is an access number?

An access number is a local telephone number (hopefully!) that the AOL software

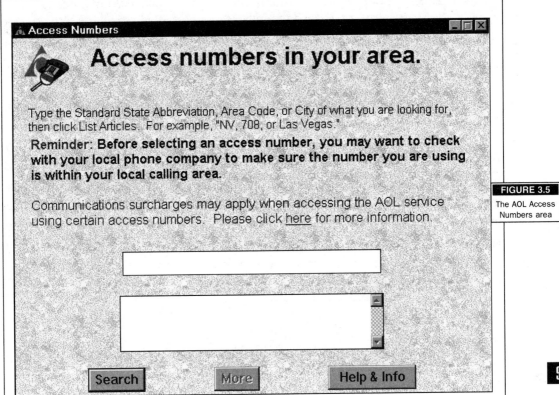

FIGURE 3.5

The AOL Access Numbers area

and your modem use to connect to AOL. This saves you the cost of making long-distance telephone calls to Virginia, where America Online corporate headquarters are located. Check out the AOL Access Numbers area (keyword: **Access**), shown in figure 3.5, for more information on how they work. From the Access Numbers window, choose Search Access Numbers and pick the access numbers in your area.

Besides giving you a list of numbers, the Access Numbers area can tell you how they work, and can lead you to technical help on connecting to the AOL service, using international access numbers and the AOL 800 and 888 access numbers, and reporting a problem.

What is a commercial online service?

Commercial online services offer huge amounts of information and access to the Internet for a fee. The leading commercial online service is America Online. Commercial online service software is free, and you can even try out the service free of charge for a limited time. After the trial period, the online service will offer a specific number of hours per day or month for a set fee. Or choose unlimited use for a flat rate, such as the AOL Unlimited Use Plan. If you exceed the total number of hours in an hourly fee plan, you are charged for every extra hour you use the online service.

All the commercial online services provide e-mail, public forums, shareware, international news, and access to searchable databases.

What is an ISP?

ISP is short for Internet Service Provider, which is a company that provides access to the Internet via dial-up telephone lines. Most ISPs offer a variety of service plans in which you pay a set fee for a certain number of hours of access per day or per month. If you exceed the total number of hours, you're charged for every extra hour you use the ISP. Some ISPs offer unlimited access to the Internet for a set fee, but you need to watch out for hidden charges or restrictions. If you subscribe to a commercial online service, you don't need an ISP.

GET CONNECTED WITH ISDN

Integrated Services Digital Network (ISDN) is a type of connection service available in many parts of the United States. The service can be somewhat expensive to set up and operate, but it offers significantly higher speeds than plain-old telephone service (POTS), which is what modems use.

ISDN service may cost anywhere from $25 to $75 per month, plus a line charge of 2 to 5 cents per minute. Setup costs include the phone company's setup charge, any special wiring or other installations at your end, and the cost of the ISDN terminal adapter. (Technically, ISDN modems are not modems, but adapters.) In addition, you will have to pay your ISP extra for ISDN-speed Internet access.

ISDN adapters create three separate digital channels for communications: two 64K channels that carry data or voice (called B channels) and one 16K channel that routes and handles information (called a D channel). The B channels can be combined for 128K communications, or you can use one line for data at 64K and the other for voice communication. Each B channel has its own telephone number, so it's like having two lines for a little more than the price of one.

ISDN lines, are the first step up in digital phone lines, but they are expensive and hard to configure. In phone lines, the next steps up are T1 and T3, at 1.54M and 44.75M respectively. But these are way out of the average person's price range, costing thousands to set up and thousands per month to operate.

You can read more about ISDN at AOL's ISDN area (keyword: **ISDN**), which provides more information on "Future Connectivity Options."

Note: Through AOL's Bring Your Own Access Plan, you can connect to AOL through your ISP. For further details, use keyword: **BYOA**.

I'd like to get faster access to information online. I've heard about ISDN lines. What are they?

An ISDN line, which stands for Integrated Services Digital Network line, is a high-speed connection to the Internet and a fast way to transfer data worldwide. You can use AOL with an ISDN line if you have a SLIP (Single Line Internet Protocol) or PPP (Point-to-Point Protocol) account, which are two standard methods of connecting to the Internet. Rather than use a modem and a regular phone line, you use the ISDN line. ISDN transfers information between the Internet Service Provider (ISP) and your home about four times faster than a modem. It is especially good for people who work at home and want fast access to information at the office. You can find a list of ISPs on the Internet or in your local yellow pages.

You can read more about ISDN at AOL's ISDN area (keyword: **ISDN**), which talks about "Future Connectivity Options."

How can I transfer data between computers?

You can use infrared data links. These work in exactly the same way as the remote control for your TV or stereo. The sending device converts data to an electrical signal, then uses the signal to rapidly flash an infrared light. The receiving device senses the light, converts it to electrical impulses, and then converts the signal back into data.

You can't see the light because infrared wavelengths

MODEM HELP

If you're having problems with connecting to AOL or with your modem, go to the High Speed Access area in AOL (keyword: **High Speed**). Here you can get help with new modems, read an overview of high speed, get to modem Web sites, and look at modem troubleshooting hints, modem companies, and frequently asked questions about modems. High Speed Access features information on the following connections:

- BYOA
- ISP
- LAN
- Cable Access
- X2
- V.90
- K56Flex

High Speed Access can also help you find a new access phone number to improve your AOL connection.

are beyond the spectrum of light visible to the human eye.

Most laptop and computers (and quite a few handheld PCs) are now shipping with infrared data links. This makes it very easy to transfer data from one to the other, or to a printer, without the hassle of cables.

What can I do to stop getting disconnected from the Internet or AOL?

There are several possible culprits if you keep getting disconnected from AOL:

- If you have call waiting on your phone line, an incoming call will break the connection. You can disable call waiting by going to the Setup screen in your AOL software before you sign on and choosing the *70 option to turn it off. When you sign off from AOL, call waiting will automatically be re-enabled.

- If someone picks up another extension on the phone line, the connection will be broken. Just sign on again.

- If you're using the wrong modem profile, the connection could be broken. Change the modem profile in the Setup screen.

- If you're having trouble with an access number and see the error message "For some reason, the host has failed to respond" shortly after signing on, write down the access number. Then report the problem at the Access area in AOL (keyword: **Access**). Choose Report a Problem. AOL will report the problem to the appropriate access company.

- If you are running a memory resident program, such as a memory manager, a device driver, or a terminate–stay resident (TSR) program it can cause the Windows modem connection to fail. Remove any memory resident programs and then add them back in, one at a time, until you find out which one is causing the disconnection. Get more information about memory resident programs in the DOS Forum (keyword: **DOS**).

How can I speed up my online surfing?

Since your computer can process information much faster than 28.8K, the phone line and modem combination is really the bottleneck. That's one of the major reasons it can take so long to get around online. The faster your connection, the smoother your online experience. And there are some applications (voice and video, 3-D Internet games, downloading files) that aren't practical at present speeds.

Your best bet for a faster connection is a cable modem, if you are lucky enough to live in an area where they are being offered. Cable modems operate at around 10Mbps, but cost roughly the same as standard Internet service over an ordinary phone line.

Cable modems require you to have an existing cable service at your home (or live in the service area), have a network card installed (they run about $50), and have a cable modem installed. You'll pay around $100 as a setup fee and about $30 to $60 per month. The big advantages are that you get super fast speed at the same price as a standard Internet connection and you don't need a second phone line because the cable system is always on with no per-minute charge.

How do I connect to AOL with a cable modem?

First call your cable company. Assuming they offer cable modem service and you subscribe to it, leave the cable modem software connected and open the America Online program. On the Sign On screen, click on Setup. Click on the Connection Devices tab. Choose TCP/IP, and then click on Close. You are returned to the Sign On screen. Click on Sign On and you will connect to AOL through your cable modem. Now you'll receive a signal over a cable line when you're online. For further information, use keyword: **Modem**. This area includes a section on cable modems.

How do I improve the speed of AOL and the Web?

You can improve the speed at which you access the AOL service and the Web by streamlining your browser. AOL's Web browser is the Microsoft Internet Explorer, which is built into the AOL software. There are two things you can do to streamline your browser: (1) turn images off and (2) clear your local cache. Here's how you can make these changes:

Before you decide to turn images off, you should know that the buttons you click on in an AOL area and on web pages are usually images. If you turn off images, it might be difficult to get around a Web site, especially if you're looking for specific text. Nonetheless, this is how to turn images off if you're using AOL for Windows 95. Click on the My AOL icon on the toolbar and choose Preferences. In the Preferences window, click on the WWW button. In the WWW Preferences window, click on the General tab, uncheck both the Show Pictures check box and the Play

Videos check box. Click on OK. As a result of this change, your Web browser will display Web pages with generic image icons where Web images and videos would normally appear. If you want to see an image behind the generic image icon, double-click on it.

If you're using AOL for Windows 3.x, turn images off by clicking on the My AOL icon on the toolbar and choosing Preferences. In the Preferences window, click on the WWW button. In the WWW Preferences window, uncheck the Show Images check box and click on OK. Now your Web browser will display Web pages with generic image icons. If you want to see an image behind the generic image icon, click on it.

Your AOL browser comes with a "cache" (pronounced like the stuff you put in your wallet). The cache stores images and text on your hard drive from Web pages you visit, so that if you return to them while you're still logged on, your AOL software can quickly reload them. When the cache becomes full, performance can slow down. To clear the cache, go to your Windows File Manager or Windows Explorer. Find the AOL 4.0 folder in the All Folders list on the left side of the window. Double-click on the AOL 4.0 folder, double-click on the Organize folder, click on the Cache folder, and then click on the username that matches your own. You should see a list of files in the Contents list on the right. Delete all the files in the folder. Now you've cleared the cache. Or click on the Prefs button in the AOL browser toolbar, and then click on the Empty Cache button.

When I try to get on the Web, I receive an error message: "Unable to connect to a specified site." Why can't I get on the Web?

There are a few possible reasons why you're having trouble. The browser may be unable to find the server or computer that stores the Web page you want. The Web address you entered may be wrong. The server on which the Web page is stored may be shut down or busy. Or the Web page may no longer exist.

When you receive this error message, check the Web address you entered and make sure it matches the Web address you were given exactly. Look carefully at the spelling and punctuation of the address.

If you know the Web address is correct, the server may be offline for maintenance, or maybe too many people are trying to access the server at once. Wait a minute or so then click on the Reload button to try connecting to the site again.

If neither of the above solutions fixes the problem, the Web page may simply no longer exist. Many Web pages come and go without a trace.

Why does my computer freeze when I'm online?

When you're online and your computer freezes, don't panic. There could be too much traffic on the AOL service or on your network. One way to unfreeze your computer is to press Ctrl+Alt+Del, choose America Online (the first item in the list), and click on End Task. If your computer still doesn't respond and displays another dialog box, choose Shut Down. Open America Online, and connect to AOL using a different local access number.

You can also purge the AOL cache in the Windows 3.x File Manager or Windows 95 Explorer. Or, if your computer freezes when you're browsing the Internet, click the Reload button. If that doesn't work, wait a while and try again.

How do I get a Web browser, such as Netscape Navigator or Microsoft Internet Explorer, to work with my AOL service?

After you install your Web browser software, sign on to AOL. When you see the Welcome screen or hear the "Welcome" sound, you'll know you've signed on. Next, open Netscape Navigator or Microsoft Internet Explorer and start surfing.

Make sure you open the AOL software before the Web browser software or you may run into trouble using the browser.

Keep in mind that once you sign off from the AOL service, your Internet connection is lost.

How do I fix GPF/Illegal Operations errors?

A GPF (General Protection Fault) error occurs when a program, or driver tries to access memory outside the range that Windows has assigned to it. Go to either Member Services (keyword: **Help**) or GPF Help (keyword: **GPF Help**) when you receive GPF errors on AOL. That's where you'll find a way to fix the error. Some GPF errors you might see when using AOL include:

- AOLMAN.AOL

- SUPERSUB.DLL

- MANAGER.AOL

- MGAPDX64.DRV

- MMSYSTEM.DLL

- S3xxxx.DRV

- STEALTH.DRV

- USER.EXE

When you're in Member Services, choose Error Messages, and then choose GPF Help. Scroll to the error message in the GPF Errors list and double-click on it. Read what the error message means and follow the instructions for fixing the problem.

There are a number of reasons for GPF errors. For example, an AOLMAN.AOL may be caused by trying to print some blank forms online. The solution is to exit AOL and restart Windows. If you want to print a form, fill in portions of the form, then print it.

You can also report GPF errors to AOL. In the GPF Help list of error messages, choose Report GPF errors to get a GPF Error Reporting form. Fill in the form, giving the date and time of the error, whether the error is repeatable, the AOL version and Windows version you use, the error message, the steps that caused the error, and any additional comments. After you send the report, AOL staff will respond via e-mail to let you know how to fix it.

Member Services

AOL Member Services, shown in figure 3.6, offers loads of AOL help and information. In the Welcome window, click on the Member Services button on the right side of the window to bring up the AOL Member Services window. Or use keyword: **Help** to get there from another AOL area.

If you have questions about a particular area in AOL or you aren't sure what the area offers, you can get help from AOL Member Services any time you're online.

Member Services provides comprehensive articles on how to do just about anything on AOL. Click on any of these 10 AOL Help topics in Member Services for additional help:

- Connecting to AOL

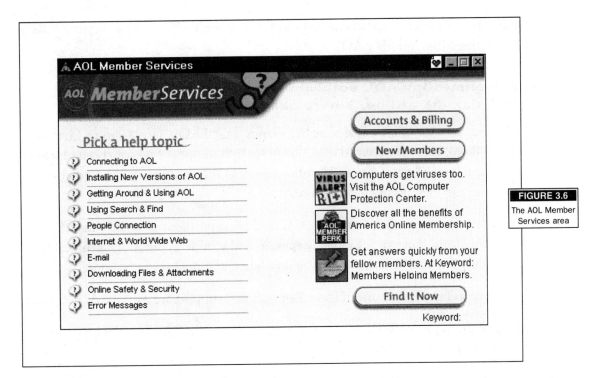

FIGURE 3.6
The AOL Member Services area

- Installing New Versions of AOL

- Getting Around and Using AOL

- Using Search & Find

- People Connection

- Internet and World Wide Web

- E-mail

- Downloading Files and Attachments

- Online Safety and Security

- Error Messages

I'm a new AOL member. Is there a place where I can get information on how to use the AOL service?

Member Services provides services for new AOL members. In the Welcome screen, click Member Services then click New Members. You'll find lots of new member information to get you familiar and comfortable with AOL. Or use keyword: **Help** to get there from another AOL area.

Sometimes my AOL software will lose the carrier and kick me offline. Where can I go for help?

Member Services offers a real-time help forum called AOL Tech Support Live (keyword: **Help**). Use the keyword to get to AOL Tech Support Live, or choose Help in the menu bar and then choose Member Services Online Support. Here you can ask staff for help in a modified chat room.

Another way to get help with an AOL technical problem is to fill out a System Response form (keyword: **System Response**) and send it to the AOL Technical Support staff. The staff will check out the problem and e-mail you a response.

If you're still stuck, visit one of these four technical support areas on the AOL service:

- Use the keyword **MHM** to post your questions on the Members Helping Members message board.

- Send your questions to an AOL Technical Representative (keyword: **Help**) via e-mail.

- Speak to an AOL Technical Representative online in one-on-one help rooms, 7 days a week from 7 a.m. to 2:45 a.m. Eastern Standard Time.

- Access the offline help available from the Help dropdown menu on the toolbar.

Finally, for technical support, call 1-888-265-8006 (1-703-264-1184 outside the U.S. and Canada).

How can I change my AOL billing plan?

The Accounts & Billing area in Member Services lets you view and change information on your AOL account (keyword: **Billing**).

I pay my AOL bill with a credit card. Is there a way to see my current monthly AOL bill before I receive my credit card bill in the mail?

Sure. The keyword **Billing** takes you to the Accounts and Billing area in Member Services, where you can see your monthly bill. For sales and billing questions, you can also call 1-888-265-8003.

Chat

AOL is an online community made up of millions of members. One way to communicate with other members is to chat with them in a chat room. You don't actually talk. You type a message and someone else in the virtual lounge types a response. There's almost no lag time between sending a message and receiving a response. You can discuss various topics in small groups. Most of the chat rooms focus on a specific subject.

After you leave a chat room, you can print out a copy of what was discussed by choosing the Chat Transcripts option.

If you haven't chatted online yet, it may seem a little strange at first, but give it a whirl. It's a great way to meet new people, learn new ideas, and get more involved with your AOL online community.

Is there a limit to how many people can fit in a chat room?

An AOL chat room can hold 23 people. If the chat room is full, wait a few minutes for a spot to open up. Or go into another chat room while you're waiting for a space to open up in that one.

How do I get into a chat room?

Start with the People Connection, (keyword: **People**) which is an area for chatting and the doorway to other chat areas. From the People Connection area, you can choose to go to either Community Center, Find a Chat, Show Me How, or Chat Now. The Community Center lets you see what's up and join a chat. Find a Chat lists the chat categories available and the featured chats under each chat category. From here, you can get directly into a chat room. Show Me How explains how to use the Chat feature. And finally, if you already know which chat room you want to enter, Chat Now gets you directly into that room.

What kinds of chat rooms are there on AOL?

There are dozens of different chat rooms on AOL that enable you to talk with other

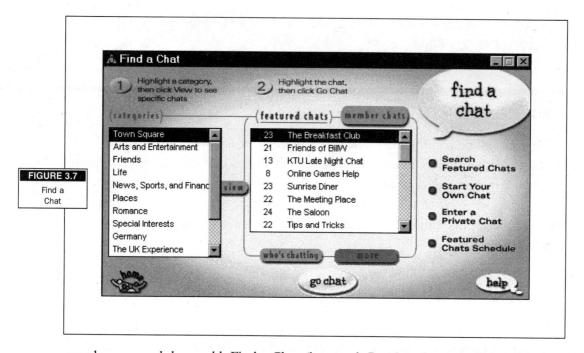

FIGURE 3.7

Find a
Chat

members around the world. Find a Chat (keyword: **People**), shown in figure 3.7, lists the different categories available, but to give you an idea of the scope of what's available, look at just the computing chat rooms. For almost every computing support forum, there is a chat room. And if there isn't a chat room, there's a message board where you can post your questions and other members will respond to them on the board.

Here are the computing chat rooms to visit:

• Animation & Video

• Applications

• Business Applications

• Consumer Electronics

• Database Applications

• Desktop & Web Publishing Forum

• Development

• DOS

• Education & Reference Applications

- Family Computing

- Games

- Graphic Arts

- Hardware

- Home & Hobby

- Home Finance Applications

- Lotus Notes

- Mac Support Forums

- Music & Sound

- OS/2

- Personal Digital Assistants

- Productivity Applications

- Spreadsheet Applications

- Windows

- Word Processing Applications

There are also regularly scheduled events in the AOL Live area, where large groups gather to discuss significant issues of the day and communicate with special guests of AOL. These events are live, too.

Here is a list of the Top 10 AOL Live Personalities:

- 16,818—Rosie O'Donnell

- 16,100—Michael Jackson

- 13,345—(Pop band) Hanson

- 9,176—Michael Jordan

- 8,000—Koko (the gorilla)

LISTEN TO SOUNDS WHILE YOU CHAT

You can now listen to sounds or WAV files while you're in a chat room if your computer has sound capability. To do this, you and the people in the chat room must have the same WAV file in the AOL 4.0 folder. Then, to hear the sounds other members are sending to the chat room, click on the My AOL icon on the toolbar, choose Preferences, click on the Chat icon, and click on the Enable Chat Room Sounds check box (if it's not selected already). If you don't want to hear the sounds, make sure the Enable Chat Room Sounds check box doesn't have a check mark in it. This will turn off the sound in a chat room.

112

- 6,947—O.J. Simpson (Civil Trial Verdict)

- 6,860—Alicia Silverstone

- 6,854—0(+ >: The Artist

- 6,270—Dennis Rodman

- 6,172—Spice Girls

Are there any new enhancements to chat rooms in AOL 4.0?

Chat rooms recently had a makeover. They're even better looking and more fun. What you type in chat rooms can be enhanced with bold, italics, or underline. You can also change the font and font color to emphasize your words. Or insert links into a chat so that you can point people to places you recommend on the AOL service or the Internet.

I would like to chat with other musicians about MIDI. Where do I go to do this?

Just go to the PC Music & Sound Forum (keyword: **PC Music**).

Is there a chat room for discussing computer basics?

There sure is. AOL has a chat room called PC Help Desk Chat (keyword: **Help Desk**). It will give you live help on basic questions about using your computer. You can also chat with the pros and get the answers you need by going to PC Help Chat (keyword: **Computing Chat**). Check out the Event Schedule on the right side of the screen.

FIGURE 3.8

The AOL
Mail Center

E-mail

The AOL Mail Center (keyword: **Mail Center**), shown in figure 3.8, is one of the most frequently visited sites on AOL. It's an economical and convenient way to send e-mail messages to anyone anywhere, as long as the recipient has an e-mail address. The AOL Mail Center lets you send, read, and delete mail; reply to a message; and attach one or more files to a message. Once you know the fundamentals of the AOL mail system, you can use such features as Automatic AOL, the personal filing cabinet, message boards, faxing mail, and sending paper mail. You get to all the mail features by clicking on the Mail Center icon on the toolbar.

Do I have to be online to compose e-mail?

You can compose mail online, but you will be charged for the time unless you use the AOL Unlimited Access Plan. To compose mail offline, open your AOL software, click on the Write icon on the toolbar, and fill in the Write Mail screen just as though you were composing mail online. Click on the Send Later button and then, when you're ready, activate Automatic AOL to send your mail.

A message will advise you that your mail has been sent. Click on OK. If you're offline, click on the Mail Center icon on the toolbar and choose Read Offline Mail. If you want to see what mail you received, choose Incoming/Saved Mail. When the list of messages appears, double-click on a message to read it.

Do I have to type an e-mail address with exactly the right upper- and lowercase letters?

E-mail addresses, like keywords, are not case-sensitive. So no matter what case you type it in, your AOL software automatically corrects the case before your recipient gets the message. The correct version of the address appears when the mail is received.

How do I find AOL e-mail addresses or screen names?

If you're not sure of an AOL recipient's screen name, look it up in the AOL Member Directory by clicking on the People icon on the toolbar and choosing Search AOL Member Directory. You'll see the Member Directory dialog box. With the Quick Search tab selected, enter any interests your friend has in the Search Entire Profile for the Following box—for example, jogging. You can also enter optional information such as the member's name, location (city/state), country, and language. Next, click on the Search button and the Member Directory Search Results window will display a list of members. The list contains screen names, member names, and their location. If you don't get any search results, change the search criteria until you see your friend's name in the list. Not everyone chooses to be listed in the member directory. If you don't see your friend's name there, you may have to get the screen name the old-fashioned way—by calling your friend on the phone!

How do I find the e-mail address of a non-AOL user?

To find an address for someone who uses another commercial online mail system (say, CompuServe), go to the Mail Center (keyword: **Mail Center**), choose Find an Address, and then choose Internet White Pages. This will bring you to the AOL NetFind E-mail Finder. You should be able to find the address you want here, or again you may actually have to resort to the phone.

How do I send the same message to more than one person?

Just type all the screen names in the To box and separate them with commas. Do the same for multiple carbon copies in the CC box. If you want to send a blind carbon copy, enclose the CC name in parentheses. Then your recipients won't know that you sent a carbon copy to anyone.

I'm not much of a typist and I often make mistakes when typing e-mail addresses. Is there a way to automatically enter e-mail addresses that I frequently use?

Absolutely. Store commonly used e-mail addresses in the AOL Address Book shown in figure 3.9. The Address Book feature is similar to a paper address book or list. It keeps track of all your addresses so you don't have to memorize them all.

You can add e-mail addresses to the Address Book in two ways: (1) from a Write Mail form, click on the Address Book button; or (2) click on the Mail Center icon on the toolbar and choose Address Book. In the Address Book dialog box, you can add addresses of individuals with the New Person button. Or use the New Group button to create a group e-mail address, then enter the names and

115

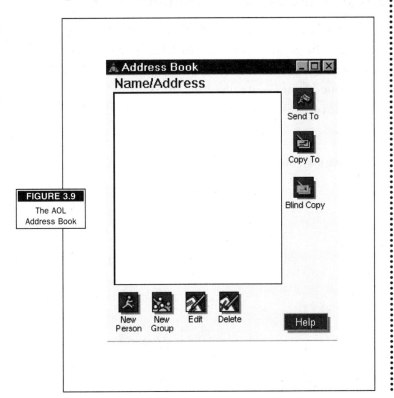

FIGURE 3.9
The AOL Address Book

addresses of each group member. This allows you to send the same piece of e-mail to everyone in the group without adding each person's separate e-mail address.

To make changes to a group name and its screen names, double-click on the group name you want to change, and then click on the Edit button. If you no longer need a group name and its screen names, double-click on the group name or screen name you want to delete, and click on the Delete button.

How do I use the e-mail addresses in the Address Book when I'm composing mail?

When you're in the Write Mail form, click on the Address Book button. Then double-click on the group or individual you want to send e-mail to. If you want the address to appear in the To box, either click on the Send To button or double-click on the screen name. If you want the address to appear in the Copy box, select a screen name and click on the Copy To button to insert a carbon copy address. If you want to insert a blind copy address, select a screen name and click on the Blind Copy button.

How can I enhance the text in my e-mail messages?

You can dress up your text in a number of ways with the AOL mail text enhancements. You can bold, underline, and italicize text. You can also change word sizes and colors, and add pictures. To make use of all these features, highlight the text you want to enhance, and then click on one of the Text Enhancement buttons. One of the most dramatic ways to enliven your text is to use one of the great eye-catching stylized fonts now available in AOL 4.0.

Here are all the text enhancement buttons you can use on your message text:

- Font

- Font Size

- Bold

- Italics

- Underline

- Align Left

- Center

- Align Right

- Text Color

- Background Color

- Insert a Picture

- Insert Favorite Place

- Spell Check

How do I use the spell checker in AOL 4.0 e-mail?

In AOL 4.0 e-mail, you no longer have to be embarrassed about spelling or even grammar errors in the e-mail messages you compose. Nor do you have to use your word processor's spell checker. You now have a powerful built-in spell checker that finds and fixes mistakes in spelling, grammar, punctuation, capitalization, and spacing before you send mail.

To check the spelling in your e-mail message, click on the Spell Check button (the last

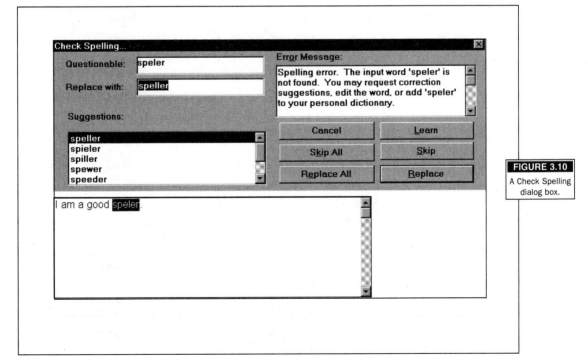

FIGURE 3.10

A Check Spelling dialog box.

one) on the Message toolbar. If Spell Check finds a spelling or grammar error, a Check Spelling dialog box (see figure 3.10) will appear showing the word in question. The Replacement box will suggest a correct spelling of the word, followed by a list of suggested words in the Suggestion list, and an explanation in the Error Message box.

There are six buttons in the Check Spelling dialog box which give you the following choices when spell checking:

- Cancel—closes the Check Spelling dialog box without making any changes

- Skip All—skips the spelling of the word in question in every occurrence

- Replace All—replaces all occurrences of the word with the correctly spelled word

- Learn—teaches the spell checker the spelling of a word

- Skip—skips this occurrence of the word in question

- Replace—replaces the word in question with the correctly spelled word

Can I insert graphics and photos in my e-mail messages?

Yes. Click on the Insert a Picture button (the camera) on the Message toolbar, and choose Insert a Picture from the menu to insert clip art or a photograph directly in your e-mail message. Or choose Background Picture from the menu to insert a picture in the background of the message text.

Can I insert a memo or letter that I created with a word processor into my e-mail messages?

Absolutely. That's one of the great advantages of using e-mail. You can insert any text file that contains a letter, memo, report, or any other document that you created with a word processor. Just click on the Insert a Picture button on the Message toolbar, and choose Insert Text File to insert the text file.

What is a Favorite Place? And how do I insert a Favorite Place in my e-mail messages?

A Favorite Place is an AOL or Internet site that is of interest to you and that you visit often. The Favorite Places feature lets you mark and return to those sites. To do this, when you're at a site you want to mark, first make sure the site's window is not maximized. If it is, click on the Restore button (the two overlapping boxes) in the upper right corner of the window. You should see a red heart icon in the upper right corner of the site's window. Click on this icon and AOL will ask you if you want to add the site to Favorite Places. Click on yes.

To look at a list of favorite places, click on the Favorites icon on the Toolbar and choose Favorite Places. To go to a site, click on the site in the Favorite Places list, then click on the Go button.

Inserting a Favorite Place in an e-mail message is easy. Click on the Insert Favorite Place button (the heart) on the Message toolbar, and choose one of your favorite places. The Favorite Place text will be blue and underlined in your e-mail message— a hyperlink. That way, the recipient can click on the hyperlink to see a Favorite Place of yours on AOL.

What is a hyperlink, and what is the purpose of having hyperlinks in e-mail messages?

Hyperlinks allow the reader to jump from your message to a Web site on the Internet or an AOL area. The hyperlinks are distinguishable in a message because they are underlined and in a different color than your text. Readers can click on a hyperlink in your message, and go directly to the area you choose to link them to: one of your Favorite Places, say, or URLs (Uniform Resource Locator, an Internet address used by the World Wide Web to specify a certain site), or documents that are stored in your Favorite Places folder in AOL.

How do I add hyperlinks to my e-mail messages?

There are two ways to add hyperlinks. One is to drag-and-drop an item from your Favorite Places folder to the body of your e-mail message. The name of the Favorite Place shows up as underlined text in a different color in your message. The other way is to highlight the text in your e-mail that you want to serve as a hyperlink. Right-click on the text and select Create Hyperlink from the dropdown menu. An input box then appears, with the text you've just highlighted as its title. Type the URL for the hyperlink in the input box and click on OK.

Remember that the body of the e-mail message is the only field that accepts a hyperlink. You cannot place a hyperlink in the To, CC, or Subject fields.

You can fax mail from your own computer to anyone else's computer or send mail to most U.S. or Canadian fax machines as fax mail. Although you cannot attach files to fax mail, you can send the same message to multiple fax mail, Internet, and paper mail addresses. You can also mix and match fax, AOL, and Internet addresses.

Here's how it works. When you're online, go to the Write Mail window and type the addressee's name in the To box, followed by an @ and then the fax area code and telephone number. The addressee's name can have a maximum of 20 characters, including letters, numbers, and any punctuation except commas and parentheses. Compose and send your message as you normally would. You will be advised that fax mail incurs an extra charge on your AOL bill. Click on Yes to accept the charges. A message will then inform you that your fax mail has been sent. Most likely, it will be sent within the hour.

I would like to embellish my e-mail messages with artwork. Is there a way to do that?

Mail Extras let you add all kinds of nifty things to your mail. To access this feature, click on the Mail Extras button in the lower right corner of the message window. You'll see the Mail Extras dialog box containing the list of Mail Extras that you can insert in your mail to enhance it. Here are some possibilities:

- Colors & Style

- Smileys

- Photos

- Hyperlinks

- Online Postcards

- Stationery

Can I attach more than one file to my e-mail messages?

With AOL 4.0, you can attach one or more files to an e-mail message without using a file compression program—multiple attached files are compressed automatically in this version. This means you can send a word processing file, a spreadsheet, a database, and any other file all together in one message.

Before you send an attached file, make sure that the recipient has the program that was used to create the file. For example, if you're sending a Word for Windows file, confirm that the person to whom you're sending the attachment has Word for Windows as well. Otherwise the recipient won't be able to open the file.

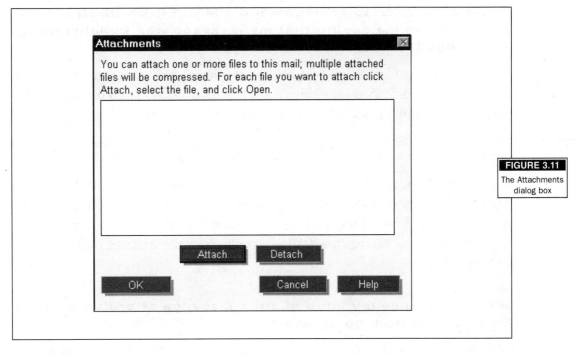

FIGURE 3.11

The Attachments
dialog box

Attachments

You can attach one or more files to this mail; multiple attached files will be compressed. For each file you want to attach click Attach, select the file, and click Open.

Attach   Detach

OK   Cancel   Help

How do I attach more than one file to an e-mail message in AOL 4.0?

Create the message and click on the Attachments button in the lower left corner of the message window. Then click on the Attach button in the Attachments dialog box (see figure 3.11) and choose the files you want to attach. If you make a mistake or change your mind, you can detach the file. Select the file in the list and click on the Detach button in the Attachments dialog box.

How do I read an attached file that someone sent me in an e-mail message?

When you're online, double-click on the message in the mail list that you know has the attached file. Click on the Download File button to transfer the file to your computer. Select a drive and folder for the file and click on OK. A dialog box opens to show you the progress of the file transfer. When the file transfer is complete, AOL notifies you. Click on OK. To look at a file that was transferred to you, open the Windows Explorer. Go to the folder that contains the file and double-click on the file name. The program that was used to create the file starts, and the file will open on-screen.

I sent a message to someone and a MAILER-DAEMON returned it to me saying that my message was undeliverable. What does that mean?

Occasionally e-mail may not be delivered. Sometimes you'll get a warning message like the one you described informing you when messages don't go through. When this happens, verify the address and try resending it.

How do I know that the recipient read my message?

While you're online, click on the Mail Center icon on the toolbar and choose Sent Mail. Click on the message you sent, then click on the Show Status button. If the message was read, you'll see the time and date it was read; if the message wasn't read yet, you'll see "not yet read." You can only check the status of mail sent to an AOL member.

What if I change my mind about a message after I've sent it? Can I stop it from being sent?

If it was sent to another AOL user, you can usually get it back from the AOL Mail Center. While you're online, click on the Mail Center icon on the toolbar and choose Sent Mail. When the list of messages appears, click on the message you want to retract, then click on the Unsend button. If it has not already been read, you can head it off. If the message was sent to a non-AOL user, you're out of luck.

I receive lots of junk e-mail. Is there a way to stop it?

Definitely. When you're online, click on the Mail Center icon on the toolbar and choose Mail Controls. Then click on the Junk Mail icon and tell AOL what you want to do about those unsolicited messages.

Can I review my old mail?

Click on the Mail Center icon on the toolbar and choose Old Mail. In your Online Mailbox dialog box, there are three tabs: New Mail, Old Mail, and Sent Mail. In the Old Mail file, click on a message and then click on the Read button. Click on the Keep As New button to mark a read message as unread. After you have read your old mail, you can reply, save, or delete it.

I can't find a message that I received about a month ago. What could have happened?

AOL automatically deletes mail after a set period. You have 27 days to open your mail. After that 27 days, any unread mail (i.e., mail you never opened) is deleted. Once you've read your mail, however, you need to decide pretty quickly what to do with it. You can either save it, print it, or delete it. If you do nothing after you've read it, it will automatically be deleted 3 to 5 days after it was received. If for some reason you're away from your computer for an extended period of time and don't read your email, messages get deleted after 22 days.

I would like to save my mail. How can I do that?

It's easy to save your mail to a file. Just click on the message that you want to save, use the File, Save command to give the message a file name, and then store the file in the folder of your choice.

I need help organizing my online communications. Any suggestions?

Use your AOL Personal Filing Cabinet. It helps you organize documents you have downloaded, incoming mail, newsgroup messages, and those documents readied for Automatic AOL (files to be downloaded, outgoing mail, and outgoing newsgroup messages). There is a Personal Filing Cabinet for each screen name, stored in a file on your hard disk. For example, if your screen name is Doxie, the Personal Filing Cabinet information is stored in a file named Doxie in the Organize subfolder within the AOL 4.0 folder. If you sign on as a Guest from another member's computer, however, you will not have access to your Personal Filing Cabinet.

The organization of the Personal Filing Cabinet is a simple tree structure of folders and files. To access it, click on the Personal Filing Cabinet icon (My Files) on the toolbar. To search for a specific folder or file, click on the Search button, type the search text, choose some search options if desired, and click on the Find Next button. AOL will find the text in the Personal Filing Cabinet list and highlight it. To add folders, click on the Add Folder button, type a folder name, and click on OK. To move files to a different folder, use drag-and-drop. To open a file, click on it, and then click on the Open button. To delete a file, click on it, click on the Delete button, and then click on Yes.

Another convenient feature of the Personal Filing Cabinet is the ability to rename folders that you created in the Favorite Places folder. To rename a folder, click on it, click on the Rename button, type the new name, and click on OK. If you want to go to the Automatic AOL setup, click on Automatic AOL. To compress the space in your Personal Filing Cabinet to make more room for additional files, click on the Compact PFC button, then click on Compact Now.

What is Automatic AOL?

What used to be called Flashsessions in AOL 3.0 is now called Automatic AOL in AOL 4.0. It's just as fast and efficient as ever. Automatic AOL can save you time and money and can handle your mail for you when you're unavailable to handle it yourself. You may want to use Automatic AOL to go online and retrieve mail at night or while you're at work. Automatic AOL signs on to AOL for you, sends and retrieves mail, downloads files, and then automatically signs off. Among other things, Automatic AOL enables you to retrieve and reply to unread messages offline and to download files when you're not on your computer so that you don't have to wait around for a long download.

How do I set up Automatic AOL?

Set up preferences for Automatic AOL when you're online or offline. Click on the Mail Center icon on the toolbar, choose Set Up Automatic AOL, and then read the instructions onscreen (see figure 3.12). You'll be asked a series of questions about how you'd like Automatic AOL to handle incoming and outgoing mail, downloading files, and sending and receiving newsgroup messages. If you're new to this AOL function, go through all the questions. But if you already understand how Automatic AOL works, click on the Expert mode button to move right along. Doing so prevents the program from prompting you to set up each Automatic AOL option.

How do I run Automatic AOL?

To run Automatic AOL, click on the Mail Center icon on the toolbar and choose Run Automatic AOL Now. To run this feature from the Automatic AOL dialog box click on the Run Automatic AOL Now button.

Can I schedule when I want to send and receive e-mail?

You can define a schedule for Automatic AOL when you set up preferences or at any time thereafter. For example, you can run Automatic AOL in the morning before you go to work and again at night after dinner. To tell AOL to run Automatic AOL at a scheduled time, click on the Mail Center icon on the toolbar, choose Set Up

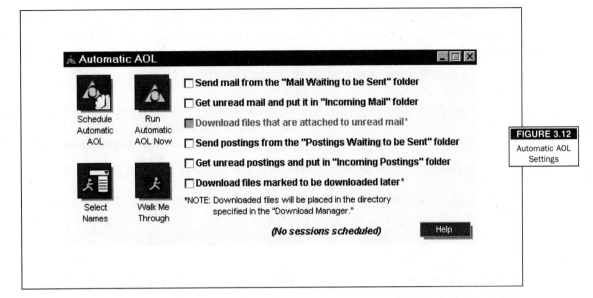

FIGURE 3.12
Automatic AOL
Settings

Automatic AOL, and choose Schedule Automatic AOL. Then pick all the days of the week that you want Automatic AOL to run, what time you want it to start, and how often. Be sure to keep America Online open when you've scheduled Automatic AOL.

How do I read mail that AOL retrieves during Automatic AOL?

After you run Automatic AOL, you'll see a list of the Automatic AOL mail activities that just took place. To read your e-mail, go to the Automatic AOL mailbox, click on the Mail Center icon on the toolbar, choose Read Offline Mail, and then choose Incoming/Saved Mail. You can also choose Mail Waiting to Be Sent or Copies of Mail You've Sent to read your mail offline.

Downloading and Uploading Files

The basic idea behind downloading and uploading is simple. Downloading transfers files from another computer to your computer. Uploading transfers files from your computer to a different computer. With the AOL service you can download a wealth of information, and share what you have with others by uploading.

You can upload or download any type of file, such as a word processing document, a spreadsheet, a database, a picture, a video, or a sound file.

If you have an hourly billing plan, you will be charged for the time it takes to download all files in the Download Manager, whether or not those files originally came from the unlimited use area. If you don't want to be charged for downloading files located in the unlimited use area, click on the Download Now button while you are in the unlimited use area.

AOL will charge you for the time it takes to upload files that you attach to a message. But remember that AOL will compress attached files automatically. A compressed file takes less time to upload, so it costs you less money.

There is no charge for uploading software, because the upload process takes place in the unlimited use area on the AOL service. This lets you attach the program files to messages and send them to your colleagues, family, and friends.

I'm not sure which file I want to download. How can I see what's available?

Search for the file with the Find command, then download it. In every AOL Channel, you can find collections of downloadable files called software libraries. Generally, buttons or listbox items display a stack of floppy diskettes that indicate a software library. You can use the Find button on the AOL toolbar to search for these downloadable files.

With the Find command, you can click on Past Month or Past Week to get a list of the newest files, or leave All Dates selected. To narrow the search, select one or more categories. To narrow the search even further, type your search criteria at the bottom of the window. Click on the List Matching Files button. The Find Results window will appear. Scroll to find a file that you want. (Click on the List More Files button, if available.) Click on the file, then click on the Read Description button.

If you can't find a file you want, return to the Find window and repeat the previous steps. Carefully read the estimated download time, the computer equipment and/or software necessary to use the file, and the general description. If you see what you want, click on the Download Now button. Specify the drive and directory location and click on OK to download, or click on OK to accept the drive and directory that are already there and download.

If the downloaded file ends with ZIP or ARC, this indicates that the file is stored in a compressed format to save transfer time. A window will open to show you what file or files have been decompressed from the compressed file.

How can I keep track of files that I want to download, and then actually download them?

The AOL Download Manager allows you to arrange all of your file downloads at the end of your AOL session; it also allows you to find files you have downloaded.

To set up the path for downloading files, click on the My Files icon on the toolbar and choose Download Manager. Just above the icons along the bottom of the screen, you'll see the path to where files are downloaded. For example, the default path is C:\AOL40\download. However, you can change the default path any time by clicking on the Select Destination button in the Download Manager window.

To see the files you've already downloaded and find out where they are located on your computer, click on the Show Files Downloaded button in the Download Manager window. Then, open the Windows File Manager or Windows Explorer to see where the files are downloaded. From there, you can open a file by double-clicking on it.

When you're online, first find the file(s) that you want to download using the Find command or a software library. Click on the Download Later button to add the selected file to your download list then click on OK. Repeat these steps for each file you want to download. Then click on the My Files menu on the toolbar and choose Download Manager. A list of the files you selected will appear in the Download Manager window. Click on the Download button to start the download process.

The length of a file transfer depends on the file's size and your modem's speed. The File Transfer dialog box tells you the approximate time it takes to download your file(s). If the download is time-consuming, you can check the Sign Off After Transfer option in the File Transfer dialog box. Your AOL software will automatically sign off when the download is complete and decompress any compressed files.

When the download is finished, and you're finished using AOL, you can sign off without exiting AOL. Any ZIP or ARC files will be automatically extracted from those compressed files. Now your downloaded files are ready to use.

I'm very busy at work and don't have the time to download files attached to messages that colleagues send me. Is there a way to have AOL automatically download files without my being there?

You can tell AOL to automatically download files during Automatic AOL, but it is

127

not advisable, given the possibility of someone sending you a virus as an attached file. You're better off just clicking on the Mail Center icon on the toolbar and choosing Set Up Automatic AOL.

If you want to download all the files at one time, click on the Download Files That Are Attached to Unread Mail check box. If you want to schedule Automatic AOL to download the files at a later time, click on the Download Files Marked To Be Downloaded Later check box. These files will be downloaded to the directory specified in the Download Manager. Close the Automatic AOL dialog box by clicking on the Close (X) button in the upper right corner of the Automatic AOL window.

To download a file yourself, click the Download Later button at the bottom of the message that contains the attached file. Then, when you either sign on or run another Automatic AOL, your AOL software will download the file at that time.

How do I upload a file in AOL?

If you want to share a game, a graphic, or a program with other AOL members, upload it to one of the software libraries on the AOL service. The upload process is free because you're contributing valuable resources to the online community. When you upload software, be sure to send a complete set of program files, including executables (EXE) and any documentation. That way, the recipient will get a complete, functional program. It's also a good idea to compress all the files that go with a program into one compressed file. One file will take less time to upload and download. You can find a file compression program such as PKZIP or WINZIP in the Download Software area (keyword: **Download Software**).

Once you're online, type UPLOAD in the text box on the toolbar. Then click on the Go button to see a list of forums. Click on a forum that is appropriate for your upload, and click on the Open button, then the Upload button. Enter information to further describe your upload and click on the Select File button. In the Select File dialog box, identify the file, click on the directory where the file is located on your computer, and then click on OK. Click on the Send button to begin uploading, and click on OK.

As when downloading, the length of the file transfer for an upload depends on the file's size and your modem's speed. AOL tells you in the File Transfer dialog box the approximate time it will take to upload your files. If the upload is lengthy, feel free to check the Sign Off After Transfer option in the File Transfer dialog box then walk away and do something more important. Your AOL software will automatically upload your files and sign off.

Buddy Lists

Buddy Lists (keyword: **BuddyView**), shown in figure 3.13, are a great way to communicate with your AOL pals. First, create a list of your friends' screen names within Buddy Lists. When those AOL members come online, you'll be notified. From there, you can find out which chat room they are in, send them Instant Messages (more on Instant Messages later in this chapter), or send them a Buddy Chat Invitation (which we'll explain shortly).

How do I create a Buddy List?

Go to the keyword: **BuddyView**. Choose a Buddy List Group, and click on the Create button. Enter your friends' screen names, and you've got your Buddy List.

A quick way to add screen names is to click on the Member Directory button in the Buddy List window. You'll see a list of AOL members that you can choose from.

Can I change the screen names in a Buddy List?

Yes. While you're in the Buddy List window, choose the Buddy List Group that contains the screen name you want to change. Click on the Edit button, choose the screen name, and make any changes.

How do I delete a screen name from a Buddy List?

From the Buddy List window, choose the Buddy List Group that contains the screen name you want to delete. Choose the screen name, and click the Delete button to delete the screen name from the Buddy List.

How do I view the screen names in a Buddy List?

Click on the View button in the Buddy List window to view any Buddy List in a Buddy List Group, or go to the keyword: **BuddyView**. AOL then displays a list of all the screen names in the Buddy List.

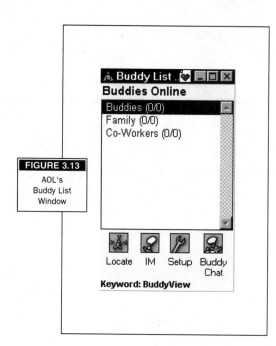

FIGURE 3.13

AOL's
Buddy List
Window

How can I organize my Buddy lists so that I can quickly access any screen name?

AOL gives you three Buddy List Groups to help get you organized: Buddies, Family, and Co-Workers. Use these groups to place your personal friends, family members, and business associates into separate lists, making it faster to find them when you need to. Not only can you use the pre-defined Buddy List Groups, but you can create your own groups, too. For example, if you have a group of online friends who share a common interest in the stock market, you can create your own Buddy List Group and call it Stock Pals.

What is a Buddy Chat Invitation?

A Buddy Chat Invitation is a way to ask your Buddies to visit with you in a private chat room or an AOL keyword or Favorite Place. To use this feature click on the Buddy Chat button in your Buddy List window. Choose the screen names of the buddies you want to invite. Type a messgae in the message to send box, and choose a chat location (a chat room, keyword, or favorite place). The Buddy List service will notify you when Stock Pals or other Buddy List members are online, so you can send them a Buddy Chat Invitation and hang out with them in a private chat room.

How can I tell when a Buddy is online?

When you first sign on, AOL shows you the Buddy List window listing the Buddies who are online. You can choose to close the window or leave it open while you visit other areas of AOL. If you leave it open, you will have a current, real-time list of all the people in your Buddy Lists who are online at that moment.

Can I control who adds me to their Buddy Lists?

Buddy List Preferences settings let you do several things: limit who adds you to their Buddy List window, control who can send you Buddy Chat Invitations, and determine whether the ding sound plays when Buddies sign on or off. To set your preferences, click on the Buddy List Preferences button in the Buddy List window and make the necessary changes.

How can I change the ding sound that plays when my friends sign on and off?

You need to download and install the Buddy List Sound Installer. Go to the Sound Library on your Buddy List Preferences form to find the installer. After you install the sound files you prefer, AOL will notify you via the sound that you selected when people in your Buddy List Groups sign on and off.

Can I prevent other AOL members from knowing when I'm online?

Use Privacy Preferences if you don't want other AOL members to know you're online. Click on the Privacy Preferences in the Buddy Lists window, and choose the options you want.

Instant Messages

You can have a one-on-one quick chat by sending an Instant Message (IM) to another AOL member. Unlike chat room talk, IM's are private—only you and the other AOL member know what you're discussing.

To send and receive an IM when you're online, click on the People icon on the toolbar, and then choose Instant Message or press Ctrl+I. In the Send Instant Message dialog box, type the person's screen name. To confirm that the recipient is signed on, click on the Available? button. If the recipient is online, type your message, then click on the Send button.

If the person is still signed on and accepting IMs, a dialog box tells you that your IM was sent. Your message should pop up on the other person's screen. The person receiving your message can reply by clicking on the Reply button. That message then appears on your screen, and you can start a conversation.

Why would I use an Instant Message rather than e-mail?

Instant Messages are like typed phone calls: you don't have to wait to get a response, as you do with e-mail. Communication is instantaneous—and private. No one can read the messages you and the other person send back and forth.

Can I enhance the text in Instant Messages?

You can use the text enhancement buttons on the IM toolbar to add the following flourishes to IMs:

- Text Color

- Background Color

- Reduce Font Size

- Reset Font Size

- Enlarge Font Size

- Bold

- Italics

- Underline

How do I know when someone has sent me an Instant Message?

The IM shows up on the screen and you hear a ding sound. Type a response and click on Send to continue the conversation.

When I'm online and want to send IMs to my friends, how can I tell if they're online?

Add them to your Buddy List, then whenever they sign on, their names will appear in your Buddy List window. To send them an IM, highlight their names and click on the IM button in the Buddy List window.

Instant Messenger

In AOL 3.0, you could use Instant Messages and Buddy Lists to communicate with other AOL members. With AOL 4.0, you can use the new Instant Messenger service (keyword: **Instant Messenger**), shown in figure 3.14, to send and receive Instant Messages with anyone on the Internet from your Buddy List window.

As an AOL member, you don't need to do anything special to take advantage of the Instant Messenger service. You can already send and receive IMs to and from any Internet user who subscribes to the AOL Instant Messenger service. You can limit which Internet messages you want to receive. When an Internet friend who is using the AOL Instant Messenger service sends you an IM, you will first be asked if you want to receive a message from the Internet. You can then opt to accept or decline the message. If you accept it, you can continue the conversation as you would with the AOL Instant Message feature described earlier. If you decline it, you will not receive another IM from that user during that AOL session.

So tell all your Internet friends about the new AOL Instant Messenger service, and then add them to one of your Buddy List groups (see the next question for instructions).

Your Internet friends will need the Internet Messenger software in order to participate in this service. They can download the software at no charge from AOL's Web site—www.aol.com.

133

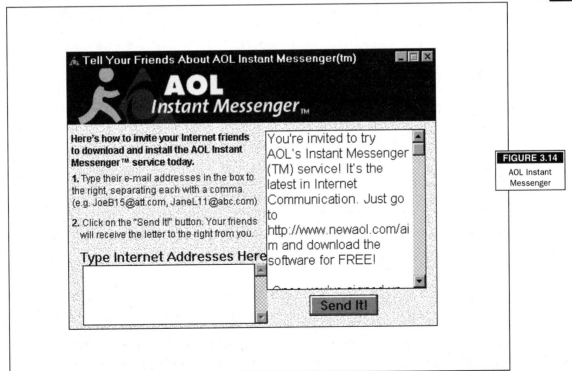

FIGURE 3.14
AOL Instant Messenger

How do I add my Internet friends to a Buddy List group?

Adding Internet friends to Buddy Lists is very easy. At the bottom of your Buddy List window, click on the Buddy List Setup button, then click on the Edit button. Choose the Buddy List group you want, type the e-mail address of the AOL Instant Messenger subscriber, and click on the Add Buddy button. Then click on the Save button.

How do I remove the screen name of an AOL Instant Messenger subscriber from a Buddy List group?

At the bottom of your Buddy List window, click on the Buddy List Setup button, then click on the Edit button. Choose the Buddy List group you want, click on the name of the AOL Instant Messenger subscriber you want to remove, and click on the Remove Buddy button. Then click on the Save button.

Conferencing and Videoconferencing

Instead of traveling to attend a conference, you can sign on to the AOL service and attend a conference without leaving your home or office. AOL holds all types of conferences daily in the Computing Events area (keyword: **Computing Live**), shown in figure 3.15.

What is an AOL conference room?

A conference room is an AOL chat room that can hold more than the standard 23 people. These are commonly used in high-traffic areas and in online classes (keyword: **Online Classroom**).

Where can I get a conference schedule?

Computing Events (keyword: **Computing Live**) gives you a schedule of events, with the conference names and times. Additionally, from Computing Events you can find out about upcoming events, go to an open chat room, and view and print chat transcripts.

Is there a way to have a videoconference over the Internet?

Videoconferencing allows you to conduct a conference between two or more participants at different sites. It uses computer networks to transmit audio and video

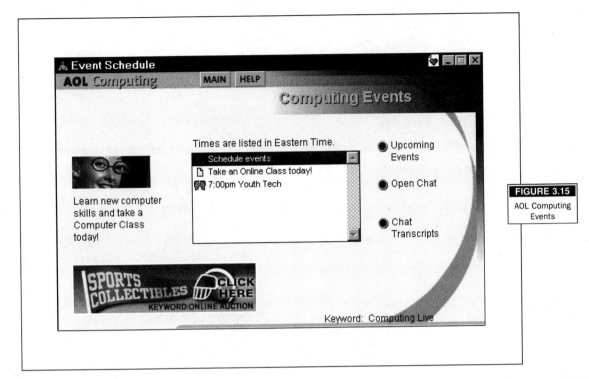

FIGURE 3.15
AOL Computing
Events

data. For instance, a point-to-point (two-person) videoconferencing system works much like a video telephone. Videoconferencing enables you to have face-to-face conversations with other people on a network, whether they are nearby or on the other side of the country.

Is there any special equipment I need to run a videoconference?

You'll need videoconferencing software and hardware so that you can see and hear the people with whom you're communicating. Each participant has a video camera, microphone, and speakers mounted on his computer. As each person speaks, his voice is carried over the network and delivered to the other participants' speakers, and whatever images appear in front of the camera appear on the participants' screens. The Connectix QuickCam VC camera and videoconferencing system is an inexpensive way to bring videoconferencing to your home or office.

Videoconferencing technology is still being refined and it requires a very fast connection (at least 28.8K) to work. But it's worth checking out.

4

MULTIMEDIA: ALL THOSE SPECIAL EFFECTS

The special effects of today's multimedia computers have captured the imaginations of computer users everywhere. Today people can play music through CD-ROM drives, watch and listen to full-motion video, and run 3-D video games, all from their desktop PCs. Never before have the tools for using audio and video files been so readily available and inexpensive.

But most of us still don't know how to use the equipment that comes with many computer systems, including color monitors, fast CD-ROM drives, and video cards. This chapter will teach you how to evaluate what you have and how to make the most of your computer's multimedia capabilities online and offline. This book's Glossary will explain any new or unfamiliar terms.

Be sure to look up digital imaging (keyword: **Pictures**) and where to go on the AOL service to learn more about this hot topic. See the sidebar "Multimedia Places to Go."

Monitors

When it comes to computing, most people couldn't care less about what happens inside the box—it's what's on the screen that counts. And understandably. Today pictures have become a critical part of the computing experience. And AOL is now brimming with multimedia features such as full-motion videos, pictures, and other images that beg for bigger and better screens.

So you'll want to shop carefully to find a monitor that's right for you. You'll find that many vendors advertise computing systems that don't include monitors, leaving it up to you to choose. The AOL Buyer's Guide (keyword: **Buyer's Guide**) has advice and reviews on monitors to help you decide which monitor meets your needs.

MULTIMEDIA PLACES TO GO

There are many multimedia areas to visit on AOL. Go to the AOL PC Animation & Video Forum (keyword: **A&V Forum**) to learn about animation, video, audio, and downloading video and audio software files. You can get answers to your multimedia questions from other AOL members at the message boards in this area.

Visit the PC Hardware Forum (keyword: **PC Hardware** or **PHW**) to get help with multimedia hardware problems, and exchange information on multimedia hardware with other AOL members.

At the AOL Store's Digital Shop (keyword: **Digital Shop**) and Hardware Shop (keyword: **Hardware Center**) you can purchase multimedia equipment. The AOL Store's Software Shop (keyword: **Software Shop**) sells PC games as well as software that takes advantage of your computer's multimedia capabilities. Visit the AOL Download Software area (keyword: **Download Software**) to download retail multimedia software and shareware.

For the latest information about computers and the Internet, visit the AOL Computing Channel's Webopedia (keyword: **Webopedia**). You'll find definitions of multimedia terms and links to multimedia sites. The AOL Online Classroom (keyword: **Online Classroom**) offers a course on multimedia.

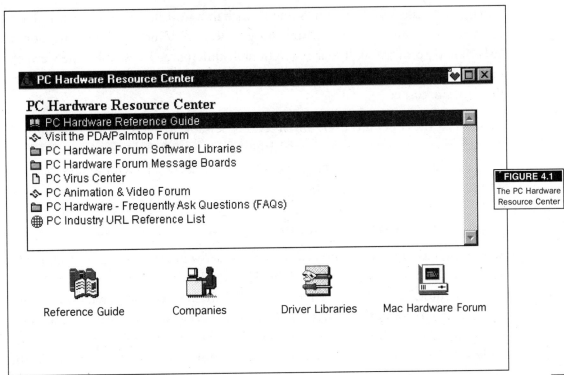

FIGURE 4.1

The PC Hardware Resource Center

What brand of monitor should I buy?

The brand of the monitor you buy is not nearly as important as the *kind* of monitor you choose. Its size, the resolution of its display, and the power of the video card (which generates the images you see on your monitor) all have the potential to dramatically improve your productivity and enjoyment. Read about the most current offerings st the PC Hardware Reource Center (shown in figure 4.1) at the PC Hardware Forum (keyword: **Hardware**). When you're ready to buy, a good place to shop is at the AOL Store's Hardware Shop (keyword: **Hardware Center**). If you're interested in purchasing used equipment, look in the AOL Computing Classifieds (keyword: **Classifieds**).

How is monitor size measured?

As with TVs, monitor size is determined by the diagonal measurement of the screen. This screen is called a CRT, or cathode ray tube. Most computer monitors have plastic framing that covers up a portion of the CRT, so you don't actually see its full diagonal length. So a 17-inch monitor's CRT isn't fully viewable.

The important thing for you to consider is the *viewable image size* of the CRT—the area that's actually visible to you. Some 17-inch monitors have a viewable image size of 15.5 inches, others have a viewable image size of 15.9 inches. While a fraction of an inch may seem trivial, it makes a noticeable difference. To establish the viewable image size, measure the screen diagonally, from one corner of the plastic framing to the opposite corner.

Remember, the larger the CRT, the larger the viewable image size of the monitor. A 21-inch monitor is great for multimedia and desktop publishing because it gives you a big viewing area and workspace. But be forewarned, a 21-inch monitor can take up over 4 square feet of space on your desk!

What size monitor do I need?

Screen size has a lot to do with how much you derive from your online multimedia experience. A bigger screen (17-, 19-, or 21-inch) lets you see more information at once. Monitors range from 14 inches to 26 inches. Most computers today come with a 15-inch monitor, although the 17-inch size is becoming much more popular. If you spend a lot of time scrolling around, your monitor is probably too small and a bigger screen might speed things up considerably. Even a small increase in the diagonal size can lead to a huge increase in what you see.

If you do detailed, visual work on your computer, buy the biggest monitor you can afford. For example, if you edit full-motion videos on your computer, you need to be able to view the full video picture and easily make changes to it.

And if you love to have lots of windows open at the same time *and* be able to see an entire document at once, think about getting a full-page display. That is, look for a monitor that can display an $8^{1/2}$ x 11-inch page in full. A 21-inch monitor can handle a page this size.

But for the average user of CD-ROMs and online multimedia, who likes to view videos and photographs, or play 3-D games, a 17-inch monitor will fit the bill just fine.

How much will I have to spend for a monitor?

Monitor prices vary widely. Depending on the size of the screen and other features, prices range from a couple of hundred dollars for a small monitor to a few thousand dollars for a high-end, professional-quality display.

What is an SVGA monitor?

Every monitor displays your image in pixels, which are horizontal and vertical dots. (Pixel is short for picture element.) An SVGA (Super Video Graphics Adapter) monitor can display 1,028 x 768 pixels. The more primitive VGA monitors can only show 480 x 640 pixels on screen, so your images won't be sharp and you can't cram as much information on screen at a time. While you may not always need a high-resolution image, an SVGA monitor gives you that option. SVGA is de rigueur.

What is dot pitch?

Dot pitch, frequently referred to as horizontal dot pitch, is the distance between the tiny dots that make up the images on a screen. A smaller dot pitch makes for crisper images because the tiny dots that comprise an image on the monitor are less noticeable. Most monitors have a dot pitch of .28mm. Higher-end monitors have a dot pitch of .25mm and .22mm, but they cost more. If you're a graphic artist or frequently work with pictures and other images, then a smaller dot pitch is well worth the extra expense. You can pay as much as $300 extra for the .25mm horizontal dot pitch, and $500 extra for the .22mm.

What is an interlaced monitor?

An interlaced monitor displays high-resolution images, but at the cost of increased screen flickering. Screen images may not be immediately refreshed, and rapidly moving images may appear to streak or flicker. You won't find too many interlaced monitors today.

What is a non-interlaced monitor?

A non-interlaced monitor displays high-resolution images without much flickering or streaking. Most monitors today are non-interlaced. They're more expensive than the outdated interlaced monitors, but worth the extra cost because they reduce eye strain. To read about the new non-interlaced monitors, go to the AOL Computing channel's Newsstand. It offers computer magazines with reviews on hardware and the best hardware buys. Search back issues of PC World and PC Magazine online and check out the Magazine Outlet (shown in figure 4.2) to find advice and the latest reviews on monitors.

You'll find definitions of dot pitch, non-interlaced monitor, and other monitor terms in this book's Glossary.

Does it matter what the refresh rate of my monitor is?

142

FIGURE 4.2

The Magazine Outlet at the AOL Computing Newsstand

A monitor works just like a TV set in that it is lit by a series of tiny lights. Some monitors refresh the entire screen very quickly, while others take a little longer. With a screen size of over 15 inches, the refresh rate matters a lot. A slow refresh rate can be distracting and may make you dizzy. If you spend long stretches of time glued to the screen, keep in mind that with a faster refresh rate there is less flicker, and your eyes will be better off. Refresh rate is measured in Hertz (Hz). The number refers to "screens per second," or how many times per second the screen is entirely refreshed. The minimum acceptable rate is currently 70 screens per second (70Hz), and 75Hz is the new international standard. Most quality monitors can achieve 70Hz or better. A refresh rate of 72Hz or better will help reduce eye strain.

Is there a way to make the images on my screen look better?

Look below the screen frame (or on the back of your monitor) for a set of knobs, similar to the ones on an old TV. Most monitors have controls for brightness and contrast, and some monitors enable you to change the vertical and horizontal position, or stretch and shrink images displayed on screen.

Is it necessary to have a tilt-and-swivel base?

If you're staring at a monitor for a good portion of the day, a tilt-and-swivel base is great because it lets you change your sitting position by changing the angle of the screen.

Adjusting the monitor can also reduce glare from a window or overhead lights. Experts suggest keeping the monitor at least 15 degrees below eye level, so the top of the screen is even with your eyes, and tilted back so that the bottom is closer to you than the top is. Keeping your monitor comfortably adjusted can protect you from eye, neck, and back strain, as well as reduce headaches and fatigue.

Most newer monitors come equipped with tilt-and-swivel bases. If the monitor you're purchasing doesn't, you might want to get one.

Should I be concerned about radiation coming from a monitor?

Your computer uses electricity and your monitor emits a small amount of electro-magnetic radiation (EMR), just like your TV set or any other electrical device in your home. To reduce any risk, buy a monitor that meets MPR II guidelines, a standard published by the Swedish government, with which computer monitors comply. MPR compliance means that a monitor has been tested and shown to have low emission.

To further reduce the risk, leave at least 30 inches between you and your monitor, if possible. Turn it off when you're not using it. But be aware that the front of your monitor emits the least EMR, not the sides or the back.

Does my monitor draw a lot of energy and increase my electric bill?

The EPA (Environmental Protection Agency) has created an energy-saving program called ENERGY STAR, which reduces wasted energy and the pollution it causes. Newer monitors meet ENERGY STAR guidelines, so when you don't use your computer for a little while, the monitor and computer go into "sleep" mode. To wake them up, simply move the mouse or press a key on the keyboard. In other words, you can leave your computer and monitor on all night, without worrying about excessive electric bills.

Is it necessary to use a screen saver?

It's no longer necessary to use a screen saver, but it can brighten up a rough day at work. Screen savers automatically run a picture or pattern across the screen anytime your computer is inactive for a specified amount of time. Screen savers were good for older monitors, because they prevented fixed images from burning into the screen. Now monitors are built to prevent screen burn.

Even though screen savers are no longer needed, they're still fun to use. You can use the screen savers that come with Microsoft Windows, or buy a software package for more variety. You can even customize a screen saver with a favorite quote or photograph. To purchase a screen saver package, check out the Cyberian Outpost (keyword: **Cyberian Outpost**).

What is a glare filter, and do I need one?

A glare filter is a see-through screen that fits over your monitor to cut down on glare and reflections. You should have a glare filter if the sunshine through a window near your monitor makes it difficult to see what's on your screen, or an overhead fluorescent light causes a glare on your screen. If you don't want a filter, try putting up curtains or position the monitor at a different angle.

Video Cards

Your computer's video card generates the images you see on your monitor. Even the best monitor on the market needs a quality video card to look good.

The Animation & Video Forum (keyword: **A&V Forum**) has information on video cards. There are message boards, and links to the AOL Store and the Computing Superstore, where you can purchase a video card.

Does every monitor need a video card?

Yes. The video card plugs into the computer's motherboard and signals all of the images you see on your monitor—from black-and-white text to full-motion clips. Most monitors and laptops come with the card already built in, but some don't.

Make sure you find a video card your monitor can handle. Your monitor won't work to its full potential unless you match the video card correctly. For instance, many video cards have a 120Hz refresh rate at 1024 x 768 resolution, beyond the capability of all but a handful of very expensive monitors.

Check the speed of the video card—the speed at which it can move data to the

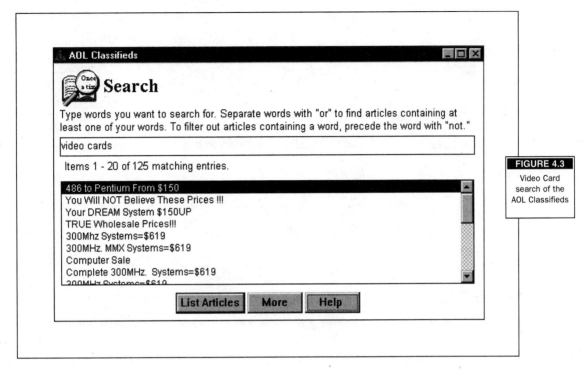

FIGURE 4.3

Video Card
search of the
AOL Classifieds

screen. Also pay attention to the amount of video memory. At least 4MB is recommended for high resolution and color selection. If you're unsure whether to upgrade your video card, use this guideline: If it is more than two years old, you may be able to speed up your overall system performance significantly by upgrading.

Decent video cards cost just over $100, and high-quality ones run about $300. Most multimedia users will do just fine for around $200. Only monitors used for professional graphics and high-end video editing call for the more expensive cards.

Many video cards now support special features that really give some punch to three-dimensional graphics, making games like JetFighter and 3-D Pinball even more realistic.

Search the AOL Computing Classified (keyword: **Classifieds**), to get hardware bargains on new or used video cards (the search dialogue box is shown in figure 4.3). You can also shop for new video cards at the AOL Store's Hardware Shop (keyword: **Hardware Center**) and the AOL Computing Superstore (keyword: **CSS**). Manufacturers include STTS and Voyetra.

To discuss video cards with other AOL users, go to AOL Chat & Messages on the Computing channel (keyword: **Computing Chat**), shown in figure 4.4.

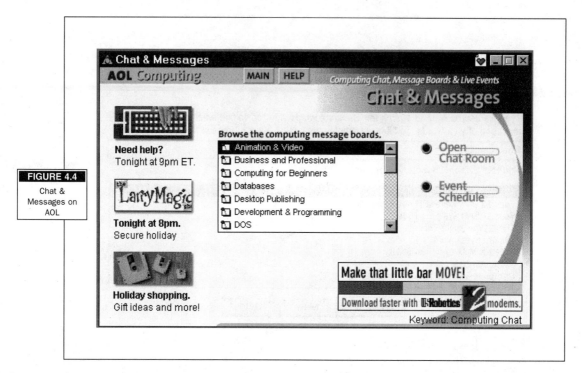

FIGURE 4.4

Chat & Messages on AOL

How can I control the quality of what I see on my monitor?

Match the characteristics of your video card with the characteristics of your monitor to ensure you get the display quality you want. For instance, does the video card support a high refresh rate? Your monitor may have the best capabilities in the world, but if the video card can't send signals fast enough, you'll be stuck with a flickering image. And a good video card should support SVGA, the highest standard of resolution. Otherwise, your supermonitor won't support its full color range. If possible, buy your monitor and video card at the same time.

To decide what sort of video card–monitor combination to buy, consider the programs you'll be using most. A CD-ROM game, for example, might be optimized for one card but not another. Or your version of Quark might work best in high resolution. If you know what you need, you're much more likely to make a decision you'll be happy with.

How much memory do video cards use?

A video card needs memory to display images. The more memory included on the video card, the better the display. Resolution, quality, color depth, and display speed all depend on getting the right amount—and kind—of memory.

VRAM (Video RAM), which provides high on-screen quality and speeds up the image display, is the type of memory you want your video card to have. Look in the Glossary for definitions of VRAM and other video terms.

If you're surfing the Web, you don't need to support millions of simultaneous colors—the AOL service only puts a few hundred on your screen at once. But once you start downloading multimedia files, you'll be glad you spent a little extra to get enough VRAM to display all those colors. You'll need at least 4MB to handle your basic multimedia needs.

What is a video accelerator?

A monitor's video card can't always keep up with the rendering and updating of the images you see. Video accelerators delegate some of this work to a specialized processor, designed to hurry graphics to the screen, leaving your video card free for other connections.

A video accelerator can dramatically increase the efficiency of your computer. If you're using hundreds or thousands of colors and a reasonably sized monitor, you may not need one, but once you start pushing the envelope in resolution, it's worth a look. For example, if you are doing full-motion video editing, if you're a graphic artist or photographer doing image editing, or if you're an architect using AutoCad or creating complex blueprints on your computer, you should consider purchasing a video accelerator.

Video accelerators are available through the AOL Store's Hardware Shop in the Multimedia area (keyword: **Hardware Center**). The cost depends on the amount of memory you want. A 1MB video accelerator costs about $45, a 2MB accelerator can cost anywhere from $53 to $99, and a 4MB accelerator will run you about $150.

I've installed my video card and monitor but they're not working. What now?

There's more than hardware involved in getting your PC to handle a new monitor and video card. For example, the video driver is necessary for the video card to run on your PC. It contains the instructions that tell the operating system how to communicate with the card.

The video driver makes a big difference in system stability and performance. If you're having trouble with the quality or speed of your display—especially with cer-

147

tain programs such as graphics, presentation, and image editing packages—the culprit could be the video driver. Windows video drivers are revised regularly. If you have a problem driver, a later version is probably available.

Contact the video card manufacturer to find out if newer drivers have been released. These drivers are usually provided to you at no cost. Many vendors even let you download them from the America Online Software Library (keyword: **Download Software**) or from their own Web site. A working driver from the same manufacturer as that of your video card is preferable because it will give you better performance than a Windows video driver.

Sound Cards

When you play PC games or work with multimedia presentations, you hear voices, sounds, and music via your computer's speakers. On the AOL service, you will hear a male voice that says "Welcome" when you sign on, "You've got mail" if you have e-mail, and "Good-bye" when you sign off. Other audio files available to you through AOL include event soundtracks and chat room noise. The sound card makes these sounds possible. The sound card lets you hear and record sound effects,

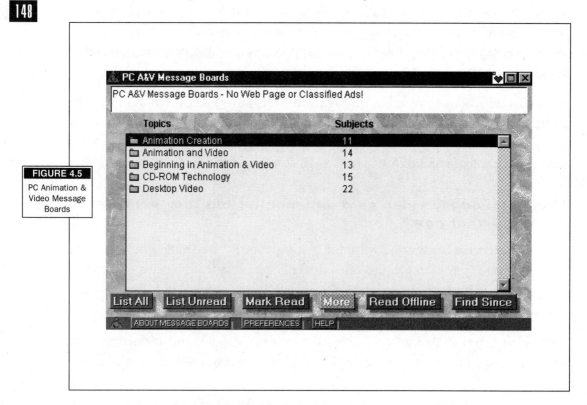

FIGURE 4.5
PC Animation & Video Message Boards

speech, and music—for everything from alternative rock to R&B. Check out keyword **PC Music**. The sound card also enables you to add sound to your documents and presentations. On the AOL service, there are tons of files to help you make the most of your sound card. You can listen to special radio broadcasts (e.g., from National Public Radio), Disney sound clips, music CDs, and even movie soundtracks, which are available at keywords: **PC Music** and **Download Software**.

Sound cards are available through the AOL Store's Hardware Shop and in the Hardware area at the Computing Superstore.

The growing art of recording and playing music on a desktop computer made its way into the personal computing world in the 1980s. If you're a musician or aspire to be one, you can compose music on your computer using a sound card, music recording software, and a keyboard attached to your computer. In fact, many famous recording artists use PCs to record and store sounds. The AOL PC Music & Sound Forum (keyword: **PC Music**), offers helpful advice and tips on how you can create professional-sounding music.

Most new computers are equipped with a sound card and speakers—ready for you to make your own kind of music. Music professionals will want to buy a top-grade sound card, high-quality speakers, and a microphone to turn their computer into a mini-recording studio, creating digital-quality audio. You can buy all this equipment in the multimedia section of the AOL Store's Hardware Shop (keyword: **Hardware Center**).

To get more acquainted with the features on your sound card, take a look at the back of your computer. Locate the edge of the sound card—it has a port and jacks where you can plug in external devices. The port is where you can connect a joystick or a MIDI (Musical Instrument Digital Interface) device, such as a musical keyboard. The jacks should be labeled *Spk Out, Line Out, Mic In,* and *Line In.* Connect speakers or headphones to the Spk Out jack to listen to sounds. Connect a microphone to the Mic In jack to record sounds and speech. Connect a cassette or CD player to the Line In jack to play music.

Sound card questions are answered in the AOL PC Animation & Video Forum (keyword: **A&V Forum**), where AOL members post questions and answers regarding sound cards on the message boards (shown in figure 4.5).

What kind of sound card should I buy for better sound quality?

When choosing a sound card, consider the sampling size and rate. A sound card

150

with a 16-bit sampling size and a 44.1KHz sampling rate will give you a high-quality sound. Before you buy anything, listen to the sounds generated by different sound cards to get a feel for what's available.

When you buy a sound card, make sure it's Sound Blaster–compatible to have full sound capabilities. The AOL Store's Hardware Shop and the Hardware area in the Computing Superstore carry sound cards.

What's the difference between FM synthesis and Wavetable synthesis?

Both FM synthesis and Wavetable synthesis are simulations of musical instruments through the MIDI processor, but Wavetable synthesis is much more realistic than FM. High-quality sound cards use Wavetable synthesis.

What is the difference between a full-duplex and a half-duplex sound card?

A full-duplex sound card lets you have a conversation over the Internet. A half-duplex sound card lets only one person talk at a time.

Speakers

Just like the ones on your stereo, computer speakers are output devices that produce sound. Speakers with built-in amplifiers between 10 and 30 watts will strengthen the sound signal and improve performance. Connect speakers to the *Spk Out* jack located at the edge of the sound card at the back of your computer.

Speakers are available through the AOL Store's Hardware Shop. The PC Hardware Forum (keyword: **PC Hardware** or **PHW**) has information on speakers, and you can get answers to your questions on speakers from other AOL members by using the Hardware Forum message boards.

Should I buy a multimedia monitor that has speakers attached to it?

If you're just using speakers for business audio and not for music recording, then the speakers built into a multimedia monitor will suffice—and will save you valuable desk space.

Take some time to talk with other AOL members at the AOL Hardware Forum message boards to find out what multimedia equipment others are buying.

I've connected my speakers but there's no sound coming from them.

MUSICIANS' SOURCES ON AOL

Stop by the Composers Coffeehouse on AOL (keyword: **Composer**), shown in figure 4.6, to exchange MIDI stories and chat with other composers. Or join the Creative Musicians Coalition (keyword: **CMC**). And if you play guitar, check out the Guitar Special Interest Group (keyword: **Guitar**).

151

FIGURE 4.6

The Composers' Coffeehouse

152

What now?

First check the connection. Your speakers should be connected to the Spk Out jack located at the edge of the sound card at the back of your computer. If you're using Windows 95, check the volume control settings by double-clicking on Volume (the speaker) on the Windows taskbar. (The Volume Control window lets you change the volume for Wave, MIDI, CD, and Line In.) If you still don't hear any sound from your speakers, go to the AOL Computing Tips area (keyword: **Computing Tips**), for solutions to many computing problems.

If you're using Windows 3.x or a Macintosh, you'll find answers to your speaker and sound problems in the Computing Tips area, too, but you might also want to check out the message boards at the PC Music & Sound Forum (keyword: **PC Music**), shown in figure 4.7. Here you'll find questions and answers on sound and speaker problems from other AOL members. You can also get help with speaker problems on the PC Hardware Forum (keyword: **PC Hardware** or **PHW**) message boards. Check the Hardware Store's Hardware Shop (keyword: **Hardware Center**) Accessories section for good deals on speakers from manufacturers such as Altec Lansing.

My speakers have an on/off switch and a volume control button. Is this how I turn my speakers on and off and change the volume?

No. Leave the speaker on/off switch set to off and turn the volume control knob to the minimum setting. Your sound card, sound card software, and Microsoft Windows will take care of the rest.

FIGURE 4.7

Music & Sound
Message Boards

Microphones

A computer microphone is like any other—it amplifies and delivers sound to and from a processor, in this case the sound card. When you buy a PC, a microphone either comes with it or you can buy one separately.

I can't get any sound from my microphone. What should I do?

Make sure the microphone is plugged into the Mic In jack at the edge of the sound card at the back of your computer. If it's plugged in properly, look for help at one of the Support Forums at the PC Help Desk (keyword: **Help Desk**), shown in figure 4.8.

What is voice dictation and recognition software?

Special software for voice dictation and recognition lets you give vocal commands to control some operations of the computer. For example, voice dictation and recognition software comes with a headset and microphone so you can read directly into a word processor. The technology behind this software is improving rapidly.

Voice dictation and recognition products are available through the AOL Store's

Software Shop (keyword: **Software Shop**). Recommended products include Voice Pilot SE, Naturally Speaking, Via Voice, and Worldbook Voice.

Scanners

Scanners, like those used to check prices at supermarket checkout counters, can read pictures and text into a computer. You use a scanner to process photographs, logos, and drawings right into your documents, or to scan text using Optical Character Recognition (OCR) software.

AOL 4.0 allows you to put images right into your e-mail messages. To do this, scan the image, then save it in JPEG, TGA, or TIF format. Once you've composed your e-mail, click on the camera icon on the Write Mail toolbar, select the scanned image from the drive and directory where it's saved, and send it off! You can also include pictures that you've downloaded from the AOL service.

For helpful information about scanners, see the AOL Image Scanning area (keyword: **SCANNING**), shown in figure 4.9. You'll find out how to include scanned images in AOL e-mail. Check out OCR & Text Scanning and Scanning Services in

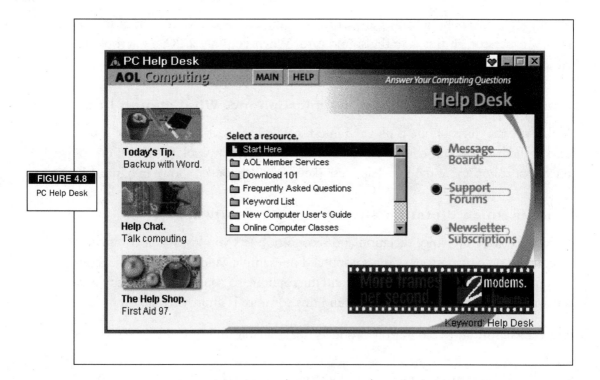

FIGURE 4.8
PC Help Desk

this area. You can also access the scanning message boards, Graphic Arts forum, AOL Computing Superstore (keyword: **CSS**), and AOL Buyer's Guide (keyword: **Buyer's Guide**) for advice and reviews on scanners.

Through the AOL Store Hardware Shop (keyword: **Hardware Center**), you'll find deals on color scanners. At under $300, today's models are cheaper, better quality, and much smaller than older flatbed scanners.

What does scanner software do?

Most scanners come with two kinds of software. Image editing software enables you to change the looks of a scanned graphic, and OCR software scans text into a document that you can edit with a word processor.

What type of scanner should I buy and where can I buy it?

There are various scanners to choose from—hand-held, sheet-fed, flatbed, grayscale, and color. The kind you want depends on what you will use it for. See the questions that follow for descriptions of each type. Scanners are available through the AOL Store's Hardware Shop. In the Hardware Shop, choose the Scanners option to see a list of scanners you can purchase online. Also, there are several areas in the Hardware Shop that provide more information on purchasing scanners, such as Upgrade Tips, Rebates & Promos, Tech Support, Hot Deals, and the Feature Item.

What is a sheet-fed scanner?

A sheet-fed scanner scans by feeding single sheets of paper. Thus, if you wanted to scan a page in a

YOU'VE GOT PICTURES!

Through AOL and Kodak's new "You've Got Pictures" service, *all* AOL members can use digital pictures, whether they have a scanner or not. The service, scheduled to begin in late 1998, will allow you to drop off a roll of film from any camera at more than 30,000 retailers that process Kodak film. For a small fee, you'll receive e-pictures at your AOL address. With your pictures online, you can easily share online "picture albums" with friends and family. You'll also be able to order reprints, enlargements, and a range of merchandise personalized with your pictures. Visit (keyword: **Pictures**) for the latest developments on the "You've Got Pictures" service.

155

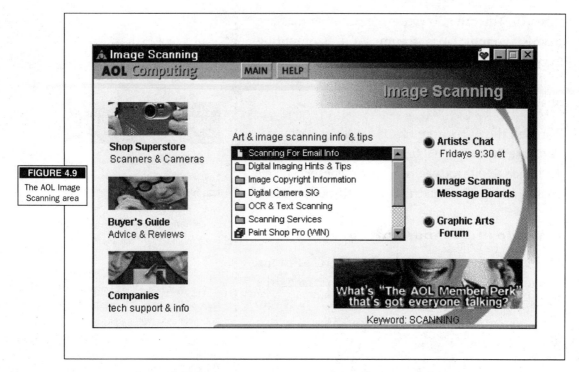

book, you would need to tear out the page. It's more reliable than a handheld scanner, and cheaper and smaller than a flatbed scanner. But a sheet-fed scanner won't work if you're working with oversized items or multiple pages. A sheet-fed scanner can cost between $80 and $199. Look for rebate offers for scanners in AOL's Hardware Shop. Sheet-fed scanners available (at this writing) in the Hardware Shop include:

- Storm SmartPage Pro

- Storm EasyPhoto Drive

- Storm EasyPhoto Reader

- Visioneer PaperPort Strobe for PC

- Visioneer PaperPort Strobe for Mac

- Umax PageOffice IIC

What is a flatbed scanner?

A flatbed scanner allows you to lay documents on a flat screen, similar to that of a copier. It's the most versatile scanner and, not surprisingly, the most expensive. A flatbed scanner can cost between $150 and $500. Check out the rebate offers for scanners in AOL's Hardware Shop (keyword: **Hardware Center**).

When we checked, flatbed scanners offered there included:

- Astra Flatbed Color Scanners for Mac and PC

- Storm TotalScan

- UMAX Flatbed Scanners

- Vivitar VSF.330 Flatbed

- Visioneer OneTouch and PaperPort Scanners

What is the difference between a grayscale scanner and a color scanner?

A grayscale scanner scans images with black, white, and shades of gray. It's best for scanning text or images that will be printed in black-and-white. A color scanner scans images with shades of red, blue, and green, so it's best for scanning color photographs and illustrations. As you might expect, color scanners are more expensive than grayscale scanners. A color scanner can range from $125 to $500.

What are scanning modes?

There are three types of scanning modes: line art, grayscale, and color. They determine the colors a scanner uses to scan an image. Line art uses black and white to scan an image. Grayscale uses black, white, and shades of gray. And color mode uses shades of red, blue, and green.

What is scanner resolution?

A scanner has a resolution measurement similar to a printer. Scanner resolution is measured in dots per inch (dpi). Some high-resolution scanners can recognize a maximum of 1200 dpi.

Can I control the scanner resolution?

You can select the scanner resolution you want to use. But when selecting a high resolution, keep in mind that a clearer, more detailed image takes longer to scan and requires more storage space on your hard drive. And there's not much point in scanning an image at a higher resolution than your printer can produce or your monitor can display. For example, if your printer prints at 300 dpi, you don't need to scan any higher than that. On the other hand, if your monitor can display at 700 dpi, you should scan your image accordingly. For best results, set the resolution on your scanner to match the resolution of your printer or monitor.

I would like to scan documents into my laptop and leave my heavy briefcase at the office. Is there a scanner out there for me?

There are small scanners that fit on your desk and range from $99 to $250. These cylindrical sheet-fed scanners are so sleek that they can fit next to your keyboard or laptop. Some small, moderately priced scanners have a detachable head for scanning bulky images, and include a 10-page document feeder.

Is there an inexpensive photo scanner that can capture snapshots?

There are photo scanners for under $100 that scan snapshots in a snap. Check them out in the AOL Computing Superstore (keyword: **CSS**).

I have volumes of documents that need to be scanned. Are there any inexpensive scanners that can handle demanding jobs?

There are several flatbed scanners that don't take up too much space, and cost from $149 to $299. These workhorse scanners offer great picture clarity and streamlined controls.

What scanners come with good photo software?

Some scanner manufacturers throw in good photo software from Adobe Systems Inc., Visioneer PaperPort Deluxe, and MGI Photosuite.

To find out more information on all types of scanners, go to the AOL Pictures Area (keyword: **Pictures**). You'll find all the details on scanners and other digital imaging products.

CD-ROMs

Built-in CD-ROM drives are getting to be like driver-side air bags—standard. A

CD-ROM drive reads information stored on compact discs. CD-ROM stands for compact disc read-only memory. In other words, you can only *read* the information stored on a compact disc, not change the information. Today you will find that most computer programs—and their manuals—come on CDs rather than floppy diskettes. This is mostly because CDs weigh a lot less than floppies and books, so the shipping and printing costs are much lower.

A CD-ROM drive is quickly becoming a necessity. If you don't have a CD-ROM drive now, you'll likely need one sooner rather than later. So when you consider this serious purchase, find advice and read reviews in the AOL Buyer's Guide (keyword: **Buyer's Guide**).

CD-ROMs are usually located inside computers, and are logically called internal CD-ROM drives. However, you can purchase external drives that connect to the computer via cable and connector. Some of the new CD-ROM drives are multidisc changers, and let you load up several CDs, similar to CD players you may have in your home or car. This allows you to run different programs simultaneously. Such multiple-capacity changers are efficient and easy to use.

How much data can a CD hold?

A CD holds a lot more information than a floppy diskette—approximately 650MB, which is more than the capacity of 400 diskettes. It can contain about 74 minutes of audio such as music, sounds, and speech, or a combination of both data and audio and video tracks.

What speed CD-ROM drive do I need?

A CD-ROM drive's speed determines how fast the disc spins and transfers the data to your computer. The speed of a CD-ROM drive is measured in kilobytes per second (Kbps). The drive's speed determines how fast the CD-ROM spins and transfers data to your computer. New computers usually come with a 16X (2,400 Kbps) or 24X (3,000 Kbps) CD-ROM drive. The 16X and 24X speed drives are available for purchase through the AOL Store's Hardware Shop (keyword: **Hardware Center**). The types of CD-ROM drives sold in the Multimedia area in the Hardware Shop are from reliable manufacturers such as GoldStar and Creative Labs.

To process information quickly, invest in a CD-ROM drive that runs at least 600 Kbps. The faster the information gets transferred, the better the performance of the CD-ROM program. For example, when you view video and animation in games

Suppose you want to back up your entire hard drive or distribute and archive information. What if you want to record music, or store pictures and other large multimedia files, such as videos? Now you can record and store large amounts of information on a CD-R drive. CD-R stands for CD-recordable. You can even record your own audio files onto a CD-R. This type of CD-ROM drive lets you read, write, and store information onto a CD, just as you would with a floppy or hard drive. However, these are write-once disks, which means that once you save information to them you cannot add to or delete it.

You can find blank CD-R media for $2 to $4 per disk, making these write-once devices great for home use, for students, and for small businesses. CD-RW drives (CD-rewritable) are more expensive, but they let you use and re-use CD-RW discs.

The Ricoh MediaMaster external CD-RW drive comes in either a PC version using a parallel port, or a SCSI version for Mac/PC. Check AOL's Hardware Shop for these and other CD-ROM drives.

and encyclopedias, a faster speed will prevent a jerky motion picture. CD-ROM speeds range from Single (1X, 150 Kbps) to Double (2X, 300 Kbps), Triple (3X, 450 Kbps), Quad (4X, 600 Kbps), Six (6X, 900 Kbps), Eight (8X, 1,200 Kbps), Sixteen (16X, 2,400 Kbps), and Twenty-four (24X, 3,000 Kbps). The 16X and 24X speed drives should be available through AOL's Hardware Shop by the time you read this.

At the PC Hardware Forum (keyword: **PC Hardware** or **PHW**), you'll find information on CD-ROM speed and models.

I bought a previously owned Compaq Presario 633 computer. How can I tell the speed of its CD-ROM drive?

Check your computer's manual or pay a visit to Compaq's AOL area (Keyword: **Compaq**). From there, you can easily get to the company's Web site, if necessary. You'll find product information, specifications, and technical support contacts with phone numbers.

I know I can find encyclopedias on CD-ROM. But are there any other applications?

There are all kinds of CD-ROM applications, including music, voice, large animation and video libraries, photographs, clip art, and encyclopedias. Take a look at the CD-ROMs available through the AOL Store's Software Shop (keyword: **Software Shop**).

Here's a sampling of some of the CD-ROMs we found in specific areas in the Software Shop:

- Games—Brain Food Games CD-ROM

- Entertainment—*I Love Lucy* Entertainment Utility CD-ROM

- Kids Only—Barbie Fashion Designer CD-ROM

- Special Interest—*Consumer Reports* Cars CD-ROM

- Home & Health—*Better Homes and Gardens* Decorating Your Home CD-ROM.

- Reference & Education—Resume Pro CD-ROM

- Sports—NBA '98 CD-ROM

There are many entertainment and educational CD-ROM titles available. Most are interactive, which means you can move through topics stored on the disc at your own pace, relate with characters and information, and find topics you want to explore in a matter of seconds.

AOL has its own line of CD-ROMs created expressly for members. Find these CDs in the CD Club area at the AOL Store's Software Shop (keyword: **Software Shop**).

What are multimedia CD-ROMs?

Multimedia CD-ROMs use everything from text to sound to animation as a way to communicate information. Most are interactive and allow users to choose their own paths through the information and what they see onscreen. There are multimedia presentations, adventure games, and educational tools—all of which can be purchased through the Software Shop.

DVD-ROM DRIVE

A DVD-ROM, or Digital Video Disc-ROM drive, is the gold standard of data archiving. It is basically a CD-ROM drive that can read very high storage capacity discs. A DVD-ROM disc can hold a minimum of 4.7GB, or 4.7 billion characters, which is equivalent to more than six regular CD-ROM discs. For example, a DVD-ROM disc can store a two-hour, full-screen movie—and has better quality than a VHS tape. And DVD-ROM drives can read CD-ROM discs. Eventually DVD will replace CDs, CD-R, and magnetic tape because it's bigger, cheaper, and faster.

To get more information on CD-R and DVD-ROM drives, visit the AOL Computing channel's Webopedia (keyword: **Webopedia**). For definitions of CD-ROM technical terms see this book's Glossary.

161

There are multimedia CD-ROM versions of every type of reference resource, including dictionaries, encyclopedias, maps, and magazine articles. Reference titles on CD-ROM can be found in the Special Interest, Home & Health, and Reference & Education areas in the AOL Store's Software Shop. When we visited Special Interest, we found the following titles:

- I Can Do Magic

- Invention Studio

- Multimedia IQ Test

- Popular Photography

Examples of Home & Health reference titles are Health Advantage, Family Album, and FloorPlan Plus 3-D.

Education titles are available in the Reference & Education area of the AOL Store's Software Shop. We found we could learn a new language with Berlitz Spanish or Self-Study Spanish for Windows 95, and go exploring with IBM's Worldbook Discoveries.

There are likely to be multimedia games for everyone. For action lovers there's Jedi Knight, and for sports and gaming fans there's Bradshaw Football '98 or casino gambling. Multimedia game CD-ROMs are available in the Games area in the AOL Store's Software Shop. For more information on CD-ROM games, visit the AOL PC Games Forum (keyword: **PC Games**).

Entertainment CD-ROMs, such as Titanic: Adventure out of Time, *BillBoard Magazine*/Blockbuster Movies CD-ROM Set, and The Best of Saturday Night Live Triple Pack, may be found in the Entertainment area of the AOL Store's Software Shop.

And here are some examples of multimedia CD-ROM titles we found in the Kids Only section of the Software Shop.

- Curious George Adventure

- Elmo's Preschool CD-ROM

- Crayola Magic 3D Coloring Book

- Lego Island

Some CDs contain time-sensitive information that will become outdated, such as telephone numbers. If you need the most current information, you can request updated CDs from the manufacturer. With some time-sensitive titles, you can access updates on the Internet.

MMX Chips

An MMX (Multimedia Extended) chip is a processor that is designed to take advantage of the more sophisticated multimedia software and hardware features available today. MMX chips can be purchased through the AOL Store's Hardware Shop under Memory and CPUs.

The PC Hardware Forum (keyword: **PC Hardware** or **PHW**) offers information on MMX chips. Find out more about these chips from other AOL members at the Hardware Forum message boards.

What is the difference between a Pentium Pro 200 and an MMX chip?

A Pentium Pro processor is designed for pure number crunching and raw computing power, such as fileservers and accounting systems. An MMX chip will give you better performance when you play games, run multimedia presentations, and record and play sounds on your computer.

Will an MMX microprocessor chip run all my multimedia applications?

An MMX chip will effectively run your multimedia applications—graphics, audio, and video—providing they are MMX enabled.

Digital Imaging

If you dislike waiting for your film to be developed, and get annoyed when your photos don't turn out well, you may want to consider a digital camera. Digital cameras save photos directly on disk, so you can immediately see the results on your computer.

Digital cameras use computer technology to store images as computer files. You shoot pictures with a digital camera the same way you do with a 35mm camera, but you don't need film. The digital camera views and records images, saving them in the camera's built-in memory, which ranges from 2MB to 4MB. And many models of digital cameras have a screen on the camera which displays the photos you take. If you don't like the picture, you can press a button to erase it.

Some models take up to 192 photos without requiring you to download the pictures to your computer. You can buy an additional memory card that plugs into the digital camera and stores the images on the card.

How do I get the digital images into my computer? And is there a way to delete unwanted photos?

Typically, you transfer or download images from the camera to your computer by connecting a cable to the computer's serial port. A digital camera comes with special software that lets you move all or selected images to your computer. Digital cameras with a built-in viewer and/or LCD display let you delete images you don't want on the fly. This frees up memory so you can continue to take pictures without having to download the images to the computer.

What can I do with digital pictures?

You can save, change, and share your picture files on disks, CD-ROMs, or over the Internet. You can even include pictures in your AOL 4.0 e-mails. Use the camera icon on the Write Mail toolbar to attach the picture file to the AOL e-mail message.

What kind of digital camera should I buy?

When digital cameras first came out a couple of years ago, they were selling for $1,000 to $2,000. Now you can get a good digital camera such as the Casio QV-700 for under $400 and an entry-level one for less than $200. Today's digital cameras offer more memory, higher image quality, and improved resolution. Learn about the most current digital camera offerings in the New Product News & PC Vendors Database at the PC Hardware Forum (keyword: **PC Hardware** or **PHW**). Through the AOL Store's Book Shop, you can purchase AOL's own guide to digital imaging entitled *You've Got Pictures*.

Digital cameras, from such manufacturers as Casio, Kodak, Vivitar, Umax, Ricoh, Minolta, and Olympus, are available at the new Digital Shop at the AOL Store (keyword: **Digital Shop**), shown in figure 4.10. At the Digital Shop you can buy digital imaging software, scanners, printers, multimedia equipment, storage devices, and books. At the Cameras & Video Hardware area you can buy digital cameras and digital imaging hardware for your computer.

Learn more about digital images and pictures in the Pictures area (keyword: **Pictures**). You'll get information on digital cameras, scanners, and graphics formats. And you'll learn how to edit images, build your own Web page, and share images via e-mail. Follow the link to the Barnes & Noble site, where you can purchase books on digital imaging. Through the AOL Store's Book Shop, you can purchase AOL's own guide to digital imaging, entitled *You've Got Pictures*.

The AOL service offers an online class on Digital Cameras (see figure 4.11). Download and read the class transcript at keyword: **Online Classroom**. The class transcript contains the lecture given in the class and any dialogue between the teacher and the students, such as questions and answers.

How do the resolution settings on a digital camera affect an image?

FIGURE 4.10

The AOL Store's Digital Shop

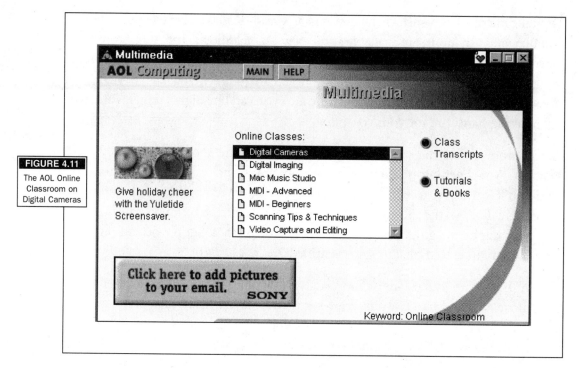

FIGURE 4.11

The AOL Online Classroom on Digital Cameras

166

The resolution settings on a digital camera determine the quality of the image. You choose a resolution setting based on what you want to do with the final images. Cameras usually have two or more settings. The higher the resolution of the image, the larger the file size. Larger files take up more camera and card memory. The lower the resolution of the image, the smaller the file size. By using lower resolution settings, you can store more images in your camera (and computer!).

What resolution setting should I use for photos to be displayed on a monitor or used in a greeting card?

A good quality photo for display on a monitor or use in a greeting card should be about 100K. At the next higher resolution setting, the photo is 500K in size. You can store approximately 12 photos before you have to download them to your computer.

What is the resolution setting for images I would print on a color printer?

If you want to print your photos on a color laser printer, a color photo printer, or a "photo-realistic" printer (ranging from $300 to $500), look for a digital camera that has at least 640 x 480 resolution. Usually, digital cameras with lower resolution that produce prints on a color ink-jet printer or a specially designed photo printer make poor quality prints. But the technology is constantly evolving and improving.

What is the resolution setting for images I want to develop at a photo lab?

If you prefer to have your digital camera images developed at a photo lab, then save the image to a floppy, a Zip disk, or a CD-R (CD-recordable) disc. By setting the resolution on your camera to 640 x 480, you'll get close to the quality of 35mm camera prints. If your digital camera offers 1000 x 786 to 1280 x 960 settings, you can get images that are virtually the same as 35mm camera prints. But be sure to stick to the 4 x 6-inch print size. If you want a larger print you'll need a high-end professional digital camera that offers 2400 x 1200 and 2400 x 3600 resolution.

As we've mentioned, the AOL Buyer's Guide (keyword: **Buyer's Guide**) offers advice and reviews on digital cameras. The AOL Store's Digital Shop (keyword: **Digital Shop**) has specs on digital cameras and digital imaging equipment, and sells a wide variety (see figure 4.12 below).

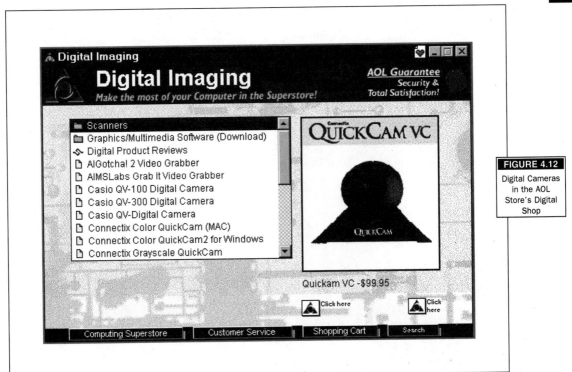

FIGURE 4.12

Digital Cameras in the AOL Store's Digital Shop

5

MAINTAINING AND REPAIRING YOUR PC

Computers will work fine with no attention for years, then they'll go on the fritz for no apparent reason. And it's usually at the most inconvenient time.

This chapter shows you how to keep your PC running smoothly, how to fix it when certain types of breakdowns occur, and where to get plenty of support and assistance. Some preventive maintenance can help you avoid certain kinds of problems, and it will also help retain whatever resale value your system has.

A good working environment is crucial to the health and life of your computer and peripherals. A clean, temperature-controlled atmosphere, and a location free from unnecessary bumps and vibration, with clean, stable power flowing to the system, works wonders.

The enemies of your computer are dust, dirt, liquids, cigarette smoke, magnetism, excessive heat, uneven power, and most of all, static electricity. Keep things clean, dry, and cool; don't smoke around your computer or allow others to do so; and don't let magnets near your computer case. Plug your components into a surge protector, and before you touch anything inside your computer's metal case, be sure to touch the case itself to discharge any static electricity you might be carrying (and, of course, to unplug the computer). If you do all that, any computer headaches you have are likely to be related to software rather than hardware.

Keeping Hardware and Software in Working Order

It's quite possible to open up your computer and look inside, and even remove and install new parts. All you need is moderate dexterity and the right screwdriver. Be sure you don't use one with a magnetized head—it could wreak havoc with your hard drive. It's also possible to take apart your mouse and even your keyboard. You'll be opening up certain parts of your printer to clear paper jams and replace ink cartridges. Even computer novices can handle these chores, which are akin to filling your car with washer fluid and checking the oil.

Some components, like your monitor, should never be opened. They generally come with stern warnings on the case to the effect that opening it will void the warranty. Pay attention to these warnings and you'll be fine.

If any of the terms used in this chapter are new or unfamiliar, you'll find their definitions in this book's glossary.

No one ever lifts a finger to maintain the computers at my office and they seem to run fine almost all the time. Does my home computer need any routine maintenance?

Today's computers are pretty hardy. However, you can help keep your computer in good shape by cleaning off dust and dirt from time to time. The interval will vary depending on how dirty your surroundings are. Perhaps your office computer is in a hermetically sealed building with an up-to-date ventilation system and a steady temperature—a good situation for a computer, and one most people can't match at home.

You'll need the following items to clean the outside surfaces:

- Cleaning solutions

- Soft, lint-free rags, brushes, tweezers, foam swabs, toothpicks

- A small vacuum cleaner with nozzles designed for computer cleaning

- A can of compressed air

Most computer stores, such as the AOL Computing Superstore (keyword: **CSS**) have these and other tools. Buy tools and materials that are specifically designed for use on computers. Cleaning solutions should be mild, contain no abrasives or harmful chemicals, and dry easily. Rags or brushes should not leave lint residue or cause scratches. Any small vacuum cleaner is fine. Just make sure the attachments fit the crevices you are trying to clean and won't zap your system with static electricity buildup.

Each peripheral should come with basic cleaning instructions, so read your manuals before starting. You should be able to use the following procedures with good results.

First, check for viruses and then back up all your critical files. Next, shut down the computer and disconnect the power from the wall. Examine the outlet for evidence of shorts or damage.

Next, disconnect each cable (remembering where and how it was connected, of course), dust it and clean it, and inspect it for shorts, kinks, frays, and broken or loose connectors. If you see any problems, replace the cable. While you're at it, make sure the cables are not wrapped around each other, knotted, or protruding into a traffic area. Consider getting a cable management device if necessary.

When all the cables are clean and properly arranged, use the cleaning solution, rags, and brushes to clean every exterior surface of the computer and peripherals. Apply the solution to the rag or brush, not the computer itself. Don't let anything get saturated, and don't allow the solution to run inside the system.

Before you clean each component, disconnect it from the system, and make sure the component and its connectors are completely dry before reattaching it. Use extra caution when cleaning the monitor screen or any display portion of your devices (such as the LCD screen on your printer or laptop) to ensure you don't cause scratches or streaks.

Clean the dust from any exterior surface or cooling vent with rags, swabs, and tooth-picks. Examine your system for damage, overheating, and unusual contamination as you go. (The kids won't always tell you when they spill their sodas on your system.)

Finally, make sure everything is clean and dry, there's no grit, lint, or other cleaning residue left, and everything is plugged back in the way it was when you started. Turn on your system and check it out. If anything doesn't work, recheck your cables first, then try it again. Cleaning the outside of your system is routine and shouldn't harm it. But there's always that possibility, which is why the first step is to make a thorough backup of all your critical files.

Post a question on the AOL Hardware/OS Forum (keyword: **Hardware**) to find out how other AOL members clean and maintain their PCs. Check out AOL Computing Tips (keyword: **Computing Tips**) for cleaning tips and hints.

I can see crumbs, hair, and dust between the keys in my keyboard. It doesn't seem to be affecting the performance any, but I'd like to get rid of it. How do I do that?

You can probably dislodge quite a bit of it with a small clean paintbrush, like the kind used with watercolors. If that doesn't work, disconnect the keyboard from the computer. Turn it over and shake it gently, or tap it lightly on the back. Then vacuum it with a small vacuum cleaner designed for computer use, or squirt the crevices with compressed air. That should get most of the debris out.

While you're at it, you can also clean finger grime off the key caps. Moisten a lint-free rag with a little cleaning solution (water will also work, though not as well) and clean each key individually.

I spilled coffee all over my keyboard, and now everything is stuck. Help!

When your keyboard sustains this type of disaster, it's theoretically possible to clean it but probably not worth the trouble. Keyboards are relatively inexpensive—a new one will set you back only $20 to $80.

How do I clean my monitor screen?

Spray some window cleaner or cleaning solution on a lint-free rag or paper towel and wipe the screen. Never spray anything directly on to the screen, and don't let any liquid run to the edge.

What about cleaning the inside of my computer? Do I need to do that? And if so, how?

Hard-core techies with a finicky streak are probably the only ones who would bother unhooking all their cables and opening up their computers just to clean them. Most people don't, and their computers become obsolete before they get dirty enough inside to worry about, especially if they're kept in a relatively dust-free environment.

But say you're opening up your computer anyway, to install more RAM or a new sound card. Or perhaps you've had work done on your house that has spread construction dust into every crevice, and you're worried (legitimately) that your computer could sustain damage from excessive dust inside. Here's the general procedure, which applies only to cleaning inside your computer's case. For the most part, your other components (monitor, printer, modem, hard drive, floppy drive) aren't made to be opened up, except by the manufacturer or a certified technician.

In addition to the tools you assembled to clean the outside of your computer, you should have:

- An inexpensive toolkit for computer work

- A grounding strap

- A flashlight

Again, you can buy these items at a good computer store such as the AOL Store's Hardware Shop (keyword: **Hardware Center**), and you should make sure they are designed to be used on computers. The toolkit shouldn't cost more than $50, and should include several screwdriver bits, tweezers, a tool for removing chips, and perhaps a container for small screws, nuts, and bolts.

As with cleaning the outside of the case, the first step is to check for viruses and then back up all your critical files. Next, attach the grounding strap to yourself and make sure you're grounded. Then, turn everything off and unplug the power cords.

If you are very familiar with the cords and connectors entering the case, unplug them and lay them aside. If not, mark the ones you think you might forget, to make sure you can correctly plug them in again. Place your computer case upright on a clean work surface and remove the screws holding the cover to the case. Put the screws in a safe place. Clean and dust the inside of the cover, paying particular attention to the vents.

Vacuum the insides of the computer to remove accumulated dust and dirt. For hard-to-reach places, blow some compressed air in, but be careful not to drive dirt even deeper into the crevices. Don't touch anything.

When you've got the interior of the system clean, use the flashlight to inspect all the components individually. Look for evidence of breakage, corrosion, or leakage (some components may exude their contents slowly). Check for twisted, burnt, or broken wiring, or other signs of damage or decay. Any symptoms of this sort are a major, irrevocable system crash waiting to happen, and your machine should be checked by a professional technician.

I'm having trouble with some of my CD-ROM disks, but others seem fine. What's the problem?

There's only a tiny space between the surface of the CD-ROM and the drive head—so tiny that a speck of dust or a finger smudge can mess things up. Try cleaning the problem discs with a soft lint-free cloth, like the ones used to clean camera lenses. Move from the inside edge to the outside. If they're still dirty, you can clean them either with a cleaning solution for tape recorder heads, or with the fluid used to clean audio CDs. These are available at most music stores and at the electronic departments of department and discount stores.

And always handle your CDs by the edges—never put your fingers on the unprinted surface, or let the CD rest on that surface. Keep them in their cases or in a protective sleeve when you're not using them.

Check out the message boards at the AOL Hardware/OS Forum (keyword: **Hardware**) and the PC Music & Sound Forum (keyword: **PC Music**) for more information on cleaning your CD-ROM drive.

Does my printer ever need cleaning? I don't use it that much.

Actually, your printer can get just as dirty whether you use it every day or once a month, though using a dust cover will help keep it cleaner during lengthy periods of idleness. If you have an ink-jet printer, the print cartridge can dry out or become clogged. Paper lint can accumulate in any printer.

Keep the outside of your printer as free of dust as possible, and follow the manufacturer's directions for cleaning the print head of ink-jet printers. (Some allow you to clean the print heads using a series of commands from within the printer's operating software; others use buttons on the printer itself.)

The routine for maintaining a printer varies so much from model to model that it's best to refer to your owner's manual for specifics. If you don't have the owner's manual, the manufacturer's Web site may have directions.

If you find you need serious cleaning or repair work done, see a professional. You can void your warranty by doing too much, and it can be dangerous to poke around in some printers. (The toner may be toxic if inhaled.)

If you own a bubble-jet or ink-jet printer, you can extend the life of your print head and ink cartridges by always turning off your printer before turning off your computer. This allows the printer to perform its power-down operation, which "caps off" the print heads and ink cartridges, like putting the top on a pen.

To get more information on cleaning your particular model printer, post a message or look through the messages on the message boards at the AOL Hardware/OS Forum (keyword: **Hardware**). You'll find out how other AOL members clean and maintain their printers.

Sometimes my pointer arrow seems to get stuck or move erratically, and I have to roll the mouse around a lot to get the pointer to move again. The arrow keys seem to work just fine, so I think it's something to do with the mouse itself. Any suggestions?

Your mouse is probably dirty. Turn your mouse over and unscrew the little plate that holds the ball in. You can do this with your fingers. (It's best to do it over a desk or table, so that if you drop the ball you have a better chance to get it back before it rolls under something.)

Wipe the grime off the ball with a cloth dampened with either water or a cleaning solution designed for computer components. Now look inside the cavity where the ball rests. You should see two or three rollers that probably also have dust, crud, or fibers on them. You can clean the rollers with a toothpick or tweezers. You can also wipe them off with a foam-tipped swab. Don't use a regular cotton swab—they can leave a trail of lint.

Now wipe your mousepad off with the cloth. Reassemble your mouse and see if the problem is gone. If not, check with the manufacturer in the AOL Computing

Companies area (keyword: **Companies**) or post a query on the message boards at the AOL Hardware/OS Forum (keyword: **Hardware**).

I've heard my computer will last longer if I leave it on all the time. Is this true?

Electrical components, particularly motors, draw a great deal of electricity during start–up. This surge of power can shorten the life of many components in your system. The less you turn your system on and off, the longer these components should last. But don't worry too much—computers are designed to cope with start–up power surges.

Turning on your system also changes the inside temperature substantially. If your system has been off all night or all weekend, it's probably pretty cool inside. When you turn it on, the temperature inside rises to normal operating temperature, maybe 50 to 75 degrees higher than room temperature. Thermal stresses can cause chips to loosen, circuit boards to develop tiny cracks, and contacts to corrode.

Computers run best when the temperature is between 60 and 90 degrees Fahrenheit. A good rule is to maintain the room's temperature so that it's comfortable to you. Stability is the key, so try to avoid large, rapid temperature swings. While you're at it, don't expose your system to direct sunlight, and keep it away from open windows to prevent extra dust from building up.

Should you leave your system on all the time? The experts say no. A running computer and monitor pose a small but real fire hazard (just like any small appliance), and you shouldn't leave them on unattended. Turn your system on once in the morning and give it a few minutes to come up to operating temperature before use. Leave it on unless you're out of your work area, then turn it off before you leave for the evening. At home, turn your computer on when you start work, and don't turn it off until you finish for the day, unless you leave the house.

I've heard I shouldn't use my computer during a thunderstorm. Is that true?

Lightning can strike your power lines and the jolt can travel through your computer (or any other appliance) to you. It's not the most likely event, but why take chances? The National Lightning Safety Institute says 38 percent of lightning deaths occur inside buildings, when people are in contact with telephones, appliances, water faucets, and bathtubs.

To be on the safe side, you should unplug your computer during an electrical storm. Its delicate insides could be fried by a lightning-related power surge, even if it's not turned on. This probably won't happen, but it's possible, and when it does happen, it's ugly.

What about power? Is what comes out of the wall OK? Do I need a grounded plug, or can I use one of those adapters that you attach to the wall outlet?

Use a grounded plug. Have an electrician install one if there isn't one handy to your work space. If your computer, printer, monitor, and other equipment aren't properly grounded, they can be permanently damaged by electrical interference, and the adapters aren't hardy enough to do a reliable job.

The power coming out of your wall is much "dirtier" than you might imagine. Even though newer computers are designed to compensate for dirty power, maintaining a clean and safe power supply will extend your computer's life and help prevent nasty surprises.

The two major categories of power problems are surges and undervoltage conditions (too much power and too little power). Surges, because they are caused by too much power in a short time, can fry your system and even cause fires. You should have surge protectors for both your electrical outlet and your phone line. You can get a surge protector that's built in to the power strip where you plug in your components, or incorporated into an uninterruptible power supply (more about this below). Phone line surge protectors prevent damage to your modems, answering machines, cordless phones, and other communications equipment.

How do uninterruptible power supplies work?

An uninterruptible power supply (UPS) can help with the three basic undervoltage conditions: blackouts, which are the complete absence of power; brownouts, which are a temporary reduction of power long enough for you to notice; and dips and sags, which are intermittent reductions of power too brief for you to notice, although your computer does. Undervoltage conditions such as these can cause lost data or, even worse, can scramble all your data.

Computers operating on alternating current (AC—the kind that comes out of your wall) draw power 120 times per second (the cycle rate), so the power is constantly being interrupted even in normal operation. The computer smoothes things out with a capacitor (an internal energy storage device), which is recharged each time the computer draws power, and discharged during the period when power is not being drawn (about 50 milliseconds).

When power is reduced or eliminated beyond this limit, the UPS senses the power failure and switches to battery power, giving you an opportunity to save your files. In addition, if you are in the process of writing files to your hard drive, the UPS will prevent the data from becoming scrambled across the drive by the power failure.

There are basically two types of UPS. For personal use, an inexpensive UPS (perhaps $250) will keep your system running for about 10 minutes. That's enough time to get your files backed up and Windows shut down, which is really all you need to do.

The other kind of UPS is for mission-critical operations (a network server, for instance) that can't go down or stay down for any extended period of time. These are much more expensive and will keep a system running for hours. Some come with special connections and software to alert the system operator remotely when power to the system is compromised.

Employing a UPS and a surge protector—preferably as a combined unit—ensures the power environment will be optimum at all times. Some UPS makers offer damage coverage. American Power Conversions (a major UPS maker) offers up to $25,000 damage reimbursement if its unit fails to protect your equipment during a surge or blackout.

Keep in mind that because the UPS contains a battery, it will eventually fail (just like the battery in your car), so checking it regularly should become part of your long-term preventive maintenance plan. The documentation that comes with your UPS will explain how to do this.

Visit the AOL Store's Hardware Shop and look through the AOL Computing Classifieds for products from American Power Conversions and other manufacturers of uninterruptible power supplies.

I've heard that you should back up your data regularly, but I have trouble keeping track of what I need to back up, and I end up not doing it. Is there an easy routine that I could do, say, weekly? And what about data that changes every day, like my incoming e-mail?

Backing up files is a tiresome process, and it's easy to forget to do it. But if you've ever lost a hard drive, or know someone who has, you know why regular backups are so important. Considering the hourly rate most people charge for information-type work, you can easily build enough data on your computer in a week to exceed the cost of a new system. Losing that data is just like losing thousands of dollars.

Backups are meant to help you out in emergency situations. That means if your hard drive ever fails unexpectedly, you'll have to buy and install a new one and then restore everything that was on the old drive. At the very least, you'll have to reload your operating system and the backup unit's software before you can restore the rest of your files. Plan on spending a few hundred dollars and a few hours getting ready for recovery no matter which backup method you employ. And make sure you know exactly where your operating system and backup unit disks are, and how to reinstall them.

Many people can simply reinstall their application's software, rather than restore from a backup copy (assuming they have all the original installation disks and documentation in one place, as they should). This might not be appropriate for you, particularly if you've got lots of customized user settings in your applications.

Incorporate a backup routine into your daily habits. It's a pain the first few times, and you'll probably forget at least once or twice, but keep at it. Soon you'll do it without even thinking about it. And if anything nasty ever happens, you'll be glad you backed up.

It's much easier to keep track of what you need to back up if you store all your data files in one directory. If that's not feasible, keep it to two or three directories, rather than scatter files all over the place. In particular, never store data files in the same directories that hold your software. Then back up those data directories, and only those, every day.

Make sure that your software hasn't automatically put some essential data, such as your e-mail folder, calendar, or address book, somewhere other than your data directories. If that has happened, either move them to your data directories (the simplest option) or remember to back them up separately (if moving them confuses your software, as sometimes happens). If necessary, keep a Post-it note on your computer with a list of what you need to back up.

As to which backup medium to use, that's a personal choice. A Zip drive or Jaz drive operates just like any other drive on your system, just a little slower than your hard drive. Backups using these devices are quick and painless. If you want to get a good deal on a Zip drive or Jaz drive, visit the AOL Store's Hardware Shop and the AOL Computing Classifieds.

If you need to back up everything on your drive, and you want it done automatically at a certain time each day, check out tape backup units. They are inexpensive and hold vast quantities of data, and you can set up the software to perform unattended backups of specific files and directories at the time of your choice. They tend to be a little slower than disk–type media, however, and finding and retrieving specific files tends to be just a bit more difficult, although they have significantly improved.

Windows 95 comes with a program called Microsoft Backup that helps with the backup process. The program isn't automatically installed, but you can install it by choosing Settings from the Start menu, choosing Control Panel, double-clicking on the Add/Remove Programs icon, clicking on the Windows Setup tab, and checking the Disk Tools box. You should then receive installation instructions.

Microsoft Backup will keep track of the files you've already backed up, and will do what's called an "incremental backup" of only the material that's changed since the last time. This saves a lot of time and disk space. Go to the AOL Windows Forum (keyword: **WIN**) to get more information on Microsoft Backup.

If you don't use Windows 95, software is available from other vendors, that does the same thing for other operating systems. Check the AOL Store's Software Shop for good deals on backup software.

What's the best way to protect my system against computer viruses? Do I need to run my anti-virus program every time I work on my system? And how does the program keep up with new viruses?

Virus-checking software is a must for any PC. If you're lucky, your system came bundled with a virus checker—the best-known ones are Norton Anti-Virus, sold by Symantec, and VirusScan, from McAfee Associates (now owned by Network Associates). If you didn't get a virus checker with your system, a number of good ones can be purchased from the AOL Store's Software Shop. Prices range from $30 to $70, depending on manufacturer, format, and frills.

You can set a good virus checker to operate continuously or only when you activate it. Continuous operation is safest if you can afford the overhead. The processor and the RAM must be capable of performing all your normal work and running the virus checker as well, and you'll know pretty quickly if continuous operation is overtaxing your resources. Otherwise, when you set your anti-virus program to search files at startup, remember that the more comprehensive the search, the longer it takes.

If you're not running your virus checker continuously, it's a good idea set it to run on start-up. Also, run it whenever you receive data or programs from any outside source: files attached to e-mail, downloaded software (don't even download attatchments or software from strangers), shrink-wrapped software that you've installed (yes, it can be infected, too), or data files that you've brought home from the office on a floppy or Zip cartridge. Be careful about e-mail attachments or software from strangers. If you're just working in your local word processing program or spreadsheet, and not communicating with outside computers in any form, you should be safe from new infections.

Whatever virus checker you choose should come with either a certain number of free updates or a very low-cost yearly subscription for regular updates, or both. Updates can generally be downloaded from the vendor's Web site, and some vendors send them automatically. For more information, check the AOL PC Virus Information Center (keyword: **VIRUS**) and the vendors' Web sites by using AOL NetFind (keyword: **NetFind**) or the AOL Computing Companies area (keyword: **Companies**).

How can I find information about current viruses?

The AOL service maintains the PC Virus Information Center (keyword: **VIRUS**), specifically to help members deal with common (and not so common) virus problems. You'll find everything you ever wanted to know about viruses, including what they are and how they work, what they can and can't do, what kinds there are, how they infect your system, and how to avoid them.

There are also message boards, software, and the latest information about how to rid your machine of viruses and repair the damage they cause. Don't miss the Top Virus Questions and Answers (shown in figure 5.1) where you'll find all the most frequently asked questions about viruses—and their answers.

Here's a sampler of what's available at the AOL PC Virus Information Center:

- Message Boards—Post a message to other users like yourself, if you have questions about a particular virus, or symptoms that you think point to a virus on your system. If you've survived a virus, you can help others by bringing your experiences into the forum.

- Software—Download virus protection or anti-virus utilities, many for free.

- References—Find everything you ever wanted to know about computer viruses, but were afraid to ask.

- Virus Companies—Get updates and support direct from the companies that make virus protection software.

- Shop for Protection—Find great deals on virus protection programs.

A friend of mine says I should get something called Norton Utilities to keep my hard disk in order and save my life when I lose data. What is she talking about? Is she right?

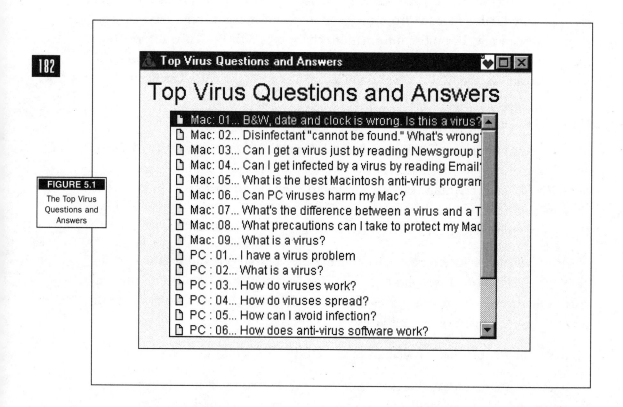

FIGURE 5.1

The Top Virus Questions and Answers

Disk utilities can work miracles when you're in a tight spot—a system crash has wiped out some of your files, or you've inadvertently deleted something you needed. They can frequently restore erased files, especially if you invoke them very soon after the erasure, and can fix various kinds of hard disk problems. You can also use them to create a diskette containing everything you need to recover from a failure or disaster, including boot sector information (without which your computer will not start up), operating system files, and small versions of essential utility programs.

Norton Utilities, sold by Symantec, is a very good program, and is by far the most popular utility package for Windows machines. At this writing, it costs less than $100. It includes a disk defragmenter as well, though as mentioned elsewhere, there's also one built in to Windows 95. The Windows 95 ScanDisk program performs some of the same functions as the Disk Doctor program in Norton Utilities, but doesn't have the same file-rescue skills. For additional information, check the PC Windows Forum on the AOL service (keyword: **WIN**). Visit the AOL Store's Software Shop to buy utility software for Windows.

My disk drive is acting up. I can't seem to get diskettes to read properly. What's going on?

The first thing to check whenever a disk drive acts up is the disk itself. Disk drives are real workhorses, and once they are installed and working properly, they usually last a long time.

Try reading a few diskettes that you know are OK. Write-protect them first, so that the drive can't erase anything. (To do this, slide the small plastic tab in the upper right-hand corner up so that you can see through the notch.) If all your floppies are exhibiting similar problems, then the problem is probably with the drive.

A problem with the drive itself, or with related hardware, may mean a trip to the shop. A bad cable or a dirty disk-change sensor can prevent your drive from recognizing when you've pulled one floppy out and replaced it with another. This could potentially erase the contents of the second disk. The solution is to clean the disk-change sensor or replace the cable. But these are technical solutions that should be performed by a qualified technician.

For more help, check the Hardware/OS Forum (keyword: **Hardware**), the Computing Help Desk (keyword: **Help Desk**), and Computing Tips (keyword: **Computing Tips**) on AOL. If you want to purchase a disk drive, check out the prices at the AOL's Hardware Shop and the Computing Classifieds (keyword: **Classifieds**).

I'm borrowing my brother's printer, and he says I'll need to download the latest version of the driver. How do I do this, and what do I do with the driver once I have it?

The PC Hardware Forum (keyword: **PC Hardware** or **PHW**) is where you'll find a Web site for downloading drivers. Look in the Recommended Utilities folder. The driver file libraries have a broad selection of hardware-type files and updated drivers for most of the common operating systems.

You can download whatever you've found—not just drivers, but shareware and freeware (any freely distributable files). Drivers generally come with installation instructions. The PC Windows Forum staff will try to answer any questions you might have on a particular file or driver.

Detecting and Diagnosing Problems

Before you can accurately diagnose a problem with your system, you must have good documentation on all your components and you must refer to it. You might be able to temporarily fix a problem without knowing what was wrong or how you fixed it, but sooner or later that method will come back to haunt you. Knowing what you're doing, why you're doing it, and what component you're doing it to will give you tremendous insight into your system and confidence in your repairs.

Whenever you buy a new system, you should make sure you have the documentation for each component, not just the system as a whole. The sound card, CD-ROM drive, hard drive, monitor, modem, and printer should have individual manuals, and each manual should contain important information about configuration and troubleshooting. Store these manuals in a safe but easily accessible place near your computer. If you bought your system second hand, the previous owner may not have passed along the manuals. If that's the case, you'll have to get documentation from secondary sources, such as the manufacturers.

How do I know the manufacturer's name for a particular component, and how do I find the documentation if it didn't come with my computer?

You can find clues by opening up your computer. Usually, the name is printed on the component's case, or the chips in a circuit board. While you're writing down names, keep your eye out for model numbers or other identifying information on the components.

If you can't find a name on a given part, you'll have to find someone who really knows their parts to identify it for you. (Local computer shops can sometimes help with this.) The computer's maker might also be able to tell you something about its sources for the components.

The AOL Computing channel has a Companies department (keyword: **Companies**). The Internet is the best place to start looking for documentation. The vast majority of component and system manufacturers have Web sites, and many of them use the company name as their domain name. Try typing the name of the company into your Web browser, in the format www.name of company.com. If that doesn't work, go to AOL NetFind (keyword: **NetFind**) and type the name.

Once you find the Web site of the company, look for the Technical Support or User Support pages. When you've found the right page, bookmark it in case you need to find it again later. Get the technical specs, the performance characteristics, diagrams, jumper lists, user manual, and any drivers available. It's often helpful to print the pages out while you're at the site.

185

User manuals are occasionally offered in a file format called PDF. If you run into one of these, download both the file and a free piece of software, called Adobe Acrobat Reader, for reading and printing it. Web sites that offer PDF files frequently have a hyperlink to the Acrobat Reader download page, but if there isn't one, visit Adobe's home page (www.adobe.com), where you'll find clear directions to the download page.

OK, I've identified all my components and I've got the documentation. How do I figure out what's causing a problem and how to fix it?

Diagnosing a problem with your computer system is called troubleshooting. Two words describe the basic premise of troubleshooting: isolate and eliminate. First, isolate the possible causes of the trouble, and then eliminate them one by one until you are left with only the actual cause. There are three steps:

- Detection—Noticing a problem, preferably before it becomes a major problem

- Diagnosis—Determining the cause

- Resolution—Performing maintenance or making a repair

Computer problems can occur at any point in your system's life cycle, from initial installation, to regular use, to upgrades, to the eventual failure of components from old age. They occur in software and hardware, and they can masquerade as benign glitches while slowly destroying your system. Early detection of a minor problem is your first defense against major problems down the road.

With normal use, you'll find you can detect some problems easily while others can go undetected for months. Failure of the system to power on or boot up, or failure of any frequently used peripheral, is something you'll notice right away—it's hard to ignore a blank monitor.

Less obvious signs of impending problems are unusual noises, lots of hard drive activity when you're not saving files, and the smell of wires frying. Unless a fire breaks out, this last symptom can easily be mistaken for the smell of the computer when it's warm, particularly if the smell increases very slowly over time. Performance problems, like longer boot-up times or file access times, slower response from the CPU, dimming of the image on the monitor, and just about anything else out of the ordinary can also indicate potential trouble.

For more information on detecting and diagnosing hardware problems, check the message boards at the PC Hardware Forum (keyword: **PC Hardware** or **PHW**).

Your problems won't always stem from hardware. Software programs create their own problems, either by themselves or in conflict with your operating system or other programs.

Is there an easy way to see how my computer and components are all set up?

Yes, your computer can actually show you that. If you use Windows 95 as your operating system, go to the Control Panel (under Settings) and open the System folder. You'll find the System Properties dialog box. There are four tabs in this dialog box:

- General—displays the operating system and computer type

- Device Manager—shows the devices running on your system and their properties (IRQs, DMAs, I/O, and memory)

- Hardware Profiles—enables you to set hardware profiles for running different devices in different configurations at start-up

- Performance—tells how much memory you have, the current CPU usage, and file system and virtual memory types; and offers options for reconfiguring virtual memory, graphics acceleration, and the file system

If your operating system is MS-DOS 6.0 or higher (and/or Windows 3.x but not Windows 95 or NT), it includes a program called Microsoft Diagnostics (MSD). You can access this program from the C:\ prompt (the command line) by typing MSD. This will display a screen that shows how the system is configured and how the system resources are allocated. You'll find data about:

- The Computer—BIOS, CPU, keyboard, and bus types

- Memory—conventional, extended, expanded, and upper memory blocks

- Video—adapter and display types, manufacturer and model, video BIOS

- Network, OS Version, Mouse, Game Adapter—presence and type

- Drives—letter, type, free space, and total size

- LPT Ports—address and usage data

- COM Ports—address, configuration, and usage data

- Windows Information—active files and installation dates

- IRQ Status—number, address, and usage data

- Terminate and Stay Resident (TSR) Programs—name, size, and attributes

- Device Drivers—name, device, and attributes

Running MSD or getting a system readout from Windows 95 won't actually diagnose or troubleshoot problems for you. But it can give you quite an education about your system and help you find memory conflicts, determine whether your system meets recommended performance requirements, and give you clues to problem causes.

For more on Microsoft Windows, check the message boards at the PC Windows Forum (keyword: **WIN**).

My system won't power on. What should I do?

The most likely cause of failure to power on is lack of power. Usually somebody forgot to put the plug back in the outlet, or reset the circuit breakers, or flip the switch on the power strip or surge protector, or press the power switch on the system itself.

Check all the switches and connections to make sure they're on; check the cables to make sure they're not burned out, smashed, or cut; and check the circuit breaker that serves the outlet you're using to make sure it's set.

If power is present and getting to the system but nothing happens, then your computer's power supply is probably dead and will need to be replaced, which is a job for your local computer store. If you've previously had problems, such as memory errors, inexplicable rebooting, system brownouts, or electrical shocks, it's likely that your power supply has been ailing for a while.

My system boots up just fine, but I keep getting interference on my monitor. What's making this happen?

A monitor that uses a cathode-ray tube, like those typically used with desktop computers, works by directing a stream of electrons to the screen, controlled by a magnetic field. Any other devices in the area emitting radiation in the same frequency range can generate electrical interference, so look at what's in the vicinity of your monitor.

A common source of interference is unshielded speakers. Speakers contain large magnets, and if you put them too close to the monitor they can cause distortions on the screen. Try moving your speaker system a few inches to the right or left of the screen, and remember to look for shielded speakers when you upgrade. A shielded speaker protects the monitor and other computer components from the magnetic field that generates sound.

My system powers on, and I can hear the hard drive spinning, but nothing appears on the screen. What should I do?

The most frequent cause of this problem is lack of power to the monitor. Make sure everything is properly connected and the monitor's power switch is on before doing anything else.

If the monitor is getting power and is on, but no picture appears, try adjusting the manual controls, especially if other people use your computer when you're not there. Kids sometimes play with these controls, and they may set the contrast so dark that the picture is invisible. If they don't know how to get the picture back, they might just turn it off and leave, to avoid getting in trouble. Naturally, this is a big surprise for you, but it's very easy to fix. The controls are usually located below the framing.

If that doesn't work, see if you can find another monitor to attach temporarily. If the other monitor doesn't work, it's a good bet the problem is in the video card. If it does work, the problem is probably in the monitor.

As a consumer you really aren't in a position to perform repair work to a monitor or video card. The solution is almost always to get a new monitor or video card. You might spend $100 to $200 for service (assuming the component is out of warranty), while good video cards are under $100, and good 14-inch monitors are under $200. Of course, if you have a 21-inch, $1,400 monitor, by all means take it to the shop.

My hard drive is taking longer to respond, and it sometimes makes odd grinding noises. My worst nightmare is that it will go bad and I will lose all my files and software. How can I tell if it's getting ready to fail, and what should I do about it?

Those grinding noises are not a good sign. In fact, neither is any noise that's loud enough to get your attention, such as loud whirring or chattering. Frequent disk-error messages or an inability to read or save files are also signals of impending disaster. You should back everything up immediately and double-check the location of all your original software disks and CD-ROMs. If you're using shareware or other software downloaded from the Internet, it's best to back the programs up onto a cartridge drive, unless they're small enough to fit on one diskette. Then start shopping for a new hard drive. They just give up sometimes, and the money you'd spend getting a diagnosis from a technician is generally better spent on a new drive. Visit the AOL Store's Hardware Shop for good prices on hard drives.

The only exception is if the drive is still under warranty. If that's the case, back up your data and demand a new one. Just as with cars, it's possible to get a computer component that's a lemon. Unreliable mass storage is the last thing you need.

As we've discussed in chapter 2, it's important to defragment your hard drive regularly. Not only does this process make it operate more efficiently, but it also minimizes wear and tear because the read/write heads have to make fewer seeks from track to track. See chapter 2 for instructions on defragmenting your hard drive.

My computer keeps crashing. What causes this to happen, and what can I do to prevent it?

A number of things can cause your computer to crash: bad power, bad memory, a bad CPU, not enough RAM, old programs, low system resources, poor memory management, a virus, and so on. If you've eliminated the first three, which are the mechanical possibilities, it's time to check the others one by one.

A quick way to increase RAM is to increase the virtual memory, which is a chunk of your hard disk that's allocated to hold the contents of RAM when your RAM chips aren't sufficient for all the programs and files you want to have open at once. That chunk of hard disk is also called a "swap file" because the computer keeps swapping its contents in and out of RAM. The drawback is that hard drive access is much slower than RAM access, and so program operation slows. And if your swap file is set too small, you could run out of memory entirely.

In Windows 95, you can access virtual memory settings from the System Properties dialog box in the Control Panel. The default is for the system to control memory management for you, but you can always choose to modify the settings for yourself. If you set the minimum and maximum virtual memory settings to be the same number, you will minimize the amount of time Windows 95 spends accessing the hard drive for operations related to virtual memory.

Sometimes older programs cause crashes. That's because some of the older programs (DOS or Windows 3.x) don't work all that well with memory or system resources. Well-behaved programs hand back memory and system resources to the operating system when they're through. If programs keep memory or resources locked up, even after they are terminated, eventually you will run out and the system will crash. The best way to avoid this scenario (or recover from such a crash) is to reboot the system occasionally. Make sure to save your work before you do.

Viruses are another sometimes-overlooked cause of system crashes. Viruses don't always work as their makers intended, and mysterious crashes can be an indication of a virus infection. Try running the latest version of an anti-virus program to eliminate this possibility.

Look in on the message boards at the AOL Hardware/OS Forum (keyword: **Hardware**) to find out what other AOL members have to say about problems they've experienced, and how they handled them.

MAKING AN EMERGENCY SYSTEM DISK

If your computer quits booting from the hard drive, you can sometimes gain access to your entire system again by using an emergency system disk. The emergency system disk contains files that constitute enough of an operating system to get your computer started again.

When you install Windows 95 or NT, you have the option to create an emergency system disk, as well as when you install any of the popular utility programs. You can also make a system (bootable) disk from within MS-DOS or Windows. To make an emergency system disk in Windows 95, open the Control Panel and go to Add/Remove Programs (at the Startup Disk tab). You'll need a floppy and your Windows 95 CD-ROM disc. Put your floppy in, click on Create Disk, and you'll be prompted for the CD-ROM installation disc. Follow the procedures specified, and you will have created your own start–up disk.

The emergency disk will contain:

- DRVSPACE.BIN
- COMMAND.COM
- FORMAT.COM
- SYS.COM
- FDISK.EXE
- ATTRIB.EXE
- EDIT.COM
- REGEDIT.EXE
- SCANDISK.EXE
- SCANDISK.INI
- DEBUG.EXE
- CHKDSK.EXE
- UNISTAL.EXE
- IO.SYS
- MSDOS.SYS
- EBD.SY

Label the disk and put it away in a safe place for use in case of emergency. If you need to use it, you must completely turn off your system and then power it up with the floppy inserted. Your system is designed to handle this emergency. When it boots, it always checks to see if there is a disk in the floppy drive before booting from the hard drive. If it finds a disk there, it attempts to boot from that disk. You may have seen the error message "Non-system disk" if you've ever made the mistake of leaving a floppy inserted while starting your computer.

My modem connects at 28.8K, but then suddenly drops to a lower speed, sometimes all the way down to 2400bps. Why?

Modems are designed to constantly negotiate speed to maintain a good connection, and "good" means that data can be accurately received, however slowly. If noise occurs on the line—and it can happen anywhere between you and whatever computer you're connecting to—the modem will switch to a lower speed, because lower speeds are less prone to poor communications.

Another possibility is that the phone lines are overtaxed. This doesn't happen so much within the United States, but for transatlantic calls there are comparatively few phone lines for the amount of traffic they carry. If you're trying to connect to a Web site in Europe, especially at a time when Europeans are awake and using their computers, your speed may drop.

Phone companies are upgrading phone lines all over the country, and indeed, all over the world, so the network should gradually get faster and better.

I bought a 56K modem, but I can never get a connection that fast. What do I need to do?

The 56K modems are certainly fast, but rarely will you approach 56Kbps. Your best speed will probably be around 40K to 50K most of the time, assuming you have a very good phone line connection.

Check whether you are using the right phone number to dial in. Whether you use the AOL service or some local ISP, you have to make sure you are using the appropriate number for a 56K connection speed. AOL lists the correct phone numbers to dial into in the Access area (keyword: **Access**), and most ISPs have a Web page that lists theirs. Look under technical support.

My CD-ROM drive doesn't work, but I didn't change anything. What happened?

It could be a virus. Viruses can destroy access to your CD-ROM drive by changing the boot-up process. One quick and easy way to find out is to run a built-in utility called "check disk" by typing CHKDSK at the DOS prompt. Look for the "total bytes memory" line. The value should be 655,360. If it reads something else, chances are you have a virus.

FIXING SYSTEM CRASHES—TRY THIS FIRST

System crashes require your immediate attention. They happen when something upsets the entire operating system. Frequently, the failure point is one of the drivers that controls your peripherals. Drivers communicate with hardware directly, and as such are granted a high degree of autonomy. They can penetrate the operating system's defenses relatively easily and cause a system crash. The only solution is to manually shut down the machine and restart. The operating system should notice that the machine was improperly shut down and clean up the mess, but your first step should be to try to find the offending driver and replace it.

FIXING FROZEN SCREENS—TRY THIS FIRST

If the window you are working in freezes—the mouse still moves, but the buttons don't work—your screens have frozen. This means a program has crashed. This problem is more difficult to handle in Windows 3.x than in Windows 95, and Windows 95 is less helpful than Windows NT. Programs crash when they perform illegal operations such as attempting to write to areas of memory not assigned to them. Sometimes crashes happen when the operating system runs out of resources.

For Windows 3.x, press Ctrl-Alt-Del. You'll get a blue screen that tells you if any applications are not responding. Pressing Ctrl-Alt-Del again will reset the system, but you'll lose any unsaved data. If you return to Windows you may get the opportunity to save your data, and you might even be able to continue working. Even so, after a program crashes, it's best to shut down and start over.

Windows 95 performs a similar function when you press Ctrl-Alt-Del, and NT makes it even easier to deal with frozen programs with the Task Manager feature. In both cases you can display all the running programs and shut down any of them individually. You won't get your unsaved data back, but at least the process is smooth most of the time.

Individual tracks on a hard drive sometimes fail, but fortunately MS-DOS 6.0 and above have a diagnostic and repair program designed to find and eliminate these particular problems.

You can start ScanDisk by exiting Windows and typing **scandisk** at the DOS prompt (C:\). The program will perform tests on the disk and mark any bad sectors it finds. It can also usually move data from bad areas to good areas for you. Just in case, the program allows you to create an Undo file on a floppy so you can reverse changes that make things worse.

The other likely causes of CD-ROM failure are broken cables or mechanical parts, an incorrect installation of Windows, or bad drivers. Go to the manufacturer's Web site for the correct drivers by using AOL NetFind (keyword: **NetFind**). Replace the CD-ROM if it is bad, and install Windows from the original disk if that was the problem.

You can find answers to your CD-ROM drive problems at the Hardware/OS Forum message boards (keyword: **Hardware**).

I have a 4.3GB hard drive and only about 900MB of files on it, but I get "Disk Full" error messages. Why is that?

When files are deleted in MS-DOS (the operating system that underlies Windows), their addresses are freed in the file allocation table (FAT), but the data remains on the disk until it is overwritten by some other file being saved. That's why you can use utility programs to retrieve deleted files. They examine file segments on the disk and attempt to reconstruct the old FAT and files.

Microsoft, realizing that people often want to restore files they've deleted, put a Recycle Bin function in Windows 95. Whenever you delete a file from the hard drive, it's moved to the Recycle Bin, another area on the hard drive, and stored until you empty the bin. You can retrieve it anytime simply by opening the Recycle Bin and using it. You don't even have to copy it to the original directory.

The Recycle Bin is really just a special directory on your hard drive, so every file that goes there takes up space. If you're getting "Disk Full" errors, empty the Recycle Bin and see if that helps.

Another devious hard drive filler is the cache on your Web browser. Netscape Navigator and Microsoft Internet Explorer (and other browsers) have an option setting that allows you to specify a certain amount of your hard drive to use for storing, or caching, the Web pages you visit.

You want to cache them because Web pages and graphics take quite a while to download in many cases, and you don't want to have to reload the entire page every time you visit. After you've been there once, the browser copies the page to the cache, and then the next time you go back, it just uses the same page, usually after quickly comparing it to the current version to see if anything has changed. Time is saved and you are happy, until you start running low on disk space and don't know what's going on.

For Internet Explorer, look under View, Option, Advanced to find the Temporary Internet Files settings. For Netscape Navigator 4.0 (Communicator), look in Edit, Preferences, Advanced, Cache for the settings.

IF YOU CAN'T MAKE AN ONLINE CONNECTION—TRY THIS FIRST

To make an online connection, you need a computer, a modem, a phone line, and some kind of communications software (like the AOL software). The modem and its driver must be properly installed, the phone line must be connected to the proper place on the modem, the phone line must be active and have a clean dial tone, and the communications software must be installed correctly.

If anything is missing, incorrectly installed, or just plain bad, you may be unable to make an online connection. Assuming you have a computer with the operating system running and correctly installed, modem, phone line, and active AOL or Internet account, try the following things:

1. Pick up the phone and make sure you're getting a dial tone. Listen for a few seconds to see if noise or static appears on the line. If there's no dial tone or it's full of static, you should contact your phone company about it.

2. If you're using Windows 95, go into the Control Panel and look for the Modems icon. Right-click on the icon to examine the modem's properties, and make sure Windows 95 has detected your modem.

3. If you're using Windows 3.x, you can use the Terminal program (in the Accessories group) to see if your operating system is detecting the modem. Change the port the modem is connected to if it's not being detected, until you find a port that can detect the modem. If that was the problem, make sure to change the port in your other programs as well (e.g., the AOL software).

You can not only reset the cache to a smaller figure but also clear the entire cache with the click of a button. It may take a minute or two to clear out all the files, so be patient. By the way, if you're looking for an image file from one of the pages you viewed recently but haven't saved on disk, try looking in the cache files. Sometimes it's just sitting there waiting for you.

I've heard lots of scary stories about the Year 2000 problem. How can I determine if my computer is susceptible to it, and what can I do about it?

Depending upon whom you listen to, the Year 2000 problem—frequently referred to as Y2K—will either shut down every computer on the planet and cause a global panic, or will be no big deal. The truth actually lies somewhere in between.

Ever since computer programs were first written in this century, programmers have been using a shortcut for dates. The shortcut works by considering only the last two digits in a four-digit year. When the century changes to 2000, programs will assume the year is 1900 instead, and you can imagine what that might do to your bank account, credit, bills, driver's license, and anything else connected to a date.

Much of the problem is with large mainframe computers, which still run many financial systems behind the scenes. Most real-time clocks (RTCs) carry only the last two digits of the year, to conserve system resources. The solution is to build a special program or a routine in the BIOS that detects 1900 date errors and corrects them to 2000 dates. Not only are the computer manufacturers incorporating fixes, but the major OS makers are fixing or upgrading their operating systems as well.

If you're not sure the system you have will handle the turn of the century, go to the manufacturer's Web site for information on software fixes. Use AOL NetFind (keyword: **NetFind**) or go to the Computing channel's Companies area (keyword: **Companies**). Chances are, you can correct any potential problem with just a piece of software.

My printer isn't working, but the cables are connected and the lights are on. What's the likely cause?

Many printers these days have an LCD on the front that will tell you when the paper's out or an error occurs. If it's just the paper, obviously you should add more, but if it's something else, it might require a little more detective work.

The printer's instruction manual can tell you what the standard error codes mean, and usually there are lights on the front that indicate whether the printer is on and also whether it's online. Online in the printer world means the printer has established communications with the computer and everything seems A-OK.

If everything is on but nothing prints out, the first step is to try sending a test page. If that fails, check to make sure no paper is jammed in the machine and that the toner cartridge or the print head is properly inserted. Either of these errors should probably also show up on the LCD.

You've now pretty much exhausted the mechanical possibilities. Assuming your printer and computer are working the way they should, the only other causes are software-related. Go to the Control Panel and open the Printers folder, then check the properties. Make sure the printer driver you're using is the correct one for your printer. If not, get the right one and update it in the operating system. You can usually find drivers at the manufacturer's Web site, which you can locate through AOL NetFind (keyword: **NetFind**).

You need at 2MB of free space on your hard drive before you can print. If you don't have that, delete unnecessary files or empty the Recycle Bin to free space. And if you're that tight on disk space, consider upgrading your hard drive or getting another one. A full hard disk is an invitation to errors and crashes.

As a final check, open the Page Setup in the program you are trying to print from and make sure you are using the right printer. It's very possible that someone has changed the default printer to another one (or a fax modem) and your computer is trying to print to a nonexistent device.

For more information on your particular model printer, look at the message boards at the AOL Hardware/OS Forum (keyword: **Hardware**).

I just installed a new sound card, and I can't get it to function. What should I check?

Whenever you install new hardware, whether it's a sound card, a modem, a CD-ROM player, or a printer, there are several things that can go wrong. First, you have to do the mechanical installation correctly, making sure that you don't zap the component with static electricity, that you use the right slot on the motherboard, that you connect power cables correctly, and that you set the jumpers properly (if necessary).

If your computer is a late model and you're running Windows 95, chances are the operating system will detect the component once it's installed and even load the correct driver. If your computer is older and you're running Windows 3.x or MS-DOS, you'll have to run the setup program that came with the hardware. This setup program should configure the operating system and install the appropriate drivers for you.

If you've done all that and the card still misbehaves, you could have a dead card or a system conflict. Any indication at all that the card is working (low or muffled sound, the detection of the card by its software, and so on), tells you that the card works but that there is a conflict.

A dead card should be replaced, and if it's new you should be able to get a replacement at no charge from the vendor. The solution for a conflict is to check all COM ports, DMAs, and IRQs. Find out how they are assigned, and reconfigure the assignments until none of the installed devices conflict. In Windows 95, you can handle this task through the Device Manager, but if you have an older system, it's probably best to take it to the shop and have an expert grapple with it.

For additional information on sound cards, look at the message boards at the AOL Hardware/OS Forum (keyword: **Hardware**) and the PC Sound & Music Forum (keyword: **PC Music**).

When to Call for Help

Technical support can be a great asset, but it won't do much good if you don't understand your computer and its components. Technical support won't help (for long) if you never clean your computer or optimize your hard drive. Technical support can't fix a problem unless you have at least some idea of where the problem is, how it occurred, and what the proper result should be.

Computers are more complex machines than your car, your telephone, your TV, or your radio. They have innumerable functions, and though they are increasingly easy to use, you need to give them their due. Learn everything you can. Keep up with new developments. Follow the instructions in the manual. Develop a network of offline friends and online services who can advise you when bad things happen. Give your computer the respect it deserves, as a four- or five-figure investment that holds reams of information that you can't do without.

Calling technical support should be your last resort. Why? Technical support is expensive, both for you and for the company you're dealing with, and most problems are user generated and user fixable. The vast majority of problems are as simple as an unplugged cable, a bad telephone connection, or improperly installed or incorrectly configured software or hardware. Yes, bugs happen and computers do fail, but not nearly as often as people set them up wrong.

How can I tell when a problem is caused by the machine rather than by my own inexperience? When is it dire enough to call the manufacturer?

Learn as much as you can about your computer, and follow the checklists and troubleshooting techniques provided in this chapter. When a problem arises, define it as precisely as you can, and see if you can make it happen more than once by reproducing the conditions under which it originally occurred. Compare notes with other computer users, either online (see below) or among your acquaintances. Once you've eliminated everything else and done everything you can, then it's time to call for help.

When you do call, make sure you have a complete description of the problem and all the related information you can find. Sometimes problems are intermittent or random, but frequently they occur after the same sequence of events. Being able to recreate the problem accurately makes solving it much less difficult. Remember, the person on the other end can't see your computer and will be relying totally on you to provide good information to make a diagnosis. Knowing your system, its components, and its configuration is crucial for a successful resolution.

Where to Call for Help

If your computer still works and you can go online, you have the world's largest and most comprehensive set of troubleshooting and problem-solving tools right at your fingertips. There are tens of thousands of newsgroups available to you through the Internet (keyword: **Newsgroups**). Look for groups beginning with "comp." The AOL service also supports many forums, such as the PC Hardware Forum (keyword: **PC Hardware** or **PHW**), shown in figure 5.2. Try the keyword Computer Terms to go to Que's Computer and Internet Dictionary. The keyword Computer Search will bring you to Search and Explore AOL Computing. Another good resource is the AOL PC Webopedia (keyword: **Webopedia**), which will give you computer terms and definitions. From there, you can search for any specific computing area on the AOL service.

The PC Hardware Forum operates according to a defined schedule, so if you check in at the right time you'll find the subject of interest under discussion. Here's an example of a PC Hardware Forum conference schedule:

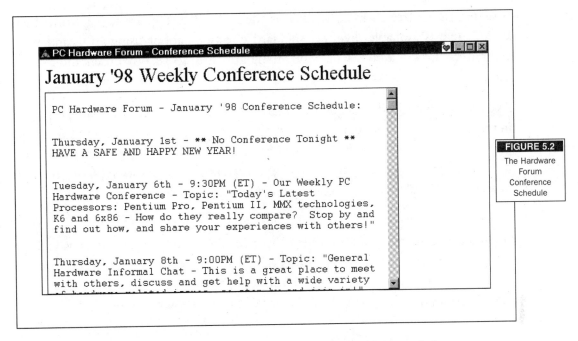

PC Hardware Forum - Conference Schedule

January '98 Weekly Conference Schedule

```
PC Hardware Forum - January '98 Conference Schedule:


Thursday, January 1st - ** No Conference Tonight **
HAVE A SAFE AND HAPPY NEW YEAR!


Tuesday, January 6th - 9:30PM (ET) - Our Weekly PC
Hardware Conference - Topic: "Today's Latest
Processors: Pentium Pro, Pentium II, MMX technologies,
K6 and 6x86 - How do they really compare?  Stop by and
find out how, and share your experiences with others!"


Thursday, January 8th - 9:00PM (ET) - Topic: "General
Hardware Informal Chat - This is a great place to meet
with others, discuss and get help with a wide variety
```

PC Hardware Forum—January '98 Conference Schedule

- Tuesday, January 6th—9:30PM (ET)—Our Weekly PC Hardware Conference—Topic: "Today's Latest Processors: Pentium Pro, Pentium II, MMX technologies, K6 and 6x86—How do they really compare? Stop by and find out how, and share your experiences with others!"

- Thursday, January 8th—9:00PM (ET)—Topic: "General Hardware Informal Chat—This is a great place to meet with others, discuss and get help with a wide variety of hardware-related issues, so stop by and join in!"

Forums are midway between a message board and a telephone call. The response is a little less immediate than a phone call, but you'll get an answer quickly in most cases. Because it's like a message board, you'll have some of the best minds in the business working on your problem, for free. For instance, if you have a hardware question, go to the PC Hardware Forum and post it. Pretty soon, some kind soul will see your question and begin to respond, perhaps with more questions that help determine the exact nature of the problem. Eventually, either an expert or someone like you who's had the problem before will figure it out. After you gain expertise yourself, you may decide to help others. It's all part of the cooperative spirit of the Internet and AOL.

What Help Desk services does AOL maintain?

Another great place to look for help is the AOL PC Help Desk (keyword: **Help Desk**). Help is available, live, for standard questions about using AOL and your computer. Check out Help Chat (shown in figure 5.3) to ask other users and experts questions.

Ask a question by sending a question mark **?** to the chat screen. Your name is placed in the queue and a consultant calls on you when it's your turn. You should also click the FAQs (frequently asked questions) button to see if your question has already been answered at an earlier time. Finally, you can post your question on the message boards. You should receive a reply by e-mail within 72 hours or sooner.

If you click on the AOL Member Services button from the AOL PC Help Desk, you'll see an interesting option called Error Messages. While this service is specific to AOL, you can find answers to lots of common problems here in the form of descriptions of what error messages mean. To get there, just click on the error messages button on the AOL PC Help Desk front page (shown in figure 5.4)

I called my modem maker's tech support line because I was having a problem getting my modem to fax a document out. They referred me to the maker of my office software, and they in turn told me to call my computer maker. This was a

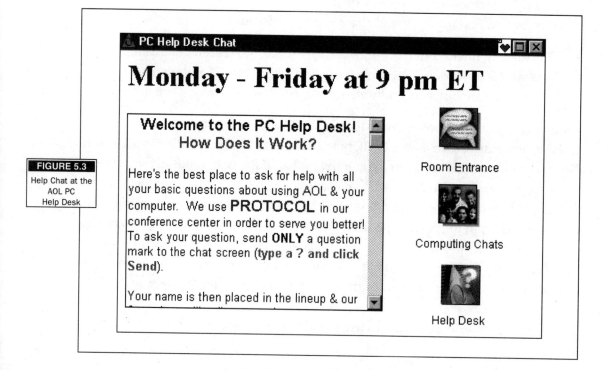

FIGURE 5.3

Help Chat at the
AOL PC
Help Desk

big pain, and I finally gave up. How can I tell which vendor is the right place to start for a given problem?

If it makes you feel better, this phenomenon is so common that information systems professionals have a name for it. It's called "finger pointing." With all the different elements that make up even the smallest computer system, it's easy for vendors to pass the buck.

Unless you've had the problem before, there often is no good way to tell where it's originating. One strategy is to compare notes with others who have used your configuration. Post your problem on an PC Hardware Forum message board (keyword: **PC Hardware** or **PHW**), or on Usenet, with as many details as you can, and chances are someone will recognize it and be able to advise you where to begin to assign blame—or better yet, how to solve it.

I hear manufacturers are putting a lot of customer information on the Web, but I don't have the Web addresses for the companies that make my equipment. How do I find them?

Try AOL NetFind (keyword: **NetFind**). Using the company name as your search term, you should turn up the corporate Web site within the first few listings. You're also likely to get lots of other references to the company, and may find sites with product

203

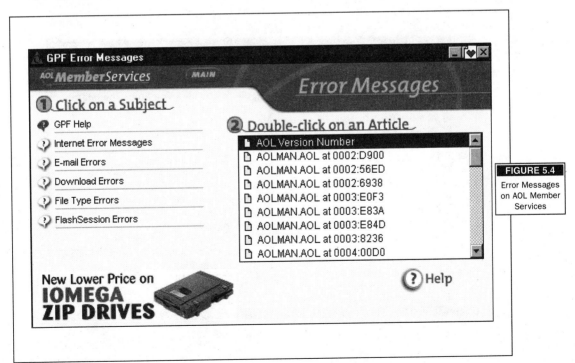

FIGURE 5.4
Error Messages on AOL Member Services

reviews and business analyses, user complaints, and other interesting background.

You can frequently find the company Web site by typing **www.nameofcompany.com** into your Web browser. But since there's no law that automatically entitles a company to a Web address the same as its name, this is far from an infallible method.

I'm having trouble downloading software from AOL. Where can I get the inside scoop on how to do it?

Check Download 101, reachable through the AOL PC Help Desk (keyword: **Help Desk**), shown in figure 5.5.

A big part of preparing to call for help is accessing the free help available first. Hundreds of AOL resources and Web sites offer free help services. The ZDNET Web site lists about 50 of the major manufacturers' Web site addresses. You can also use AOL's help sites like the Member Services area (keyword: **Help**), Flag a Techy (keyword: **Help**), or the Maven service (keyword: **Maven**). Or you can use the AOL NetFind (keyword: **NetFind**) search engine.

If you need to find reference material, look in the AOL Computing channel (keyword: **Computing**). You'll find pages leading to Computer Magazines, Consumer

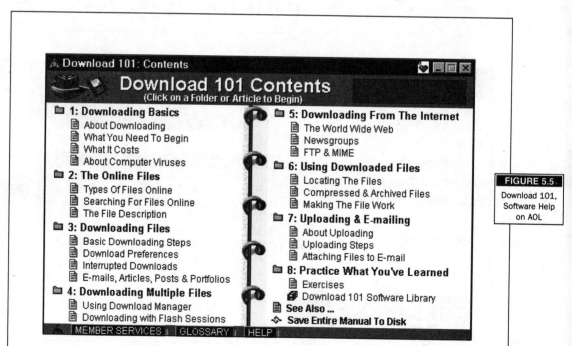

FIGURE 5.5.
Download 101, Software Help on AOL

Information, Computing News, and General Computing Information.

What if my computer's not working? It's pretty hard to go online without a computer.

If your computer's not working, you can read the manuals, call a friend, call technical support, or even rely on your own good judgment and common sense. Try the basics first. Check power cables, battery, connectors, and so on. If none of these are the cause, call your computer service person. Many new computers come with onsite repair as part of the warranty. Arrange to ship your computer back to the manufacturer or take it to a local authorized repair shop.

Where do I turn for help if my computer is out of warranty?

First, try Computing Tips (keyword: **Computing Tips**) on the AOL service, which offers a variety of helpful tips for making your system run smoothly. This site can also help you with a number hardware and operating system problems.

If your computer's manufacturer is still in business, its Web site can be a good source for some kinds of information. As mentioned elsewhere, you can usually track down the manufacturer through AOL NetFind (keyword: **NetFind**).

The AOL computing forums and the computer-related Internet newsgroups are a gold mine of free advice, and regardless of the equipment you have, someone else is sure to have the same configuration and be able to advise you about specific problems. Check out the PC Hardware Forum (keyword: **PC Hardware** or **PHW**).

It's also worth looking into computer user groups in your area, where you'll find people with various levels of expertise, and where the grapevine may lead you to a competent repair shop. Larger computing clubs are likely to have Web sites, which you can track down through AOL NetFind (keyword: **NetFind**) or a Web directory such as Yahoo. You may also be able to get leads through your local high school or community college.

205

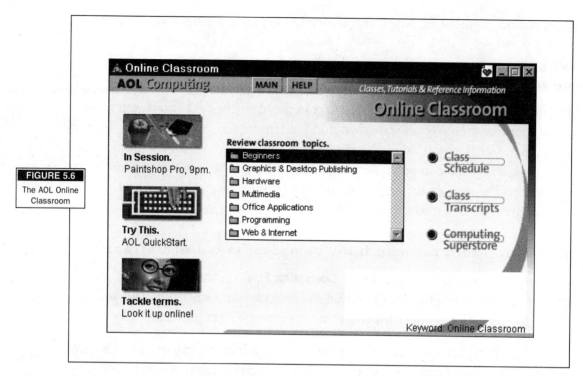

FIGURE 5.6

The AOL Online Classroom

How to Learn about Your PC

An easy and inexpensive way to get a good education about your computer is to use the Online Classroom feature of the AOL Computing channel (keyword: **Online Classroom**) (see figure 5.6).

Just about everything you might want to know about computers is covered in one of the classes at the Online Classroom, from help for beginners, to advanced programming, to hardware basics. The Web and the Internet are covered as well, as is the AOL service.

New software used to come in a shrink-wrapped box with the software disks and three or four large manuals. The manuals would tell you how to install the software, how to get started using it, and how to use it in depth—with plenty of examples. They would also offer complete references for all formulas, functions, menu choices, options, and commands. Any company that didn't provide excellent documentation as part of the software package was quickly skewered in the popular press.

Then, along came the GUI. Programs operated with the same interface and many of the same menu choices, and the manual became the last resort. Users had become familiar with the basic functions of the common programs (spreadsheets, databases, and word processors), and large manuals were viewed as a crutch for companies that couldn't design user-friendly programs. Users expected to be able to figure out the program from the main window alone, and the joke "If all else fails, read the manual" was born.

It's not uncommon today to get a thin manual or two with your new software, perhaps the install guide and another one labeled "Getting Started." Most programs also have a Help menu that you can access while you're running it. The hard-copy reference manuals, extensive user guides, and how-to books can be purchased separately, from the manufacturer or a third-party publisher. Experienced users appreciate this, because it means software prices can be lower, and new users actually have more choice about the kind and extent of documentation they purchase.

But why should I have to constantly learn about computers? Isn't it enough that I've learned the basics of how to operate my own system?

The more you know about computers in general, and your computer in particular, the more ways you'll find to use it. You may know how to use your word processor or spreadsheet, or how to send e-mail through AOL. But if you keep stretching the limits of your knowledge, you'll find out that you can use your computer to trade stocks, or create and send a direct-mail catalog for your business, or compose music, or get hundreds of comparative life insurance quotes in seconds, or track down the current phone number and e-mail address of an old college pal who lives somewhere in Europe.

Computers and the Internet constitute an entirely new way of thinking, writing, calculating, and communicating, so it's not surprising that most of us feel like we're back in school half the time, relearning the three Rs. A computer's capabilities increase daily, and it's worth keeping up.

What can I learn at the Online Classroom?

On the main window of the AOL Online Classroom, you'll find a list of the topics covered in the classes, something like this:

- Beginners—These classes cover a wide range of topics from the beginner's perspective.

- Graphics and Desktop Publishing—Artists, publishers, graphic designers, and editors will find in-depth information about the most frequently used software packages for graphics and desktop publishing in these classes.

- Hardware—Just the place if you are interested in becoming hardware proficient, and especially useful for this chapter.

- Multimedia—Designing a CD-ROM application? Complete coverage of multimedia development software and the development process is included in these classes.

- Office Applications—Send your staff to these classes without leaving the office, and watch their productivity zoom.

- Programming—Professional programmers, and programmers-in-training can start or upgrade their skills in these classes, which are taught in a user-friendly, non-threatening way by skilled instructors.

- Web & Internet—Web site design, servers, TCP/IP, and many other Internet/intranet related topics are discussed in these classes.

Classes at the Online Classroom are held online on given dates, last from 4 to 12 weeks, employ top instructors in the field, and charge a small registration fee. Each class features live, online lectures (except self-study courses), daily message boards and e-mail support, and private libraries of supplementary materials. You can sign up online and charge your AOL account for registration. There is a course fee for each online class you take. Costs vary.

How do I find out if a class is for me?

Click on any topic at the main window of the Online Classroom, and you'll bring up another window with classes under that particular topic. You can then get further information about the course by clicking on Class Details.

When you click on Class Details, a window opens that outlines the specifics of the course (see figure 5.7). You'll see when the class starts, who the instructor is, the registration fee, the meeting days and times, the duration of the class, and any prerequisites. Clicking on Course Description displays a complete course description, including any software you must have and an in-depth outline of the course contents.

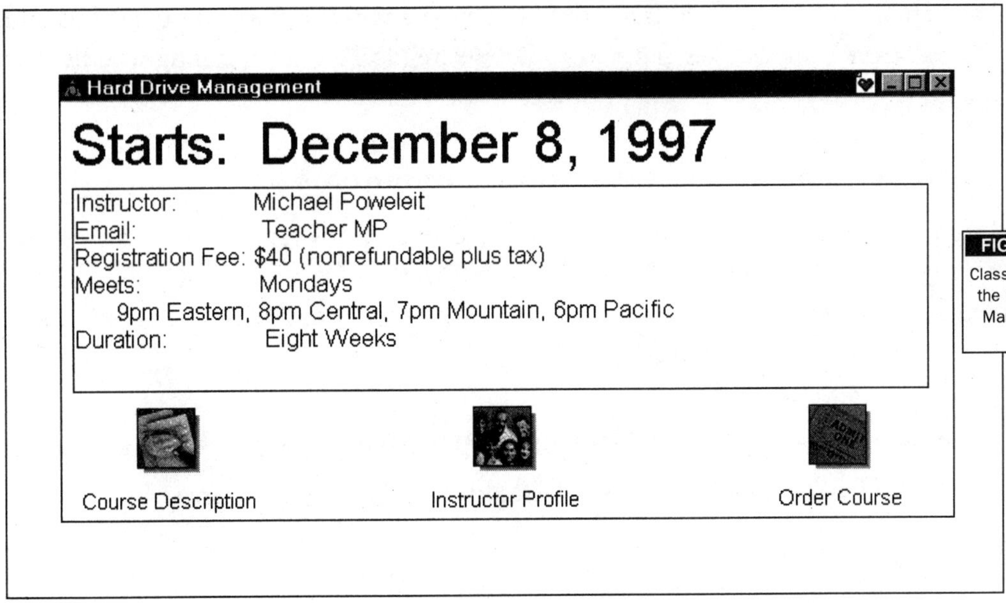

Starts: December 8, 1997

Instructor: Michael Poweleit
Email: Teacher MP
Registration Fee: $40 (nonrefundable plus tax)
Meets: Mondays
     9pm Eastern, 8pm Central, 7pm Mountain, 6pm Pacific
Duration: Eight Weeks

Course Description

Instructor Profile

Order Course

FIGURE 5.7

Class Details for the Hard Drive Management Class

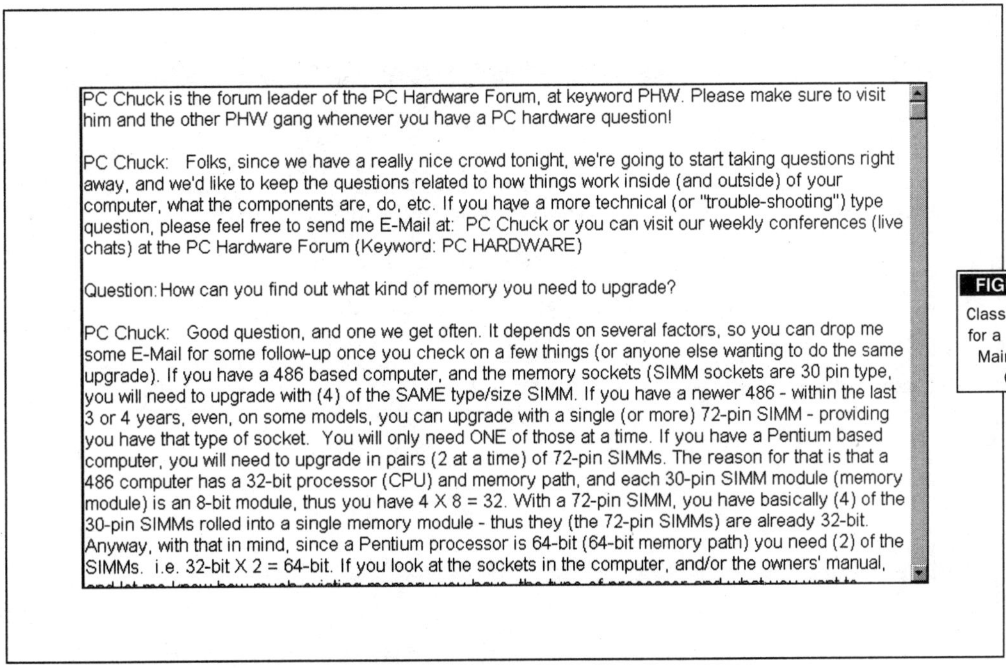

PC Chuck is the forum leader of the PC Hardware Forum, at keyword PHW. Please make sure to visit him and the other PHW gang whenever you have a PC hardware question!

PC Chuck: Folks, since we have a really nice crowd tonight, we're going to start taking questions right away, and we'd like to keep the questions related to how things work inside (and outside) of your computer, what the components are, do, etc. If you have a more technical (or "trouble-shooting") type question, please feel free to send me E-Mail at: PC Chuck or you can visit our weekly conferences (live chats) at the PC Hardware Forum (Keyword: PC HARDWARE)

Question: How can you find out what kind of memory you need to upgrade?

PC Chuck: Good question, and one we get often. It depends on several factors, so you can drop me some E-Mail for some follow-up once you check on a few things (or anyone else wanting to do the same upgrade). If you have a 486 based computer, and the memory sockets (SIMM sockets are 30 pin type, you will need to upgrade with (4) of the SAME type/size SIMM. If you have a newer 486 - within the last 3 or 4 years, even, on some models, you can upgrade with a single (or more) 72-pin SIMM - providing you have that type of socket. You will only need ONE of those at a time. If you have a Pentium based computer, you will need to upgrade in pairs (2 at a time) of 72-pin SIMMs. The reason for that is that a 486 computer has a 32-bit processor (CPU) and memory path, and each 30-pin SIMM module (memory module) is an 8-bit module, thus you have 4 X 8 = 32. With a 72-pin SIMM, you have basically (4) of the 30-pin SIMMs rolled into a single memory module - thus they (the 72-pin SIMMs) are already 32-bit. Anyway, with that in mind, since a Pentium processor is 64-bit (64-bit memory path) you need (2) of the SIMMs. i.e. 32-bit X 2 = 64-bit. If you look at the sockets in the computer, and/or the owners' manual,

FIGURE 5.8

Class Transcript for a Preventive Maintenance Class

You can also click on Class Transcripts to get to a window showing questions and answers from the class (see figure 5.8). These are ideal for determining whether the class is right for you, or is too advanced or too basic.

How can I know the instructor's credentials?

Open the Instructor Profile from the Class Details window. A picture of the instructor (and the online name) will appear, along with the instructor's real name and credentials (see figure 5.9). Most of the instructors have many years of real-life teaching experience and hold advanced degrees.

What classes are available concerning hardware?

In the Hardware window there are classes in the following categories:

- Digital Cameras

- Hard Drive Management

- Hardware Trivia

- Local Area Networks

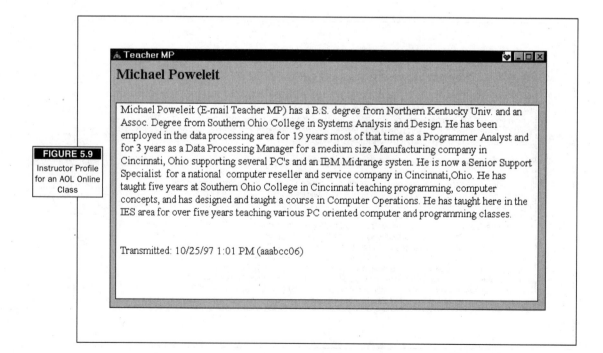

FIGURE 5.9
Instructor Profile for an AOL Online Class

Teacher MP

Michael Poweleit

Michael Poweleit (E-mail Teacher MP) has a B.S. degree from Northern Kentucky Univ. and an Assoc. Degree from Southern Ohio College in Systems Analysis and Design. He has been employed in the data processing area for 19 years most of that time as a Programmer Analyst and for 3 years as a Data Processing Manager for a medium size Manufacturing company in Cincinnati, Ohio supporting several PC's and an IBM Midrange systen. He is now a Senior Support Specialist for a national computer reseller and service company in Cincinnati,Ohio. He has taught five years at Southern Ohio College in Cincinnati teaching programming, computer concepts, and has designed and taught a course in Computer Operations. He has taught here in the IES area for over five years teaching various PC oriented computer and programming classes.

Transmitted: 10/25/97 1:01 PM (aaabcc06)

- Modems

- Personal Digital Assistants

- Preventive Maintenance

- Printers

In Preventive Maintenance, for instance, you can get general preventive maintenance tips, find out how to protect your computer from potential power line problems, and learn how to set up and properly use a backup system.

You'll also find online college courses on computers offered by universities through the AOL Research & Learn channel (keyword: **Research and Learn**).

Can I take classes on software, too?

Yes, though not all software packages have online classes. However, you're likely to find classes on the most popular office applications and on graphics and desktop publishing software. At this writing, classes were being offered in Microsoft Excel, Publisher, and Access, as well as in spreadsheet and word processing basics.

211

I know of several classes I want to take. How can I find out which one is next, and make sure to attend when it starts?

The AOL service will e-mail you before class starts so you don't forget, and you can click on the Class Schedule button from the main window of the Online Classroom to see the schedule of all current classes. (Keep in mind that the schedule hours are in Eastern Standard Time.)

6

UPGRADING YOUR PC

t happens to almost everyone. Your new computer is barely out of the box, and already you're looking for ways to improve it. It can be faster. You can add more enhancements. How do you know when to stop?

This chapter discusses the need for speed, why it's important to upgrade every so often, and how to tell the truly necessary upgrades from the wanna-buys. You'll also learn how to upgrade intelligently, because some upgrades either won't work at all or will have minimal impact unless other components are installed at the same time.

Once you've educated yourself, you can have some fun shopping. There are two computer stores located within the AOL service: the AOL Store (keyword: **AOL Store**) and the Computing Superstore (keyword: **CSS**). The stores contain all the popular brands, makes, and models of computer hardware and software: complete systems, upgrades, components, accessories, supplies, and just about anything you can think of. Plus there's plenty of information about what goes with what, and the newest gear just coming on the market. The AOL Store, shown in figure 6.1, and the Computing Superstore are fast, easy, and convenient places to shop.

The Cyberian Outpost (keyword: **Cyberian Outpost**) is another good place to shop for computer hardware and software, especially memory.

Why do computers keep changing so frequently?

It's a combination of factors, but the two most important are (1) they can, and (2) lots of people make money every time they do.

Once a big idea lands in the public consciousness, smaller ideas spring from it like ripples in a pond. The invention of the integrated circuit in 1959 made modern computers possible by dramatically shrinking the size and power requirements of the computer's brain. The changes you see are mostly variations, refinements, and extensions of that breakthrough.

214

FIGURE 6.1
The AOL Store

The Internet is the other big idea now fueling change. It's a simple notion: use your computer to access millions of other computers around the world. It was not simple to execute, but now that the basic structure is in place, it's making the biggest splash since the invention of movable type.

Processing power for PCs doubles approximately every 18 months. The newest gear probably cost less than your current machine; size continues its steady march toward microscopic; and reliability improves steadily. Manufacturers milk each innovation for a few months and then bring in another one. Of course, they have no choice, because if they don't regularly roll out new products, their competitors surely will.

All this means that whatever you have today will become outmoded soon, and you won't be able to use the latest software or hardware peripherals. It may also mean you can't run the current version of AOL software (4.0).

What components can be upgraded?

Just about anything can be upgraded, though some components are better investments than others. Upgrading means buying new capabilities you didn't have before, as well as improving what you already have. For instance, if you bought a color ink-jet printer to replace your laser printer, that's upgrading just as much as buying a faster, better laser printer to replace your current one would be.

Upgrading applies to software as well as hardware. You can upgrade from Windows 95 to Windows 98. You can also upgrade from the current version to the next version of most applications programs. In fact, to keep you from defecting to competing software, virtually all manufacturers offer inexpensive upgrades to current users. Some manufacturers will offer the same deal to registered users of competing software, to get them to switch over.

When you're ready to upgrade your hardware or software, visit the AOL Store's Hardware Shop (keyword: **Hardware Center**) or Software Shop (keyword: **Software Shop**). The AOL Computing Classifieds (keyword: **Classifieds**) is another resource to check out for good buys on new and used computer equipment and software.

Which upgrades will give me the most bang for the buck?

It depends on how hard you're pushing the limits of your current configuration. Upgrading generally means buying something that has new features; is smaller, faster, or cheaper to operate; has more capacity; operates with something else that is newer and better (meets a new standard); or simply fits your lifestyle and working needs better.

Typically, the following items fall into the upgrade category:

- RAM, motherboard, and CPU

- Modem, network card, Telephony equipment

- Hard drive, CD-ROM drive, and backup and mass storage devices

- Monitor, video card, input devices, and multimedia gear

- Operating system, applications programs, and utilities

- Printers and scanners

- Surge protection equipment

Of these, the upgrades that extend your computer's useful life the most are adding more RAM, going to the next generation of CPU, getting a larger hard drive, and adding removable mass storage. Quality-of-life upgrades include a faster modem, a faster CD-ROM drive, a larger and/or better quality monitor, an ergonomic keyboard, or a more comfortable mouse.

Whether and when to upgrade operating systems and software is a judgment call that will vary depending on whether you're bleeding edge (willing to risk bugs and system crashes to have something first), trailing edge (favoring the "If it ain't broke, don't fix it" school of thought), or somewhere in between. You will probably want to upgrade them eventually, because if you fall too far behind the curve, you'll have problems getting support from the manufacturer and sharing files with bleeding edge computer users. But remember that even though Windows 95 has been around since the year of its name, there are still people happily using Windows 3.x, and even DOS.

Most of the other upgrades—printers, scanners, multimedia peripherals—are driven by changes in the way you're using your computer.

First, put all the advertisements out of your mind and reflect carefully on the things you are unsatisfied with, new capabilities you'd like to have, and your budget over the next six months. Chances are you don't need all the upgrades overnight, and by reading some pertinent information you can gauge when you're likely to get the best deal on that shiny new trackball or color printer.

Next, make a list of every component you have: make, model, speed, size—all the important details. List everything, not just the things you know you might change, because upgrading one component often means upgrading another. Read this chapter and some of the sources cited to decide which parts are interdependent.

The AOL Store's Hardware Shop and Software Shop will give you good prices. The Cyberian Outpost (keyword: **Cyberian Outpost**) is another great place to buy computer components, as well as the AOL Computing Classifieds.

How hard is it to install upgraded components? Can I do it myself, or should I take it to a shop?

Most upgrades can be done by an interested, informed owner, but the task isn't for everybody. If you're not sure you're up to it or just don't want to take the time, add installation costs to the purchase price of the parts. In some cases, retailers will install components as part of the purchase price (at no additional charge).

Most exterior peripherals can simply be plugged in, and Windows 95 (and Windows 98) should be able to do the necessary software set up. You also may be able to handle plugging in an expansion board (such as a sound card or an internal modem) or a new motherboard, changing out RAM chips, and perhaps upgrading a processor chip or adding an extra one.

It's probably worth paying a technician to install a new internal drive (hard, floppy, CD-ROM, or

217

HOW MUCH DOES IT COST TO UPGRADE?

Here are ballpark prices for some typical upgrades, as of this writing. Remember that a garden-variety new PC is likely to cost somewhere between $1,300 and $2,000, and come with the latest version of Windows, a very large hard drive, and a built-in 56K modem. If you upgrade a monitor, a printer, a keyboard, or another peripheral device, odds are you can use it with your next computer.

- Motherboard (without CPU): $190
- 300MHz Pentium II MMX CPU: $620
- 8.4GB internal hard drive: $350
- 16MB RAM: $40
- 56K modem: $90
- 17-inch multisync color monitor: $620
- Windows 98 operating system upgrade: $90
- Color ink-jet printer: $320
- Ergonomic keyboard: $40

removable mass storage), since the plates that hold them in place don't always fit without some expert fiddling, and the drives are filled with delicate moving parts.

You should always be able to handle installation of new software, perhaps with some telephone hand-holding from the vendor's technical support staff. You can find software vendors in the Computing Companies area on the AOL service (keyword: **Companies**) or use AOL NetFind (keyword: **NetFind**) to search for the software vendor you want to call. See Appendix I for instructions on installing AOL 4.0 software.

Upgrading Your CPU

The primary reasons for upgrading your motherboard, CPU, and RAM (besides total failure of the old parts) are speed and computing power. (For definitions of motherboard, CPU, and RAM, see this book's Glossary.) Often you can replace the CPU (Central Processing Unit) or add more RAM without replacing the motherboard because many motherboards are designed to work with several CPU chips and varying amounts of RAM. If you do need a motherboard, the AOL Store's Hardware Shop (keyword: **Hardware Center**) shown in figure 6.2, has plenty of them to fit every budget or need.

The CPU is probably the single most expensive item inside your computer case, and the newest models in any given year can easily account for 20 percent to 50 percent of the cost of the whole system, including the monitor. Upgrading can significantly

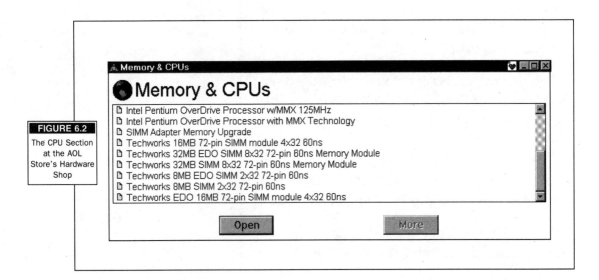

FIGURE 6.2

The CPU Section at the AOL Store's Hardware Shop

INSTALLING CPU CHIPS

If you've had the opportunity to examine the circuit boards inside your computer, you've probably noticed that some of the chips are connected to the boards by pins. The pins are inserted into holes in the board or into special mounting fixtures on the board. The pins are then soldered directly to the board, or the chip is held to the mounting fixture (which is soldered to the board itself) by friction.

The tiny contacts on CPU chips are soldered to the pins on their packaging cases, and unless you break one open you'll never see the actual chip. The packaging case is black and has hundreds of pins protruding from the bottom. While each pin requires only a minimum of force to hold it in place, the same force applied to hundreds of pins makes it very difficult to remove and replace the chip.

The ZIF socket was designed to make chip removal and replacement easy for anyone. (ZIF stands for Zero Insertion Force socket.) A lever at the side of the mounting fixture relieves pressure on all the pins when open and applies pressure again when closed. Simply open the lever to remove the old chip, insert the new chip, and close the lever once again.

By the way, some chips are Murphy-proof, meaning there's only one way they can be installed. But other chips aren't. Make sure you are installing your new CPU correctly before turning on the power. And make doubly sure you have connected the power cable to the motherboard correctly as well. The very newest chips come built in to their own circuit board, which makes installation even easier.

boost system performance when other factors are properly taken into account. Similarly, a poorly chosen upgrade can deliver no performance gains at all.

I've heard there is a bug or problem with the original Pentium chip. Has it been fixed?

Yes, there was a problem, and it has been fixed. But the question brings up a good point about computer hardware and software in general. Although we all perceive well-manufactured, high-quality products to be defect-free, in fact there is simply no such thing.

Computer chips and software always have bugs, but most of them are benign and never cause a serious problem. Automobiles are the same, in that they contain probably hundreds of small flaws or deviations from specs that never get our attention, unless the car is a real lemon. Scrutinizing any product will eventually turn up a flaw, however minute it might be. But computer software and hardware both typically contain many millions of lines of computer code. So the tiniest mistake can cause an error that gets our attention, and surprise us because we expect computers to perform perfectly.

What does MMX mean? Is it really better?

Multimedia Extensions (MMX) is the term Intel uses for a set of special instructions built in to the CPU that processes graphics, audio, and other media elements. Intel has now released a new MMX standard called MMX 2, and it's being incorporated into its latest chips.

When MMX was first released, there were few software applications designed to take advantage of the increased capability. That has changed now, and most new applications will get a significant performance boost from MMX capability. If you're buying a new CPU as an upgrade, you'll want to get the MMX chip if your current motherboard will accept it. If not, seriously consider doing a combination motherboard/CPU upgrade—the computer equivalent of a brain transplant. You'll just about have a new system right there.

Upgrading Memory

If I'm still running the same software, why should I buy more RAM?

Two reasons: first, you can have more of your programs open at once, and second, it may cut down on the amount of virtual memory your computer needs, and can therefore reduce wear and tear on your hard drive. (For more about RAM, see chapter 2. For a definition of RAM and the different types of RAM, see the Glossary.) RAM prices have dropped dramatically in the past few years. Check AOL's Hardware Shop, shown in figure 6.3, and the Cyberian Outpost for the latest prices.

How much RAM can my system handle?

The amount of RAM your system can handle is determined primarily by how many memory chips can be plugged into its motherboard, either directly or via expansion slots. The CPU, or processor chip, has a limit on how much memory it can recognize, but all Intel CPUs since the 386DX, including the 486 and the Pentium, can recognize 4GB of RAM, which is much more than the average user needs or the average PC can accept. The motherboard itself physically holds the RAM, so the

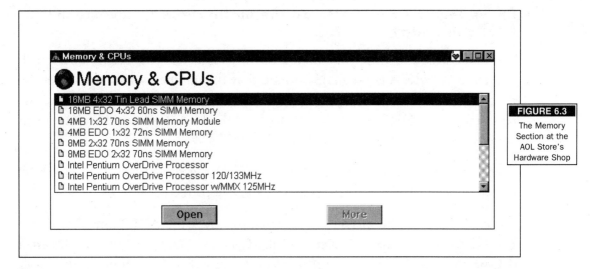

number and type of RAM slots on the motherboard limits the total RAM that can be installed. The documentation that came with your computer should tell you the RAM capacity of the motherboard.

Lower-end systems sold today still have as little as 16MB of RAM installed, especially laptops. But many users feel 32MB is indispensable, and 64MB highly desirable. More than 256MB should be necessary only for high-end graphics, video or audio work, or servers.

What are SIMMs and DIMMs?

Some motherboards allow you to install RAM directly, while other designs force you to add RAM by using expansion slots. The difference is that RAM installed in its own sockets on the motherboard can talk to the CPU much more quickly than RAM installed in expansion slots. The latter also has the disadvantage of consuming a slot that could be occupied by some other device.

The boards may be referred to as chips, but the technical name is Single In-line Memory Module (SIMM). Older 386 and 486 systems used 30-pin SIMMs, while more recent systems use 72-pin SIMMs. The latest personal computers employ 168-pin DIMMs (Dual In-line Memory Modules), which have a double row of chips.

221

I have located my SIMMs on the motherboard. How much RAM can I add?

The documentation with your motherboard should tell you exactly how much RAM you can add. A good guide is to multiply the number of memory sockets by the total amount of RAM available per SIMM or DIMM. For instance, if you currently have two 8MB SIMMs, for a total of 16MB of RAM, you could replace them with two 32MB SIMMs for a total of 64MB of RAM.

Keep in mind that whatever the configuration of your motherboard, you must fill an entire memory bank for your system to operate correctly.

Again, if you're in the market for RAM chips, check the AOL Store's Hardware Shop (keyword: **Hardware Center**) and the Cyberian Outpost (keyword: **Cyberian Outpost**) for great prices. Another place to buy RAM is through the AOL Computing Classifieds (keyword: **Classifieds**).

What about chip speed? How is it measured and what are the limitations?

Chip speeds are measured in nanoseconds (1 nanosecond equals one billionth of a second). Typical speeds these days are 50 to 60 nanoseconds, but older RAM operated in the 100 to 120 nanosecond range.

Remember that you must always buy RAM that is the same speed as or faster than what your system calls for, and don't mix and match speeds for any given memory bank. Check your documentation to find out what speed is the minimum.

What is parity checking? Should I get parity or non parity memory?

Parity is a form of error checking that automatically checks data every time it is read from memory. It can be valuable for detecting signs of problems in the early stages, while you can still take positive action.

You want a motherboard that enables parity checking so you can add parity RAM. Parity checking circuitry is built in on 386 and above CPUs. Mixing parity and non parity RAM will eventually cause errors, and adding a single non parity SIMM may disable parity checking for all SIMMs installed.

See this book's Glossary for definitions of parity and other common computer terms.

I have a fast 486 (a 486DX-4 100) with 8MB of RAM. I want to upgrade to 32MB of RAM so I can run Windows 95. How should I go about doing this, and what can I expect from my new operating system?

One of the best reasons for upgrading RAM is to make software run better. You can run Windows 95 with 8MB of RAM, but it will run quite slowly and few other programs can be open. Microsoft's own documentation says the minimum is 8MB, and strongly recommends 16MB. Running several programs simultaneously is one of the benefits of Windows 95, so getting more RAM is a good idea. You can find RAM (30-pin SIMMs) priced at only $4 to $6 per megabyte, so why not?

Once you have the additional RAM, you can find Windows 95 in the Operating Systems section at the Software Shop in the AOL Store (keyword: **Software Shop**). (And by the time you read this, it's likely you'll find Windows 98 there as well.) Or do a search on operating systems at the Computing Superstore (shown in figure 6.4).

Windows 95 must be installed as an upgrade to your current MS-DOS or Windows installation. If you're installing over MS-DOS, you need to have DOS version 3.2 or later, but 5.0 or later is recommended. If you're not sure what version you have, type **ver** at the DOS command prompt (c:\).

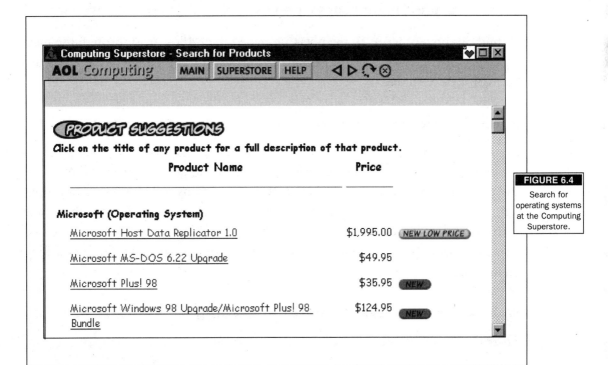

FIGURE 6.4
Search for operating systems at the Computing Superstore.

To install Windows 95 you'll need at least VGA graphics (which you undoubtedly have if your system has a color monitor), roughly 30MB to 100MB of hard drive space available (so you might also be looking at a hard drive upgrade), and a CD-ROM drive. Otherwise you'll be shuffling floppies for quite a while. Microsoft also recommends a mouse (you'll be wretchedly unhappy without one) and a modem.

The installation process should be fairly routine. If you have an older machine that doesn't support Plug and Play, you'll have to choose the correct drivers for some devices, such as network adapters, sound cards, SCSI cards and proprietary CD-ROMs. (Some of these devices are described in chapter 2.) As you progress through the installation screens, Setup will attempt to detect installed devices, which may cause your system to lock up. If so, just restart the machine and run Setup again. The detection process that caused the lockup will not be repeated, and Setup should continue normally.

When you're done, you will notice several advantages of using Windows 95 over MS-DOS or Windows 3.x. If you're upgrading from MS-DOS, the Graphical User Interface (GUI) is a major improvement for many folks, although it will take some getting used to. Overall, the GUI for Windows 95 is simpler to use than the one for Windows 3.x.

If you're upgrading to Windows 98, you'll find that install instructions come with the program. Install instructions were not available at the time of this writing.

To find out how other AOL members upgraded their 486s, read through the messages or post your own message on the message boards at the PC Hardware Forum (keyword: **PC Hardware** or **PHW**).

Can I still run my old DOS programs when I want to?

In many cases, Windows 95 will let you run DOS programs better than previous versions of DOS because it's more efficient at allocating disk resources and memory, and you can even cut and paste between DOS applications and your Windows applications. Install DOS programs by following the installation instructions that come with them, or by double-clicking on the installation program (often called install.bat, setup.bat, or go.bat). You can launch your program by double-clicking on its EXE file.

What are other advantages of upgrading to Windows 95?

There are several benefits of the Windows environment.

NAME THAT FILE

Files are fundamental to data storage in all personal computer systems. A filename uniquely marks an individual file, allowing it to be located and retrieved from anywhere on your computer system or even the entire Internet. A Web address, also known as a Uniform Resource Locator (URL), is actually a reference to a specific file on a specific computer on the Internet.

Different files can have identical names as long as they are stored in separate directories or on different computers.

Filenames frequently end with extensions. Conventionally filename extensions are three- or four-character endings that ordinarily follow a period, such as .html. The purpose of the extension is to identify the file type or format, so the computer has a clue about the format or content of the file. Extensions are often a match for the file type, but there's nothing that mandates the relationship.

Descriptive filenames and extensions make dealing with files easier, but there have been some historic limitations. MS-DOS filenames were restricted to 8 alphanumeric characters, with a three-character extension. Windows 95 allows 255 characters including blank spaces and other special characters not found in the MS-DOS world—a welcome relief for every DOS user who ever had to name a letter to his mother ltr2mom.doc.

Descriptive filenames let you determine the format, content, and identity of a file for fast retrieval later on. There's rarely any reason to use more than 20 or 30 characters for a filename. Any more than that is overkill and quickly becomes unwieldy. You're better off creating a unique set of subdirectories to classify and categorize your files.

For more information on Windows 95, go to the AOL Windows Forum (keyword: **WIN**).

225

- You can keep several programs running in open windows at the same time. You can now pop back and forth from a spreadsheet to a database to a word processor, which makes it easy to coordinate your efforts and eliminate extra steps. Also, the Cut, Copy, and Paste functions make it easy to share data between programs.

- A specific advantage of using Windows 95 versus Windows 3.x is that open programs remain on the taskbar whenever they're minimized, so you shouldn't lose track of what's running. Also, you can start programs easily from the taskbar without interrupting your current job.

- Other specific advantages include a more intuitive file management system, single clicks to activate most functions, more length and flexibility in filenames, shortcut menus using the right-click, object and properties orientation, a Recycle Bin, shortcuts, and hundreds of other improvements designed to make your life easier.

- There are practical reasons to upgrade as well. For instance, most programs are now written for Windows 95 (meaning they will run faster in Windows 95 and may not run at all under Windows 3.x). And Windows 95 has now matured to the point where most of the important bugs have been worked out.

What about Windows 98? Now that it's out, should I jump on it?

Windows 98 was released in June, 1998. Prior to that, it had been out in a test version (what computer types call a beta) for a while. About 100,000 people participated in the test. Whether or not to upgrade to the first commercial version is likely to be more of a personal choice than a requirement, because Windows 95 should get you by until the reasons to upgrade become overwhelming.

Microsoft Windows operating system packages are unique in that they are by far the most used in the personal computer world. Thousands of other software packages and hardware devices must interact properly with Windows, and each new version must maintain backward compatibility with generations of previous hardware and software. The potential pitfalls are considerable. In a demonstration of Windows 98 at the 1998 Spring Comdex conference, the largest computer trade show in the world, Microsoft chairman Bill Gates was chagrined to see his PC succumb to a fatal error while showing off one of the jazziest new features.

Visit the AOL Windows Forum (keyword: **WIN**) and the Microsoft Web site (www.microsoft.com) for additional information on Windows 98.

What is beta testing?

Developing and testing new versions of software is a monumental task. As software manufacturers write, test, debug, rewrite, and retest their software, they work with version after version (called alpha versions) until they eventually develop something that has all the intended features and seems stable under all the conditions they can devise in the lab. This version is called the beta version. It is unfinished because it has not yet been tested in the real world.

In the real world people have an amazing assortment of systems, from elderly 386s to high-powered Pentium II workstations. Every device that could be attached probably has been, and in every conceivable combination. Third-party, fourth-party, illegal, and just plain bad hardware and software are rampant, yet everyone wants the new operating system to cope with it. The real world is not a friendly place for software, and beta testing is the only way to work the remaining problems out. The vendor enlists real-world volunteers—sometimes hundreds or thousands— and has them put the software through its paces and report all problems, or bugs. Beta testers usually get the product for free, and in its first post-laboratory incarnation, it's usually worth every penny.

However, competitive pressures may lead software companies to rush through the beta-testing stage and release post-beta versions that don't work as well as they should. They may be unstable, or they may conflict with certain other programs, causing system crashes, data loss, and no end of headaches for the unwary user.

For that reason, unless you absolutely have to have some specific feature found in a new version of a software program, consider sticking with what you have for a while longer. Wait until the first set of bug fixes has been released (usually indicated by a version number that ends in .1 or .01), which generally happens within three to six months of the initial release.

227

I bought my computer and all of my software pretty recently, but I'm already getting notices from some of the software makers that I can get upgrades for what seems like not very much money. But $29.95 here and $39.95 there adds up. Do I really need to upgrade every time a new version comes out, and if not, how often should I upgrade? Does it make a difference what kind of program it is?

Deciding whether and when to upgrade depends on how much you rely on the software, how often you swap data with others who use it, how badly you want the new features, or sometimes how often you're tormented by bugs that are corrected in the new version.

Software is generally upgraded incrementally rather than overhauled all at once, and the size of the increment can be deduced from the version number of the software. For example, suppose you start out with version 2.0. If the manufacturer notifies you that version 2.01 is available, that's likely to be no more than a bug fix release, and the manufacturer may even give it to you free. Version 2.1 may have an addi-

WINDOWS 98: SHOULD YOU UPGRADE?

If you bought a computer with Windows 95 installed, you'll probably be wondering whether you should bother upgrading. Maybe, maybe not. To help you decide, here are some things Windows 98 can do that Windows 95 can't.

- *It turns your whole desktop into a Web browser.* You will be able to access all of your files, not just the Web, through the Back and Forward buttons on Explorer, or by clicking on hyperlinks from directories that Windows 98 automatically builds from what's on your hard drive. If you love the Internet Explorer Web browser interface, you'll love Windows 98.

- *It stores files more efficiently.* Windows 98 uses a file storage system called FAT 32, which makes more effective use of the space on your hard drive and could potentially free up many megabytes of disk space. FAT 32 can also handle hard drives larger than 2GB without your having to partition them into several smaller logical drives.

- *It maintains your hard disk more intelligently.* The Disk Defragmenter Optimization Wizard keeps tabs on which programs and files you use the most, and stores all their pieces near each other, resulting in quicker start-ups. The Tune-Up Wizard lets you schedule defragmenting and other disk maintenance tasks to take place at a regular time.

- *It lets you hook up more devices more easily.* Windows 98 includes support for something called the Universal Serial Bus (USB), which allows you to daisy-chain up to 127 devices off a single port, though most home users aren't likely to want to have that many. The devices have to be USB-compatible, but they can include almost anything: mice, joysticks, printers, keyboards, modems, and gadgets not yet dreamed of.

- *It actively helps you keep your operating system and software up-to-date.* An Update Wizard automatically reaches out to a Microsoft Web site to upload the latest drivers and operating system updates.

Overall, Windows 98 will probably not be faster than Windows 95. New software, whether an operating system, a desktop publishing program, or the latest whiz-bang computer game, always takes up more processing power than the older version. Microsoft does claim, however, that it will be quicker to power up and shut down your computer.

Microsoft says that you should have at least 32MB of RAM with an Intel Pentium 166 (at least), at least 200MB of free hard disk space, and a 4 x CD-ROM drive to run Windows 98. With this system configuration, you should be able to install Windows 98 in approximately 38 minutes.

The AOL Windows Forum (keyword: **WIN**) and the Microsoft Web site (www.microsoft.com) can tell you more about Windows 98.

tional feature or two, and cost you $19.95. Version 2.5 may have a number of new features, and cost you $29.95 (or $19.95 if you're upgrading from version 2.1). And version 3.0 might be different enough to seem like a whole new product, and cost you $49.95 (while new users will pay perhaps $109.95).

The longer you wait to upgrade, the more it will cost you, though it will probably take two whole version numbers (say, from 2.0 to 4.0) to put you back to the status of a new buyer.

There are two occasions when upgrading is always an excellent idea. First, if you're upgrading your operating system (say, from Windows 3.x to Windows 95 or 98, a truly major upgrade), it's a good idea to upgrade all of your most-used software at the same time to versions designed to work with the new operating system. But wait a few months for the new versions to get their kinks out. Older versions won't take full advantage of your new operating system capabilities, and may not even run properly, depending on how old they are. It's particularly important to upgrade disk utilities, since the new operating system may handle files differently. Depending on how long it's been since you upgraded, you may have fallen back to the status of a new buyer, but upgrade anyway or buy some other program. The magazines at AOL's Computing Newsstand (keyword: **Computing Newsstand**) have reviews on the latest software packages.

Second, upgrade your anti-virus software whenever the opportunity presents itself. You should get a certain number of upgrades free when you buy the product initially, but keeping it current is very cheap insurance for your system.

My office uses Microsoft Office 95, and I have it at home so I can take work back and forth. Should I upgrade to Office 97, or should I wait until my office does it, which could be a while? What's the advantage of the new version?

Internet integration is one of the biggest differences between Office 97 and Office 95. In Microsoft Access 97, for instance, there is a new data type called Hyperlink, expressly included for containing hyperlinks in the database. And you can make hyperlinks between Office 97 applications and sites on the World Wide Web. A complete description of Office 97 can be found in the Software department at the AOL Computing Superstore (keyword: **CSS**), shown in figure 6.5.

As for upgrading before your office does, the main issue will probably be the difference in file formats. It is possible, however, to save your files in the file formats

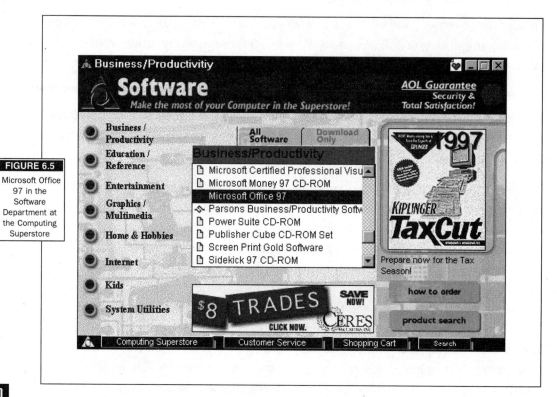

230

of earlier versions even when you're using Office 97, so if the new features sound good to you, you might as well upgrade. Just don't forget to save your files in the correct format.

Do I need to upgrade my utility programs? If so, how frequently?

Whenever you upgrade your operating system, you should also upgrade your utility programs, because many utilities are designed specifically to take advantage of the strengths and shore up the weaknesses of the operating system.

Virus checkers present a special case, because viruses mutate and evolve rapidly. Most makers of virus checkers offer free virus updates for a period of time after your purchase, and when that period runs out it's time to purchase the upgrade.

The AOL Store's Software Shop (keyword: **Software Shop**) carries utility programs at very good prices.

Upgrading Display

One of the most popular upgrades is a larger monitor. By the way, do not shop for a new monitor without checking the specs on your video card or video circuitry for compatibility. This piece of information should be in the documentation that came with your computer. It's possible that your video card or the video circuitry on your motherboard can handle a larger monitor and higher resolution than you started out with, but if it doesn't, you'll need to upgrade it, too. You'll find a great selection of monitors at the AOL Store's Hardware Shop (keyword: **Hardware Center**), shown in figure 6.6.

What should I look for when upgrading my monitor?

Monitor prices vary quite a bit, but there is a range within which most good models fall for each set of attributes. The attributes to watch for are:

- Diagonal screen size and viewable image size—Remember, the viewable image size is always smaller than the screen size, sometimes by an inch or more.

- Resolution and dot pitch—These are the number of pixels and size of the illuminated dots on the screen. Higher resolutions and lower dot pitch are better.

- Refresh rate and method—This is the screen repaint speed, either line by line or every other line.

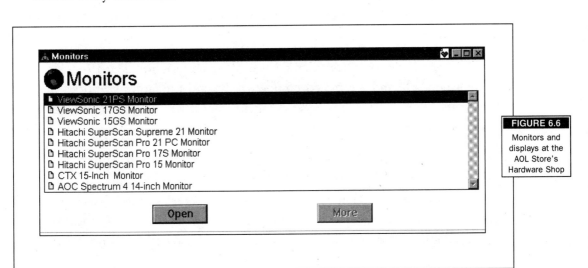

FIGURE 6.6

Monitors and displays at the AOL Store's Hardware Shop

- Picture and color quality—This varies by brand, model, and personal taste.

- Controls—These will be mechanical, on screen, or some combination of both.

- Power consumption—Energy Star compliance means a lower electric bill.

- Radio frequency (RF) radiation, glare—Some models protect you better than others.

- Flat screen—Flatter screens distort less.

For more information on monitors, see chapter 2.

I have an old 14-inch color monitor. What do you recommend as an upgrade?

Solid, entry-level monitors seem to fluctuate around a base price of $200, and these days a 15-inch color monitor is the minimum standard, with several excellent choices in the $200 range. Remember, monitors are measured diagonally across the screen unless viewable image size is specifically mentioned.

Viewable image size is measured as the size of the largest window that can be displayed on the screen, using the controls to push the image to the maximum width and height. Just a few years ago manufacturers began quoting viewable image size in their ads, because some were producing monitors with large screens (and selling them as such) when the viewable image size was actually comparable to much smaller monitors.

If your budget supports it, consider a 17- or 19-inch monitor. The 19-inch monitors are a new size and are priced competitively, and the larger size does make a tremendous difference. Once you get a larger monitor you'll never want to go back to a 14-inch again.

If you're willing to spend $1,000 or more, or you absolutely have to have a very large size monitor (if you're planning on doing computer-aided drafting, for instance), check out the 21-inch, 24-inch, or even larger monitor sizes. They tend to be very high quality, with high resolutions, high refresh rates, and excellent color and color control. Remember, though, that those larger monitors consume a huge amount of desk space. Plan on about 4 square feet of desk space for a 21-inch monitor.

Read the AOL Computing Buyer's Guide (keyword: **Buyer's Guide**), for advice and reviews on the latest monitors.

What's the difference between dot pitch and resolution?

Dot pitch is the diagonal distance between the lighted dots on the screen. On a color monitor or television, these dots consist of phosphor triads, a fancy technical term for red, green, and blue (RGB) spots that glow when the electron beam hits them. It's pretty easy to see the dots on a color TV, but much harder on a monitor, which has lower dot pitch. The lower the dot pitch, the closer the dots. Meaning you'll get finer detail and greater clarity, which is easier on the eyes.

Dot pitch is measured in millimeters (mm). The standard range of monitors currently on the market runs between 0.28mm and 0.26mm. Avoid monitors with higher dot pitch numbers, no matter how good a deal they seem to be. There's no need to opt for the really fine dot pitches (down to 0.15mm) and the extra cost involved, unless you know you'll need the extra sharpness for special applications.

Resolution is the number of picture elements, or pixels, that can be displayed on the screen at once. The more pixels you can see, the sharper the picture is and the more things you can display on the screen. However, the higher the resolution, the smaller things look on your screen, so very high resolutions are better suited to very large screens.

Pixels are arranged on a grid, and resolution is expressed as the number of pixels displayed horizontally times the number displayed vertically. The resolution for Super VGA (SVGA) is 800 x 600. This is the current minimum resolution. It's also about the highest practical resolution for a 15-inch monitor, which is the minimum size commonly used.

A multisync monitor—which is what most good models are these days—can be made to display different numbers of pixels by changing the resolution setting in the software. A good monitor might be capable of up to 1280 x 1024, though you probably won't use resolutions this high for everyday work. Conversely, if you want to display very large type on your large monitor, you can set the resolution lower than usual: to 800 x 600 or even 640 x 480. Because fewer pixels are being displayed, the edges of the letters may look ragged.

See this book's Glossary for definitions of monitor terms and chapter 2 for more information on monitors.

Isn't color quality the same for all brands? If not, how does it vary and how do I find the best quality for the money?

Differences in manufacturing processes of competing brands cause differences in picture and color quality that can't be discerned simply by looking at the specs or the price. The only way to truly tell is to look at them in person.

Things to look for are clarity, color saturation and depth, and fuzzy or color-fringed text characters or lines. Also check horizontal and vertical proportionality. To do this, draw a circle. If it doesn't look round, move on.

One useful strategy is to shop the showrooms of major computer stores, and then when you know which model you want, go to the AOL Store's Hardware Shop (keyword: **Hardware Center**) to get the best deal on a monitor.

What does Energy Star mean?

The Environmental Protection Agency (EPA) is charged with finding ways to reduce the impact on the environment of the machines we use. It has created the Energy Star specification to help consumers find computers that are moderate in power consumption. The Energy Star rating can be applied to any computer system (computer and monitor combined) that uses less than 60 watts when idle.

What about radiation?

There's been a lot of concern among computer buyers about radiation. The jury is still out as to whether it's well founded. To be on the safe side, you should be on the lookout for reduced radio frequency (RF) output. The standard to look for is called TCO, or low-emission.

Whether or not monitor radiation can harm you, lowering RF emissions also lessens the chance that your computer will interfere with other RF devices, such as radios and TVs.

I have a lot of trouble with glare. Is there any way to reduce it?

It's easy to reduce glare with an anti-glare screen, which attaches over your monitor.

It's a simple fix, and you'll find that reducing glare alleviates eyestrain and makes your screen easier to use. Some monitors are now specially finished to reduce glare automatically.

Find out how other AOL members deal with glare by going to the message boards at the PC Hardware Forum (keyword: **PC Hardware** or **PHW**).

What's the fuss about flat screens? I thought all monitors had flat screens.

From one perspective, yes, all monitors do have flat screens, but some are flatter than others. You'll want to buy the flattest screen you can get, because flatter screens show less distortion than curved screens and also reflect less glare.

By the way, *flat screen* is likely to take on new meaning in the next few years as flat-panel displays become more available and less expensive. These use a different technology than the CRT screen you likely have now, and are more akin to what's used in laptop computers. Flat-panel displays are only a few inches deep. They cost thousands of dollars now, but are likely to follow the usual cost-performance curve for computer-related equipment.

Where do video cards fit in? How do they affect display?

Video cards or circuitry reside on or in the motherboard, and they generate the signals that drive the monitor. Video cards range in price from under $50 to over $2,500, and they are used for everything from simple VGA graphics display to very fast 3-D graphics rendering. Whether or not you get the best out of your monitor (and your graphics software) largely depends on choosing the right video card, so take the time to educate yourself about these cards.

There are plenty of video card models to choose from in the Hardware department at the AOL Computing Superstore, shown in figure 6.7, and the AOL Store's Hardware Shop.

Newer motherboards frequently have adequate video circuits built in, so upgrading might mean using one of your expansion slots for a new video card. Check your motherboard documentation to see if this is the case, and also find out how to disable the onboard video circuitry if necessary.

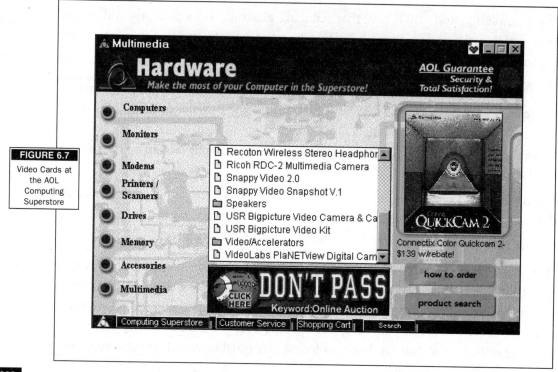

FIGURE 6.7

Video Cards at
the AOL
Computing
Superstore

236

What should I shop for in a video card?

You definitely want a co-processing chip to relieve the CPU of as much work as possible. You also want at least 2MB of RAM and preferably 4MB. With 4MB your monitor can display more than 16 million colors at a resolution of 1280 x 1024 pixels.

In your quest for the ideal video card, you'll see terms such as DRAM, SPRAM, EDO RAM, VRAM, WRAM, MDRAM, and perhaps even SGRAM. Don't be intimidated—they're all just forms of RAM, or random-access memory, and the amount you have dictates the display capability of the card.

- DRAM means dynamic random-access memory, and it's the generic name for all RAM memory modules or chips. The word *dynamic* means that the contents (data) on this type of memory disappear when the power is shut off. In contrast, other forms of memory called mass storage–hard drives, floppy drives, and so on–retain their data for years without power.

- SRAM means static RAM, simply a faster form of RAM than common DRAM.

- EDO RAM means extended data out RAM. It refers to specially manu-factured chips whose timing overlaps between successive accesses, for a significant performance improvement. EDO RAM is more expensive, and your motherboard must support it. It offers the greatest benefits to faster systems that employ Pentium, Pentium Pro, and Pentium II processors.

- VRAM means Video RAM, and it's much faster than EDO RAM.

- WRAM means Windows RAM. It's slightly faster than VRAM, and sur-prisingly, it costs a little less. Two to four MB of VRAM or WRAM is a good choice in a video card.

- MDRAM means multibank DRAM, and SGRAM means synchronous graphics RAM). Both are high-end solutions not intended for the general market. They are very fast, but very expensive. If you do lots of graphics or animation, or simply want the best card for high-end games, you could be in the market for a card with SGRAM.

I keep seeing the term *color depth*. What does that mean?

Color depth refers to the number of bits used to code the exact color for a given pixel. The greater the depth, the greater the number of colors that can be displayed. For example, 4 bits equals 16 colors, while 24 bits equals 16 million colors. True color is considered 24-bit color, and some systems use color depths up to 30 bits. Look for 24-bit color when shopping.

Do I need to be concerned about the bus when I upgrade my video card?

Probably not. Chances are, the only choice you'll have with a newer machine is a video card that uses the PCI bus. If you're upgrading an old, low-end 486, you might have to go with a VL-bus video card, but stay away from them if you can. While you're at it, make sure the card you get has 3-D acceleration built-in. It's only a matter of time before most applications will incorporate some sort of 3-D graph-ics. The most popular games and simulators already do.

I really want to be able to capture video and edit it in my computer, but I know it takes quite a bit of horsepower. What exactly do I need, and what should I watch out for?

Both television and computer display technologies use video signals, but unfortunately they are not the same kind of signals. TV in the United States and Japan uses the National Television System Committee (NTSC) standard. France uses the Sequential Couleur Avec Memoire, or SECAM, standard, and the rest of Europe uses the Phase Alternate Line, or PAL, standard. Computers use the standards we've already discussed—chiefly VGA and SVGA.

Your strategy will depend on whether you're generating the video on your computer or through standard videotaping equipment and whether you want your output to appear on your computer or your television. You'll need a special converter card if you want to output to a standard TV. Look for a VGA-to-NTSC adapter, which converts the VGA output of your computer to an NTSC signal. You'll have to set the resolution low so the characters and small details will be visible, but it will still be hard to read. These converter cards also let you output your computer screens to videotape. This is handy if, for example, you're making a videotape-based training program.

A video capture board does the opposite, capturing incoming analog video signals by digitizing them (in much the same way audio is recorded by your computer) and storing them. Then you can edit the video in your computer. Captured video is stored frame by frame, and capture rates vary widely with the capture card used, the bus employed, and your own system's processor. In every case, the faster the better.

What is MPEG 2?

Video files captured at high resolution are very large, as much as 2MB for a single frame at full-screen. Not only does this fill your hard drive quickly, but the size taxes your bus's ability to move the files rapidly for video editing. Compression solves these problems for today's systems, and Motion Picture Experts Group (MPEG) 2 compression is widely used throughout the industry.

Upgrading Disk Space

Today, you can buy hard drives of 8GB or more, and even though floppies are still limited to 1.44MB, you can buy a Zip, Jaz, or other cartridge drive (rewritable mass storage device) with anywhere from 100MB to 2GB of storage space. Storage gets cheaper by the year, which is just as well, since the computer industry is always thinking of new ways to use it up.

FIGURE 6.8

Hard Drives at the AOL Computing Superstore

239

The AOL Computing Superstore, shown in figure 6.8, and the AOL Store's Hardware Shop have plenty of hard disk options for all systems.

How many hard drives can my system hold?

The computer you have now should have at least one hard drive already on board, and that drive should be accessible as drive C. In fact, if you look at the DOS command prompt, it will read C:\. Physically, most computers have the room and connections for at least two hard drives, and if you like, you can label them drive C and drive D.

Logically, if you partition your hard drives into smaller segments, you could have four or five more entire hard drives available. They'd still be the same two drives you installed, just logically partitioned.

There are a few good reasons to do this. You'll get a little more hard drive space out of the deal, and you can run two or more operating systems if you're so minded. Read on for more details.

What is the FAT?

Aside from the fat we all know about, there's another kind. The addresses for all the files and directories on your hard drive are kept in a special table called the File Allocation Table (FAT). The FAT is placed in a secure location on the hard drive, and each time a file is read or written, the operating system looks up the correct location using the FAT.

The FAT is limited in the number of locations it can address, and the limitation is inherent in the operating system. Different operating systems use different versions of FAT, and some can access more addresses than others. In any case, since all of them can access only a limited number of addresses, the drive is chopped up into thousands of tiny file storage locations called clusters. Each cluster has its own address and is made up of thousands of bytes. The size of the cluster is determined by the overall size of the drive.

Repartitioning your hard drive into two or four smaller logical drives reduces the cluster size and frees up previously inaccessible portions of the clusters. One portion will now be labeled C and the other D. You'll still have the same single, physical drive, but it will now be split into two logical drives. It's almost like getting something for nothing.

How can I run more than one operating system on the same computer?

With smart partitioning packages like Partition Magic, you can set up the partitions correctly for different, incompatible operating systems, even on the same physical drive. If you have a 4GB hard drive currently labeled C, you can split it into two C drives of 2GB apiece. Each drive will be hidden from the other during use. Two GB is plenty to run an operating system and lots of applications.

When you want to start your computer using the other operating system, select which operating system to use and the computer will boot under that environment. It's a piece of cake. This is a very handy ability if, for example, your office environment is still running Windows 3.x and you've upgraded to Windows 95, or if you want to take a computer programming course that's based on UNIX.

Are there upgrades for my floppy drive? It seems like 1.44MB is kind of small nowadays.

There are upgrades for floppy drives, but unfortunately they aren't standardized, so there's no obvious answer. As long as software manufacturers distribute software on 1.44MB floppies and people use them for transporting files, you don't want to get rid of your floppy drive completely. For small file transfer, they are a very handy size at an extremely low price.

There are several prominent manufacturers of mass storage devices, which can accommodate files in the 100MB range and up. But the formats are incompatible and it's anybody's guess which one will win out. The demand is clearly there because so many files now exceed the 1.44MB limitation. But it's hard to figure out which device to buy.

All mass storage devices are in the $100 to $300 price range, and the media prices per megabyte are also comparable. The Zip drive by Iomega is a major contender, with wide distribution and a low price (around $100 to $150 for the drive and $20 for a 100MB disk). A competing format in this category is the LS-120, which has the added advantage of being able to read standard 1.44MB floppies at five times the normal speed. However, the LS-120 is less widely distributed than the Zip. Check out the Zip drives at the AOL Computing Superstore, shown in figure 6.9.

What styles of mass storage devices are there?

Zip drives come in two styles, internal and external, the external being about $50 more. You can specify an IDE connection (like the one your hard drive probably has) or a SCSI connection. The SCSI will be a little faster, but it requires a SCSI interface card, meaning you'll have to install the drive using one of your expansion slots, and the card itself will cost you extra if you don't already have one.

The Jaz drive, also by Iomega, comes with the same options. It is about twice the price of the Zip, but it can hold either 1GB or 2GB on each removable disk, and the disks work at speeds comparable to hard drives rather than floppy drives. The devices are actually like small removable hard drives. Again, the big disadvantage is that none of these formats are compatible with one another. But if you're not swapping data with anyone else, or if your company has one standardized format, the lack of universal compatibility doesn't really matter most of the time.

Should I get a faster CD-ROM drive? How about a DVD-ROM drive? Isn't it just an over-hyped CD-ROM player?

Digital Versatile Disks or Digital Video Disks (DVDs), whichever you prefer, are superfast CD-ROM disks. Comparatively, they hold massive quantities of data, and

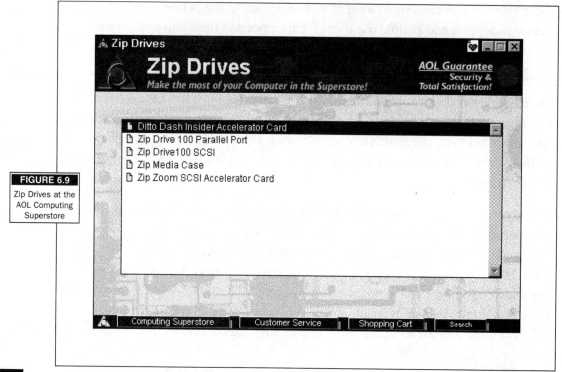

FIGURE 6.9

Zip Drives at the
AOL Computing
Superstore

can transfer data at much higher speeds than CD-ROMs. They are convenient for holding movies and long musical pieces, which makes them a medium whose time has come.

Because manufacturers rarely encode ordinary CD-ROM disks with data at more than 4X, and because the superfast CD-ROM players tend to create so much noise and draw so much power during playback, you should seriously consider upgrading to DVD rather than purchase a faster CD-ROM drive. DVD-ROM drives are being manufactured in quantity now and prices are falling as competition takes hold.

Check out the Products 2000 category in the Buyer's Guide (keyword: **Buyer's Guide**) for more information on DVD-ROM drives.

Upgrading Your Modem

You're not alone if you complain about how long it takes to connect to the Internet. In these days of instant gratification, no one wants to wait around. Fortunately, there is a way to speed up this process: upgrade your modem. You can go with either a cable modem (very expensive) or a 56K modem.

Most folks won't be in a position to connect via a cable modem for at least a year or two, because it depends not only on their willingness to purchase a cable modem, but also on their local cable provider's willingness to provide Internet connections. At this writing, Internet-over-cable is in only very limited testing. In the meantime, the practical alternative is to upgrade to a 56K modem. The AOL service offers 56K connections in most locations, so it's easy to justify the purchase.

As is currently the situation with mass storage devices, there were originally two competing formats for 56K technology. U.S. Robotics (USR) was first out of the gate with the new modems, which it called X2. Lucent & Rockwell and other major manufacturers backed a different format called K56Flex.

Recently, the two merged into something called V.90. Any 56K modem you buy should be V.90 compliant.

Check the AOL Store's Modem Shop (keyword: **Modem Shop**) for good buys on modems.

Do 56K modems actually do 56K?

Your actual average data transfer speeds will probably never be 56K, and have a limitation of 53K. The 56K technology relies on clear, crisp analog phone lines and digital connections from your phone company's switching office. If you have poor quality phone service (lots of noise) or are a long distance from the nearest digital switching equipment, you probably won't get lots of improvement for your money. On the other hand, 56K modems are cheap now, so even a little improvement is probably worth it.

I need to connect two computers in a small network. Is it expensive? Do I need a consultant, or can I do it myself for a reasonable price?

Lots of households now have more than one computer and are going through the same thing offices did years ago. It's inconvenient to transfer files via sneakernet—walking around from computer to computer with disk in hand. And it's costly to buy a separate printer for every computer in the house.

The obvious solution is to connect your computers together in a small local area network (LAN). There was a time when networking was an expensive proposition, because only highly paid consultants knew how to do it and the gear cost an arm and a leg.

These days, anyone running Windows 95 can easily set up a small network for as little as $100. All you need are two network interface cards (NICs) and some cable. The cable can be either coaxial cable, like your TV cable, or twisted-pair cable, similar to the clear plastic cable connecting your telephone to the wall. Search the AOL Computing Superstore (keyword: **CSS**) with the term **network**, and look for networking starter kits that have two NICs.

You just pop the NICs into expansion slots in both computers, connect the cables, load the drivers and install them into your operating system (Windows 95 should do it automatically), and voilà! Of course, there's always the chance that some difficulty will crop up, but you shouldn't need a $150-an-hour consultant to make it work. A local computer store or repair shop can do the installation for you. Or if you're buying new computers, you may be able to get the NICs pre-installed.

Adding Multimedia Elements or Features

The term *multimedia PC* appeared a few years ago. It refers to PCs having a particular set of capabilities, not one certain piece of hardware or software. Generally, multimedia means your computer has video and audio functions, but it also means quite a bit more than that.

Today, audio and video are everywhere, and are inexpensive as well.

CD-ROM and DVD-ROM drives play a central role in multimedia because they store so much data in a compact format. They're perfect for storing entire entertainment packages, but there's quite a bit of hardware that goes along with them. Sound cards, digital cameras, scanners, speakers, microphones, surround sound, PC cams, accelerated 3-D animation, 3-D mice, joysticks, immersive virtual reality (VR) devices, and other cutting-edge stuff is rapidly invading the scene.

What should I look for in sound cards?

The first thing you'll want to look for is Sound Blaster compatibility. The Creative Labs Sound Blaster is the industry standard, and most games and applications use this standard for audio. The AOL Hardware Shop, has a wide selection of Sound Blaster–compatible cards (shown in figure 6.10).

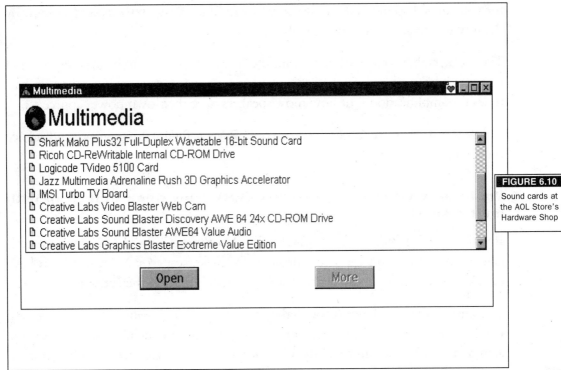

FIGURE 6.10

Sound cards at the AOL Store's Hardware Shop

The next thing to specify is wavetable synthesis. This feature uses recorded instrument sounds stored as digitized sound waves in a table on the computer, hence the term *wavetable*. Audio synthesized from this source is quite realistic.

Sound cards are relatively inexpensive (from $30 to $300) and easy to install. Even a novice can do it using an expansion slot. If you're running Windows 95 or Windows 98 and using Plug and Play components, it's unlikely you will have any difficulty with the hardware configuration, but if you're running an older operating system, setting the COM ports, IRQs, and Direct Memory Accesses (DMAs) can be difficult.

The AOL Buyer's Guide provides reviews and advice on sound cards.

Can I use stereo speakers for my computer system? What about surround sound?

You can use any speakers you like, and any audio formats you like, as long as the sound card and the software you're running support them. What comes out of your computer system is the same as what comes out of your sound system by the time it's traveling over the speaker wires, so it makes no difference. Check the wattage, dynamic range, and other parameters to make sure you're using the proper speakers for your digital sound system, just as you would for your stereo sound system. By the way, stereo sound systems are also going digital.

The speakers that come with new computer systems are likely to be inexpensive, and have medium wattage and no dedicated bass speaker. Early systems relied on batteries for amplification, but now most speakers have their own power source.

Check the AOL Buyer's Guide (keyword: **Buyer's Guide**) for reviews and advice on speakers.

I'm interested in virtual reality (VR). How does that fit in with multimedia?

If you have a fast Pentium with 32MB of RAM or more, a good 3-D graphics accelerator video card, and the latest browser from Netscape or Microsoft, you have everything you need to zoom inside a 3-D virtual world on the Internet.

To complete the experience (though they're a low priority if your dollars are limited), you can buy immersive headsets, which are the goggles and helmet used in VR game arenas or on TV. You can also buy 3-D mice, which are mice that can move you (or your point of view) on screen in many directions and dimensions. A few joysticks also have this special 3-D functionality.

What about keyboards and mice? Is it worth upgrading these items, or should I stick with what I've got?

If you're uncomfortable with your standard keyboard or mouse, consider upgrading, because there are some products available that can make life better. Some people find a trackball much more convenient to use than a mouse, especially if they're prone to shoulder or neck pain. There are also ergonomic keyboards available, some with a more natural angle on the keys, and some that actually split into two separate boards, one for each hand.

Another input device is the glidepad. It's common on laptop computers, but you can also get one as a peripheral for your desktop machine. As their name suggests, glidepads allow you to move the cursor by sliding your finger around a pad. Try one out before you buy because it is quite a different way to work.

I want to produce good-looking hard-copy output. What do I need for really brilliant color?

Color ink-jet printers are a bargain today. For less than $500, you can get one with outstanding image quality. Most use a wet process that shoots tiny bubbles of ink precisely onto the paper. A company named Alps makes a model that uses ribbons coated with a hard, dry colored wax. The ribbons press the colored wax onto the paper. Both technologies create brilliant, long-lasting color on ordinary paper, but the dry process is much more resistant to water damage.

The big differences, compared to black-and-white laser printers, are the cost per sheet and the time to print. Color printers are improving all the time, but they are still slower and significantly more expensive to operate. If you need high-speed color printing and have deep pockets, check out the color laser printers. They offer excellent image quality and high speed for around $4,000 and up.

I've always wanted a scanner, but the cost has put me off. Have these come down in price, too?

They sure have. Good flatbed scanners used to cost thousands of dollars, but now you can find them for less than $200. A flatbed scanner looks a lot like a copier. You lay a paper or book on a glass surface and the scanner passes a high-intensity light over the face of the paper to capture the image. You want 24-bit color capture and 600 dots per inch (dpi). Software can interpolate the dpi to much higher levels, so read the ads carefully to find out exactly what you're getting.

Go to the AOL Buyer's Guide (keyword: **Buyer's Guide**) for advice and reviews on scanners. The AOL Store's Digital Shop (keyword: **Digital Shop**) has good prices on scanners.

Building Your Custom PC

Building your own computer can be one of the most rewarding and most frustrating experiences you'll ever have. Doing it successfully will give you a glow of accomplishment and a crash course in hardware, but you have to be committed. If you

247

If you are building a desktop system, make sure whatever boards you buy have edge-connector contacts matching the ones in the motherboard (gold-to-gold or tin-to-tin). Dissimilar metals tend to corrode, and can quickly cause problems.

You'll need about 256K of cache memory for up to 32MB of RAM. Make sure the motherboard supports pipeline burst cache.

Intel and other manufacturers are steadily lowering the power requirements of their CPUs (and therefore the amount of heat generated), but a heat sink or cooling fan is a good investment, and is mandatory in some cases. A heat sink consists of metal blades attached to the CPU case, and a cooling fan is a small fan attached to the heat sink. Both serve to absorb and dissipate heat from the CPU.

A built-in mass storage device, such as a Zip drive or a Jaz drive, is a handy feature for backing up.

A CD-ROM drive is mandatory, because most software is now distributed on CD-ROM disc. Complete multimedia packages, including CD-ROM drive, sound card, speakers and quite a few titles are very inexpensive today. But be aware that most of the titles are usually lesser-known packages that you may or may not find useful.

248

want to try it, make sure to block out enough hours to succeed and promise yourself you won't give up.

Take a look at the magazines at the AOL Computing Newsstand (keyword: **Computing Newsstand**) for good ideas and suggestions on building a custom PC.

Companies like Dell, Gateway, and Micron thrive because they can build PC systems to order. In the same fashion, you can buy all the parts you need and put one together for yourself. If you know where to shop, you can save money as well. The AOL Store's Hardware Shop is a great place to start. In addition, you can find plenty of reference material to help you along at TechWeb's TechShopper site (shown in figure 6.11), featured on the AOL Buyer's Guide.

Just remember that you won't get technical support or a warranty with your homemade system. If anything goes wrong, you'll have to figure it out for yourself. And if something conks out on you, you'll have to rely on the manufacturer's warranty for that individual part.

Where can I get technical advice about building a computer?

There are plenty of resources available. If you need technical advice, check the computer forums on the AOL service, such as the PC Hardware Forum (keyword: **PC Hardware** or **PHW**). You can submit a question on the message boards, and within a few minutes or hours you'll receive an answer to your question, probably from someone who encountered the same problem recently. By the way, it's polite (and great fun as well) to take a turn responding to other people's questions with your

newfound knowledge. The PC Help Desk, AOL Computing New Computer User's Guide (shown in figure 6.12), and AOL Computing Tips (keyword: **Computing Tips**) can help with your computing questions and problems.

I'm a little worried about being all on my own with this, without the backup of the computer company. What if my parts burn out or break down?

Electrical components tend to follow the same rule. They either fail during the first 30 days of use, or they don't fail until the normal end of their life. That means that if you use your computer heavily for about a month anything that's going to fail will probably fail then. Rather than wait a month, you could just leave it running for a few days constantly—the so-called burn-in period.

After the burn-in period most components should last a long time. There are always a few that are bad right out of the box or after a few hours of use.

OK, I've got the bug. How do I get started?

It's as easy as making a list of the necessary items and doing a little shopping at the AOL Store's Hardware Shop. Before you make any purchases, cruise around the shop and find out what parts go with what. For instance, you need to decide what style of case you want, and then make sure the motherboard you want fits into that

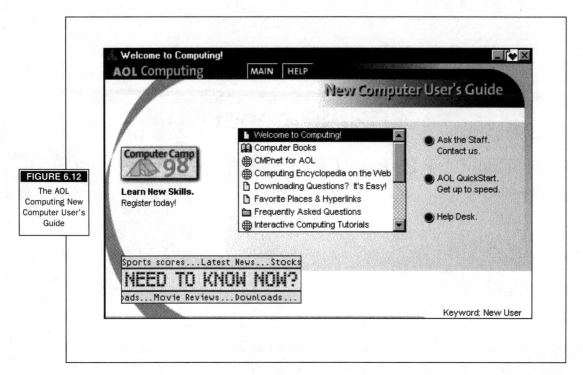

case. Fortunately, there's tons of helpful information in the shop, and also links to other sources of information. On the Web, you can find whole Web sites devoted to helping you build your own computer, and some even have software that lets you select your desired components and tells you what parts are compatible with what other parts. There are many excellent books available on the topic of building your own PC. Check out Barnes and Noble (keyword: **barnesandnoble**) or Amazon (www.amazon.com). Good luck, and have fun!

7

BUYING A NEW PC

After you've used your PC for a while, and possibly gone through one or two rounds of upgrades—more RAM, a new hard drive, a faster modem—you will eventually start itching for a brand-new one. A friend will get one, and you'll watch enviously as it tears through cyberspace and runs popular programs that scorn your computer's current configuration. Prices will drop to the point where machines two generations ahead of yours cost less than you paid, and come loaded with software and gadgets that weren't invented when you bought yours. Don't feel bad—it happens to everyone.

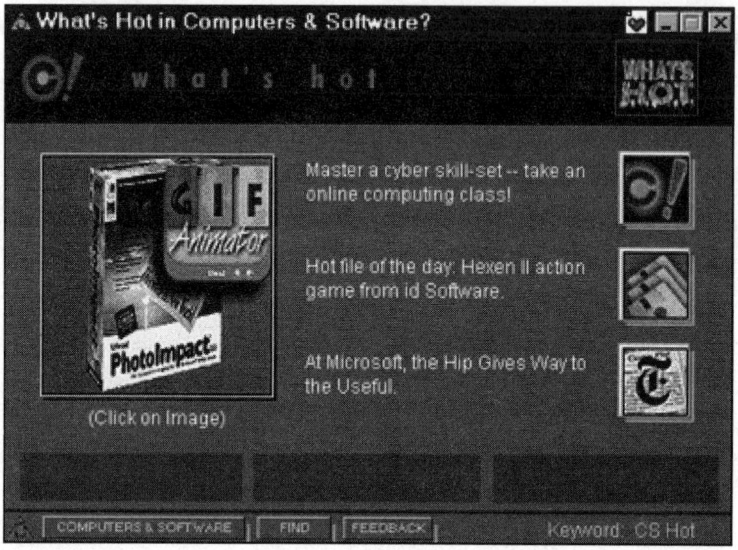

FIGURE 7.1.

What's Hot in Computers & Software?

In this chapter you'll learn all about how to buy a new computer: how to identify what you really want, what to look for and where to get it, and how to cut through the hype. There are so many choices that gaining a clear understanding of the basics is a good idea, even if this is your third or fourth purchase. The "basics" change radically every few years. Once upon a time, a 100MB hard drive was considered large; now drives with ten times that space seem cramped. Once, half a megabyte of RAM seemed like a lot; now smart computer buyers demand at least 32MB. See What's Hot in Computers & Software (keyword: **CS Hot**), shown in figure 7.1.

How Much Computer Do You Need?

Computers are designed to run software. The hardware you buy needs to be able to run your software choices today, and should be upgradable to run tomorrow's best packages as well. In addition, because new components are constantly being developed, you need to make sure the system has the room to connect to or accept them. The Gadget Guru (keyword: **Gadget**) (shown in figure 7.2), in the Computing

FIGURE 7.2
The Gadget Guru

Buyer's Guide (keyword: **Buyer's Guide**), shows off the latest goodies, so you can reappraise your needs and wants frequently. Products are listed by category area.

253

How do I decide what my needs are?

Computers are multipurpose machines, which is why they've all but displaced single-function appliances like the dedicated word processor or the game console. Identifying your central needs won't preclude using your computer for lots of other things, but it will help you figure out how best to allocate your computing dollars.

Do you want entertainment? Maybe you'll want a game machine, or a good multimedia system, and you'll want to spend extra to get the best display and sound quality. Do you run a business or do research? You'll want the fastest modem you can afford, for connecting to the Internet and the AOL service, the latest versions of whatever software you've come to depend on, and perhaps a good color printer for creating presentations—but maybe you can do without the top-of-the-line speakers.

Do you travel, and do you need your computer when you're on the road? You might want to consider a laptop computer. A fully loaded laptop computer is expensive (up to twice the cost of a comparable desktop PC) and not the most comfortable for long stints of work, but it lets you carry your office with you. Only you can say whether the trade-offs are worth it.

Are you in school? Being able to use your home-generated data on the school computers could be important, so you want to ensure "backward compatibility" even if you end up with a machine fancier than the ones at school. Obtain information about the school's configuration, particularly about which software versions it uses, and have it with you when you shop.

Should I get the fastest system I can find? How soon before it's obsolete?

Computers are obsolete virtually the moment they come out of the box, in the sense that a newer and more powerful model is probably already available. Get used to this fact of life—it's not going to change anytime soon!

At this writing, Intel Pentium and Pentium II chips are the standard, though you might find 80486-based PCs available for extremely low prices, particularly in laptop models. If all you're doing is word processing or spreadsheet calculations, an 80486 might be enough. However, if you're going to have anything to do with multimedia or surfing the Internet (as most people will eventually), it doesn't make sense to economize on processing power. Your savings will evaporate if you need to upgrade later. If you try to tough it out without upgrading, the potential for frustration is considerable.

Because the price difference between an adequate system and a fully capable system is relatively small, getting the extra features and performance you want makes a lot of sense.

If you're not happy with what you're using or it can't handle Windows 95, find out what's on the market that has the hardware and software capabilities you need. The AOL Store (keyword: **AOL Store**) has tons of information about all manner of computer systems, the specs, the prices, and performance ratings, so it's a great place to start.

At the AOL Computing Superstore (keyword: **CSS**), you can find hardware by clicking on the Hardware button (shown in figure 7.3). The AOL Store's Hardware Shop (keyword: **Hardware Center**), Modem Shop (keyword: **Modem Shop**), and Digital Shop (keyword: **Digital Shop**) are other places to shop online for hardware. You'll find information on computers and the spectrum of peripherals that make them work for you: monitors, keyboards, hard drives, video cards, sound cards, mice, modems, CD-ROM drives, printers, scanners, and backup devices.

255

If you're not sure where to go for a particular item, try the Product Search button on the front page of the AOL Computing Superstore (keyword: **CSS**), shown in figure 7.4. Enter the name of the product you're looking for, and the AOL service will automatically find it for you.

The AOL computer shopping sites are the best places to find the fastest systems and components, as well as the information to use them productively.

Only you know whether you need a cutting-edge computer badly enough to pay the price premium that separates it from models a generation or two back—which could be a couple of thousand dollars for a complete, fully loaded system. Depending on how long it's been since you've purchased a new PC, just about anything now on the market may seem overwhelmingly fast and dazzlingly sophisticated. One approach is to spend an afternoon with a friend's newish garden-variety PC—these days a Pentium MMX-based 166MHz computer with about 32MB of RAM, at a

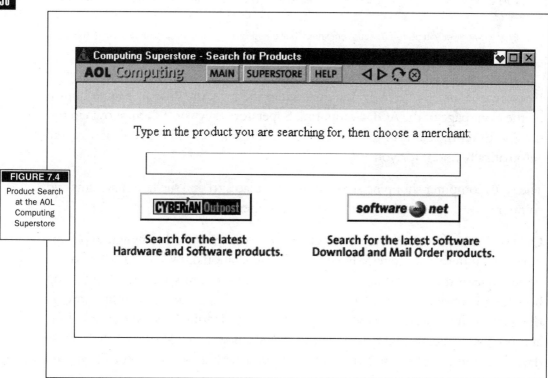

FIGURE 7.3
The AOL Computing Superstore Hardware area

FIGURE 7.4
Product Search at the AOL Computing Superstore

price of about $1,300—and run it through the tasks you find annoying, difficult, or impossible to do on your old machine. If the performance blows you away, then you probably don't need to spend more than your friend did. If it's only OK, and you have the extra cash, you may want to buy something a little more powerful.

Interpreting the Ads

To get the best deal for your money, you have to be able to cut through the hype, the fads, the gimmicky nonsense and find the real facts. Knowing what the acronyms, buzz words, and slick sales talk actually mean can save you plenty, and get you much closer to the performance you deserve for a price you can afford.

The only things that count when you're buying a computer system are performance, price, quality, and interoperability. The computer systems market can be very confusing, but it's also extremely competitive, which is why prices drop so rapidly. Speaking of price, it's not very hard to get a price quote for an entire system or individual components from several different vendors. If you stick with the major brands, quality shouldn't vary too widely. (However, the quality of the technical support is another issue altogether. That's discussed in more detail soon.)

Every vendor says their computers are the best. How can I tell who actually sells the finest equipment?

Like any other purchase, there's more to getting a good deal than just the quality, speed, and price of the system itself. Customer service, unambiguous advertising, comprehensive warranties, reasonable return policies, price reduction guarantees, on-site service, and technical support all play a role in differentiating an average purchase from a great deal.

Look for a company that is known for excellent customer service, because computer equipment can be difficult and confusing even for knowledgeable users. A pleasant and competent person on the other end of the phone can be a lifesaver when you're not quite sure what to buy. Scuttlebutt on AOL forums, such as the PC Hardware Forum (keyword: **PC Hardware** or **PHW**), can alert you to problem companies. And if you're considering buying from a particular company, you can post your choice and ask for comments at the forum's message board. Another place to check out a computer company is on the AOL Computing channel. This is where you'll find the Companies area (keyword: **Companies**), which lists computer hardware companies alphabetically and brings you to their Web sites. Once you're at a company's Web site, you'll be able to get information about the company and what they offer for customer service.

Look for extra information in ads that makes it easy to tell whether a particular feature is going to be of use to you. It's very annoying to buy a product, get it home, and plug it in, only to find out something doesn't quite do what you expected it to. You can also turn to the AOL Computing Classifieds area (keyword: **Classifieds**), which sells new and used computer equipment.

The AOL Computing Newsstand (keyword: **Computing Newsstand**) is your best source of unbiased information about new computer systems for sale. There are dozens of online magazines and newspapers to choose from, and hundreds of reviews, customer surveys, and in-depth analyses to steer you in the right direction. You can search for topics by choosing the Newsstand Search function, shown in figure 7.5.

If you're looking only for reviews of specific systems or system types, check out the Desktop Computer section at the AOL Computing Buyer's Guide (keyword: **Buyer's Guide**), shown in figure 7.6. The front page opens to a series of selection boxes in which you can narrow your choice of system. For instance, you can choose

258

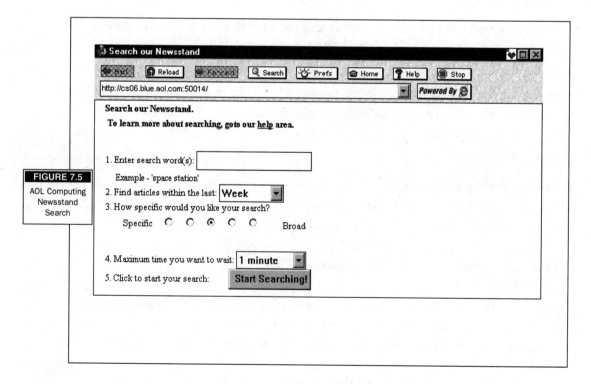

FIGURE 7.5

AOL Computing
Newsstand
Search

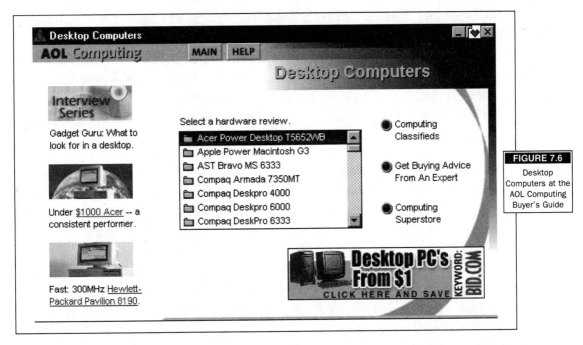

Desktop Systems, Pentium IIs, and then Dream Machines to see reviews of high-end, fully featured systems.

What kind of warranty should I look for?

Watch out for companies that offer little or no warranty of their own, expecting you to rely on the manufacturer's warranty. Some component retailers operate this way. While you may get a one-year warranty on the parts (which is more than adequate), the trouble is you have to take them back to the store and hope the next one you get isn't bad as well. In effect, you become the manufacturer's quality control system, only you're doing it at your expense. What may seem like a really good price will suddenly not look so hot.

The return policy can make or break a deal, because if you can't return the goods for a full refund within a period of at least 30 days, you may not be able to fully burn-in the item. As we discussed in chapter 5, if electrical components (and whole systems, for that matter) are going to fail, they tend to do it in the first 30 days of continuous use. Watch out for stores that have a very short return period, accept returns only for store credit, or charge a "restocking" fee. Also, be careful when purchasing sensitive components, such as RAM. Some stores allow no returns on RAM whatsoever.

Something else that can make a good deal great is a price reduction policy. Computer system prices drop dramatically all the time, and if the company you are dealing with is reputable, it will refund the price difference between the system you just bought and the same system it sells at a lower price today. How much time can elapse after you purchase the computer depends on the computer company. Often, calling the company and explaining the circumstances will result in a refund even in the absence of a formal price reduction policy.

On-site service and technical support are the cornerstones of any good computer deal. Sometimes these services cost extra, but if you want to concentrate on your work instead of becoming a computer fix-it whiz, they are invaluable. You can usually get both for a small fee (or free for a short time, in some cases), and the only caveat is that they might not actually be there when you need them. Find out the hours that the company's technical support staff is available. After all, even the best policy or warranty is meaningless if the company doesn't deliver when you need it the most. Take the time to ask around or find out about other customers' experiences before taking the plunge. Use the AOL service's Computing Chat & Messages area (keyword: **Computing Chat**) to find out, firsthand, what other people think of manufacturers.

Computer ads look like a jumble of acronyms and jargon. What are the most important specs I need to keep an eye out for?

The most difficult and complex job you face as a consumer is determining whether an advertised system will deliver what you need. Every ad you read will sound like Greek until you know what the specifications really mean. If you take a look at some common computer ads in a magazine like Home PC at the Computing Newsstand (keyword: **Computing Newsstand**), shown in figure 7.7, you might see an ad that reads something like this:

```
Brand Name Superdesktop 200—Intel 200MHz Pentium Processor w/
MMX, 64MB SDRAM, 6.4GB Ultra ATA hard drive, 24X EIDE variable
speed CD-ROM drive, 17" monitor .26 (16") 1024 x 768—Included
Standard - 512KB pipeline burst cache, flash BIOS, Integrated
100MB Iomega Zip drive, 3.5" floppy drive, 32-voice wavetable
stereo sound with speakers, USR Sportster 56K data/fax modem,
PCI 64-bit 3-D video, MPEG, 4MB EDO DRAM, Microsoft
IntelliMouse, USB Connections, Microsoft Windows 95 and MS
Plus!, Microsoft Office 97 Small Business Edition, Software
Bundle Pack, 5-year/2-year warranty. $1,699
```

Huh?

We'll take the ad apart so you can feel comfortable with each bit of it.

The first things most people look for (and one of the most prominent features advertised) are CPU brand, type, and speed. CPUs (or central processing units) are defined by the chip or processor that powers them—the "brain" of the computer. Intel dominates the market for personal computer chips, but competitors AMD and Cyrix make chips that are compatible with Intel's and run all the same software. Intel chips are considered the standard, and cost more for that reason. The AMD and Cyrix offerings represent a good, lower-cost alternative, and some user surveys show a preference for the AMD chip over Intel. AMD chips are designated as K5 or K6 chips (rather than Pentium) followed by the MHz rating (a measure of the chip's speed). Cyrix chips are identified as 6x86MX-PR and then the MHz rating.

Currently, CPUs are likely to be either Pentium or Pentium II (for Intel chips), with speeds that range from 166MHz to 400MHz. Although it's unlikely that you'll find any new CPU system without MMX technology, some of the lower-end processors (especially the lower-end laptop models) just might lack it. Look for MMX, because it's increasingly important to have for optimum performance of the latest multimedia software.

You keep mentioning the motherboard, but I don't see anything about it in the ad. How do motherboards vary? What do I need to look for?

Actually, the ad does make reference to the motherboard, but it's hard to spot unless you know the terminology. The phrase: "512KB pipeline burst cache, flash BIOS" is about the motherboard.

Cache is a special type of very-fast-access RAM that is dedicated to supporting the CPU directly, when normal RAM memory is too slow. For older DOS and Windows 3.x systems, having more than 256KB of cache RAM installed on the motherboard does not improve performance. With Windows 95 and Windows 98, however, 512KB is a good standard. Up to 2MB can result in a nice performance increase.

There are several kinds of cache available: asynchronous static RAM (Async SRAM), synchronous burst static RAM (Sync SRAM), and pipelined burst static RAM (PB SRAM). Look for PB SRAM in a new system, with at least 512KB cache.

Motherboard expansion slots aren't even mentioned in our sample ad, but it's essential to find out about them before you buy a computer. The number and type of expansion slots are crucial factors in determining your system's upgradability, because anything you buy that's labeled "internal" has to go either in a drive bay or an expansion slot on the motherboard. For example, a new video card, sound card, modem, network card, or controller card must have an expansion slot available to be installed.

There are two types of expansion slots. PCI slots are compatible with the more recent PCI bus, while ISA slots are compatible with the ISA bus. You need both types of slots because some components work better (and will only fit into) one or the other. Naturally, the more your motherboard has, the more you can expand or upgrade your system.

Also find out how many RAM expansion slots the motherboard has, and whether they're DIMM or SIMM slots. That will determine how much RAM you can ultimately install.

"Flash BIOS" means the BIOS (or basic input/output system, built into the CPU) is upgradeable. In older computers, the BIOS couldn't be upgraded.

I see the ad lists a hard drive, a CD-ROM drive, a Zip drive, and a floppy drive. Do I really need all four kinds, and how do I know if the models are reliable?

The ad describes the hard drive as a "6.4GB Ultra ATA hard drive." The size, 6.4GB, is the primary attribute to look for, and this one's currently on the large side. "Ultra ATA" means the data transfer interface is the latest version currently available. (Earlier ones include IDE and EIDE.)

There are two critical specifications that can vary among drives, and those aren't mentioned in the ad: the access (seek) time and the data transfer rate. Currently, anything under 10ms seek time and over 6MB data transfer rate suggests a very good hard drive.

CD-ROM drives are included in almost every system sold these days, and the most prominently advertised spec is the X value, as in the 24X in our sample ad. The X value means how many times faster the drive is than the standard 300K per second data transfer speed. There is a fair amount of variation between drives, so look for sustained data throughput as a better measure of overall performance. EIDE (Enhanced Integrated Drive Electronics) refers to the data transfer interface between the CD-ROM drive and the hard drive.

The Iomega Zip drive in the sample ad is by far the most painless way to back up your data. Iomega is the leading manufacturer of Zip drives and Jaz drives for mass storage. The difference between them is the size of the cartridge. Zip cartridges hold 100MB, while Jaz cartridges hold a 1GB—ten times as much. The Zip is the most common drive included with new systems. Floppy drives, which accept 1.44MB 3.5-inch diskette, are standard on all machines. They're a commodity, and any kind will probably perform reliably.

For more information about drives, see the discussion in chapter 2.

Is the monitor in this ad a decent one? What does all that stuff about the video card mean?

As a system, "video" consists of the video processing circuitry and the monitor. In our sample ad, the monitor is described as "17 inch monitor .26 (16 inch) 1024 x 768 inch." This means the monitor has a physical screen size of 17 inches, measured diagonally, but only a 16-inch viewable image size. The size of this monitor is today's new standard (17-inch), and the advertiser is acknowledging that the viewable image size is only 16 inches diagonally. The monitor is probably manufactured as original equipment for the system maker, so the brand name doesn't need to be included.

The dot pitch is 0.26mm, and can display 1024 pixels horizontally by 768 pixels vertically. The lower the number, the crisper the image. Computer monitors generally range from .30mm to .15mm. A dot pitch of .26mm will perform well for just about any work.

This type of monitor is capable of displaying SVGA and higher resolutions, and in all likelihood, even though it's not mentioned, the monitor is non-interlaced. Interlacing is a way to provide greater resolution at a lower cost—the downside is that it can cause screen flicker. Of two monitors with the same resolution, the non-interlaced one will generally be better.

This monitor is a good purchase, but it would be nice to know the refresh rate and the layout of the controls. The faster the refresh rate, the less the monitor flickers. The refresh rate for a monitor is measured in hertz (Hz), and 75Hz is standard. Some monitors are multisync, meaning they can accommodate a variety of refresh rates, which is desirable. As with TVs, monitors are controlled via external buttons or dials, through a series of on-screen icons, or by some combination of the two.

Video adapters (video cards, video circuitry) drive the monitor, meaning they supply the video signal to the monitor. In our sample ad, the video card is described as "PCI 64-bit 3-D video, MPEG, 4MB EDO DRAM."

- PCI 64-bit means that the circuitry on the card uses a PCI-style bus to communicate with the motherboard, and a 64-bit bus to transfer data throughout the card. Some higher-end cards even use a 128-bit bus internally.

- The term 3-D video is usually used in the context of a 3-D graphics accelerator, but its use here may not necessarily indicate significant 3-D graphics acceleration capability. Look for the specific term "3-D graphics accelerator" to be sure.

- MPEG (Motion Picture Experts Group) means that the hardware provides MPEG video compression and decompression (rather than rely on a software emulation of it). This type of hardware processing is faster than software processing. The key thing to look for is whether MPEG I or MPEG II—the latest version—is employed. MPEG II is the one you want.

- 4MB EDO DRAM means there is a total of 4MB of RAM on the card. This is the new standard. A card with only 2MB is adequate, but usually denotes a lower-end system. As you may recall from chapter 6, EDO DRAM simply means extended data output dynamic RAM. It's fine, but it's not the fastest. Look for SDRAM on the better video cards.

Now what about the sound system?

Like the video card and monitor, your sound card (or circuitry) and speakers work together to provide sound for your computer system. Modern motherboards usually have sound capability built in, but you'll probably want a separate sound card for the best sound.

Virtually all sound cards (or sound circuitry on a motherboard) will have audio-out, microphone-in, and line-in connectors. These are located at the rear of your system. Better sound cards will include MIDI (musical instrument digital interface) capability, but the key feature you're looking for is the kind of synthesis performed to produce sounds.

Wavetable synthesis is used in better sound cards, and it means the card uses an actual recording of the waveform of a particular sound (or instrument) for truer audio performance than FM synthesis.

You can pick and choose speakers based on the same kinds of specifications you would look for in a stereo system: wattage, frequency response, and total harmonic distortion. Keep in mind the price, whether it has stereophonic sound or surround sound, and your intended use.

- *Wattage* is a straightforward measurement of the total power the speakers can accept. Sound cards themselves may amplify the total wattage to only 4 or 8 watts, which is not enough for rich stereo sound, so you may want to get a separate amplifier or speakers with built-in amplifiers.

- *Frequency response* is a measure of the range of sound frequencies that can be reproduced; 20Hz (20 cycles per second) to 20KHz (20,000 cycles per second) is ideal, because it is very close to the range of human hearing.

- *Total harmonic distortion* refers to the amount of noise your speakers introduce. It's the difference between the signal leaving the sound card and what comes out of the speakers. Higher-quality speakers will introduce very little (less than 0.01%) total harmonic distortion.

Don't forget to get shielded speakers if you plan to mount them close to your monitor. The magnets in unshielded speakers can cause distortion on the screen. To find out if the speakers are shielded, call the manufacturer.

What does the ad tell me about the modem?

The modem in the sample ad is described as a "USR Sportster 56K data/fax modem." The USR stands for U.S. Robotics, a popular manufacturer of modems, and Sportster is the model name. This is a pretty common but good-quality brand/model combination. The data/fax part is almost unneeded, because most, if not all, modems today will transmit faxes as well as data.

A few computer system makers may still offer 33.6K modems because up until recently there were two competing standards in the 56K modem market: X2 technology which is USR's 56K format, and K56Flex, a format developed and backed by a consortium of chip manufacturers. The final standard was decided in February 1998, and is called V.90. If the modem for the system you're looking at mentions either X2 or K56Flex, find out if it's upgradable or has been upgraded to the new standard. In all likelihood it will have been, but it's worth asking.

For more information on modems, see chapter 2.

The ad doesn't mention the keyboard. How can I know what kind it is? And what can be deduced about the mouse?

In all likelihood the advertised computer comes with a 104-key Windows 95–compatible keyboard. It's so common it would be unusual to purchase a new system without one.

The Microsoft IntelliMouse has a little wheel between the two mouse buttons. When you use newer software, you can simply roll the wheel to scroll up and down the page. But what's more important is the action on the buttons, and that's something you can't really check until you get your hands on it. If you can, test it out before you buy.

I'd like to buy a laptop computer. What should I be looking for?

First of all, you should know that laptops, as a rule, are roughly twice as expensive as comparable desktop systems, and the highest rated chips usually go into the desktops before migrating to the laptops. That said, laptops are becoming more popular.

Laptops give you portability while still retaining a desktop system's functionality. Manufacturers are getting so good at this that it's not uncommon for people to replace their desktop system with a laptop when they upgrade—if they have the extra cash.

The CPU, RAM, and hard drive on a laptop are essentially the same performance-wise as the desktop models, although they may be lower wattage. The modem and other peripherals usually connect via a PCMCIA port. PCMCIA stands for Personal Computer Memory Card International Association, also called the PC-Card. This bus comes in three types:

- PCMCIA Type I—for memory expansion cards

- PCMCIA Type II—compatible with Type I, and can be used for all expansion devices, such as modems and LAN adapters (NICs)

- PCMCIA Type III—compatible with Types I and II, and is designed for computers with removable hard drives

Most laptop keyboards are nearly full-size and full-featured, but frequently the keys share functions to save space. Also, mice and trackballs have been completely replaced with glidepad or "eraser"-type pointing technologies. If you're considering buying a laptop as your only machine, give the pointing technologies an extended test-drive to see which type you prefer. Both take time to get used to, but they represent very different ways of using your hands, and you should be sure you're happy with your choice.

One of the biggest and most confusing differences is in laptop displays. You'll see ads touting 12.1-inch to 13.3-inch screens, SVGA, Dual Scan, Fastscan, passive matrix, active matrix, flat-panel, and so on. The most important attribute is active matrix. Active matrix provides brilliant sharp color under most viewing conditions. Other than that, look for the largest screen size you can afford. Any laptop you buy should offer SVGA, and they're all flat-panel displays.

One last area of concern is the battery type. Get lithium ion or, as second best, nickel-metal hydride (NiMH). Lithium ion batteries cost more, but they last longer and have less "memory effect." Memory effect means the battery tends to "learn" to take less and less charge over its lifetime. Your laptop battery will seem limited enough when you're on the road with no outlet, without taking less of a charge than it was designed for.

The Computing Buyer's Guide (keyword: **Buyer's Guide**) provides advice and reviews on laptop computers.

What about handheld PCs? Should I consider buying one?

Probably not as your main computer, unless you are constantly on the go and don't do much typing. Whether it's a useful accessory depends on how you currently maintain your calendar, address books, to-do lists, and other items you might conceivably store on it.

The first truly successful computer of this type is the PalmPilot. The PalmPilot incorporates easy-to-use functions with a docking cradle, an easier handwriting-recognition package, and a lower price (under $400) to make a highly desirable product. The AOL Store's Hardware Shop (keyword: **Hardware Center**) carries a complete selection of PalmPilot computers and accessories.

Handheld PCs, while similar to PDAs, are in a slightly different category. They use Windows CE operating system, usually have a complete but pint-size keyboard, and often come with modems, back-lit (and lately color) screens, and RAM nearing standard computer levels. These computers use much less power than notebooks, so they last quite a bit longer, and the disadvantages of the tiny keyboards will fade when they are powerful enough to be voice-activated in a few years.

For more advice and a review on handheld computers, read the Computing Buyer's Guide (keyword: **Buyer's Guide**).

I'm going to buy a printer to go with my system, and I need to know what I'll pay for the features I need. Can you help?

Assuming you're an average consumer, you probably want a printer for 8.5 x 11-inch output most of the time, with the occasional $8^{1/2}$ x 14-inch sheet size. You probably need output of about 4 to 8 pages per minute. And although most of your work is in black-and-white, you'd probably like some color now and then.

You can expect excellent black-and-white output at reasonable prices, and high-quality color as well. On the less expensive side, consider one of the better bubble-jet or dry ink color printers for around $300 to $400. Keep in mind that color printing is slower and more expensive per sheet than black-and-white, and that the best color results are obtained with special (more expensive) paper.

If you need more speed, somewhat crisper output, and lower cost per page, and can get along with black-and-white, go for the more expensive laser printers for around $700 to $800. Laser printers use ordinary copy paper well, and cost quite a bit less per sheet than their color counterparts.

For good advice and reviews on printers, see the Computing Buyer's Guide (keyword: **Buyer's Guide**). The AOL Store's Hardware Shop carries printers of all different makes and models. In the AOL Computing Classifieds area (keyword: **Classifieds**), you'll find lots of good bargains on new and used printers.

I'll need a scanner and digital camera to capture images for my new color printer. What do I need to know?

Flatbed color scanners used to be relatively expensive (over $1,000), so most people made do with handheld black-and-white scanners. The trouble with the hand-held scanners is that it is difficult to scan evenly across a page with them, even with special software that can "stitch" the image back together. Fortunately, the prices on flatbed scanners have dropped, and now you can find good scanners for around $200.

The key attributes to look for in a scanner are:

- Color depth (as in 30-bit color)

- Optical resolution (300 x 600 dots per inch, or dppi)

- Interpolated resolution (4800 x 4800 dpi enhanced)

- Bundled software—most units come with scanning software for optical character recognition (OCR), which reads the image into a file format and can save and convert the image to other formats. OCR converts image text into digitized (ASCII) text. A few basic graphics packages, such as Kai Photo Shop, let you have a little fun with your images once they're captured.

Digital cameras also capture still images, but they work just like a camera. The image quality is still low compared to 35mm, and the price is significantly higher. But as usual in the world of electronics, the price is dropping while performance is improving rapidly.

The key attributes of digital cameras are:

- Number of pixels on the charge-coupled device (CCD)

- Number of images it can capture

- Battery life

The CCD is a semiconductor that has light-sensitive elements arrayed over its surface in a square pattern. When you take a picture, light hits the CCD, is converted into digitized signals, and can then be stored at a variety of resolutions. In the same way that sampled audio files grow larger as the quality improves, higher-resolution images take up more space in the camera.

Other features to look for are the capability to accept additional lenses, LCD viewfinders, and a video-out port for viewing your pictures directly on your TV.

The AOL Store's Digital Shop (keyword: **Digital Shop**) sells scanners and digital cameras. The AOL Computing Classifieds has ads for both products new and used. If you want advice and reviews on this digital equipment, look at the Buyer's Guide.

By the way, you don't necessarily need a digital camera to get digital pictures. Many photoprocessors will put your images on CD-ROM for a price, and you can also frequently arrange to download high-resolution images of your pictures from the Internet for an extra processing fee, currently about $5 per roll. For more information, check out PhotoNet (www.photonet.com). In addition, AOL's new You've Got Pictures service combines the reach of AOL and Kodak to make digital pictures available to everyone. See the AOL Pictures area (keyword: **Pictures**) for the latest news on this exciting new service.

FIGURE 7.8
Computing Today
magazine

I need a second computer, and I definitely cannot afford a new monitor for a while. Is there anything I can do?

Many of us are in the same position. We need to buy another computer for the kids, for our spouse, or just to run the latest software, even though the old one still works fine. Check out Computing Today Magazine (keyword: **CPM**), shown in figure 7.8, for interesting tips on using your current system longer.

Should I buy, lease, or rent my next computer?

The question of whether to buy, rent, or lease actually has more to do with business than computers. Buying a computer can now be relatively inexpensive, considering that for under $1,000 you can get a very powerful system.

Leasing is probably the next least expensive way to get a system, and is usually on a par with buying a system on credit. With leasing, however, you can deduct the full cost of the lease as a business expense. If you're running a business, the tax advantages can be significant. As with cars, leasing means you'll be able to upgrade to the newest systems when they're available (most leases are year-to-year), and that's a great bonus considering how fast the technology changes.

Renting is probably the most expensive way to get system capability, and should be reserved only for short-term needs where nothing else will work, such as a convention or presentation in another town, or a contract job where special capabilities are required. Again, the rent is completely deductible, but the rates are usually so high that it just doesn't make sense except under extraordinary circumstances.

There's a place in town that buys old computers as trade-ins when you buy a new one. How much can I expect to get? Would it be better to donate it for the tax write-off?

The way prices fall and computers become obsolete, you might think used parts or systems have little value, but think again. RAM memory chips retain much of their value even when used, as long as you can still put them in a newer system. Other components don't bring as much, but just about any working system is worth at least $150 to $300.

And if the system or the components are old or unique enough, they might even be worth more than when they were new. Try posting an inquiry in one of the AOL forums if you're looking to unload a possible classic.

ERGONOMICALLY SPEAKING

When personal computers became common, a whole new field was born based on the premise that an ergonomically incorrect working environment can cause real injury. Here are some basic guidelines to help you avoid repetitive-stress problems.

The monitor has to sit at least 4 feet off the ground so you can see it from a sitting position. The keyboard has to be below the monitor. The mouse has to be conveniently positioned as well, or it's unusable.

Fortunately, office furniture makers have begun to recognize the difficulties we face. They now market a variety of computer desks, monitor and system stands, input devices, and other equipment designed to ease the strain. Probably the most fundamental element is a keyboard tray below standard desktop level, so that you can keep your wrists horizontal when typing. Some users also benefit from a wrist rest, which can be as simple as a strip of thick foam rubber placed in front of your keyboard. Another essential is a comfortable chair with good back support, to keep you from contorting into odd positions. A glare filter for your monitor eases eyestrain if your room lighting creates shiny spots on the monitor.

Beyond that, there's no one configuration that works best for everyone, so the best thing to do is just go shopping. If you have a pretty good idea of what you're looking for, go to OfficeMax Online (keyword: **OfficeMax**), which has some reasonably priced computer desks available. You can also buy chairs online, but it's best to give them a test in person. Once you've found the perfect model, use online stores and mail-order catalogs to get the best price.

If you would like to sell your computer pretty quickly, put an ad in the AOL Computing Classifieds (keyword: **Classifieds**). Hobbyists and collectors who read the Computing Classifieds are always looking for one more computer to add to their collection, or for working parts from older systems.

If you're interested in getting a tax write-off, you can donate your system or components to any legitimate charity or nonprofit organization. Be sure to get a letter on the organization's letterhead confirming the donation and assigning a value to it.

Prices

There is a saying that performance will double and price will halve every 18 months for computer CPUs. Since CPUs tend to be one of the most expensive items in a computer, the overall computer prices tend to fall constantly as well. And hard drives seem to operate along the same lines, with prices constantly falling and storage capacity constantly rising.

If prices are always falling and performance is always improving, won't I be better off if I wait another three months before buying a new system?

It's true, the longer you wait, the more the price of your system will fall. But by the time it does, the next technology will be on the market, increasing performance dramatically for about the same price your favorite system was when you started. In this time of rapid computer development, there will *always* be something better or cheaper around the corner. So buy when you need to.

Isn't anything stable in the computer market?

Monitors are much more stable, in terms of price and performance, than systems as a whole. Printers are also very stable, but lately even that's been changing, with low-cost laser printers and very high-quality color printers available at low prices.

Some of the individual components, such as cases, power supplies, floppy drives, keyboards, and mice, have been quite stable. This is because they are well-known and understood technologies, they're easy to manufacture, and their development costs have been long since recovered.

Every now and then, though, a manufacturer attempts to push devices like these back into the "new technology" realm. Ergonomic keyboards are a good example. Some variations on keyboard design, if they can be shown to have a patentable function or benefit, can bring a manufacturer a franchise in the market—if consumers accept the higher price and regard the new features as essential.

Brands

Just like the cowpoke who brands a calf to identify it with a particular ranch, marketers try to sear the name of a company forever onto a particular product. In some cases, they succeed too well and can actually lose their trademark on the name if it becomes a word rather than a product name in the public's mind—like Kleenex or Xerox.

What are the benefits of buying a certain brand, and should I

stick to brand-name products when I buy a new system?

Every product has some kind of brand name, either the name of the producer or some actual name for the product itself. The difference is, we tend to think of names as being valid brand names only when we've heard of them through advertising. We often hear horror stories about the "fly-by-night" no-name company that pops into business, promptly rips off as many people as possible, then disappears with our money. If a company is big enough to spend all those dollars on advertising, it must be a legitimate business here to stay, right?

Going with a brand-name company improves the odds of getting a good product, but you still need to investigate your purchase and the company carefully. If you're willing to shop around, compare prices, talk with your friends, and examine the pros and cons, you might find a local company producing a superior product at a lower price without national advertising.

I want to buy a second-hand system, but I can't seem to find what I'm looking for in the local paper. Do I have any alternatives?

274

FIGURE 7.9
Computing Channel Classifieds

ADVANTAGES OF SHOPPING AT THE AOL STORE

- You can shop at the AOL Store at your convenience. It's safe and secure. If you ever have a shopping problem, or even a suggestion for improving your shopping experience, e-mail AOL at screen name MARKETMAIL, and a representative from AOL's Customer Service Help Desk will contact you within one business day of receiving your message. AOL guarantees your satisfaction 100%.

- Your credit card information is secure on AOL. Since the creation of AOL's shopping area and the inception of its guarantee in October 1996, there has never been a report of a credit card that was compromised during a shopping transaction on AOL. This means that shopping on AOL is actually safer than shopping at your local mall.

- Before AOL adds merchants to its Shopping Channel, it certifies them. To become a Certified Merchant, each store is required to pass a series of rigorous tests ranging from customer service response time and member assistance, to order fulfillment and online business practices. To ensure that each merchant upholds this high level of service, these tests are conducted frequently after each merchant has become certified. To view a complete list of AOL Certified Merchants, go to Certified Merchants. AOL checks out its merchants, so you don't have to!

- For your protection, all AOL Certified Merchants offer return policies that are backed by AOL's unconditional money-back guarantee. If for any reason you are not satisfied with your purchase, contact the merchant through the store's Customer Service area. If, after contacting the merchant, you do not get a satisfactory resolution, then outline your complaint and notify AOL's Customer Service Help Desk at screen name: MARKETMAIL. AOL will intervene on your behalf to help you obtain full satisfaction from the merchant. Should any AOL Certified Merchant not comply with its return policy as stated in the merchant's Customer Service area, then AOL will provide you a credit for the full purchase amount.

- AOL is priced competitively with the market. Dependability, ease of use, newness of product, and product selection (one-stop shopping) keep bringing buyers back to the AOL store.

You can find used systems at swap meets, flea markets, garage sales, in the newspaper, at auctions, and by checking bulletin boards around town. The easiest way is probably the AOL service's Computing Classifieds, shown in figure 7.9 at (keywords: **Classifieds** and **Computer Listings**).

On the front page you'll find radio buttons that let you search listings from all over the country or any given area you choose. You can also place an ad for your own excess computer gear.

It sounds like the average person stands a better chance of getting a good deal by buying one of the major brands through the AOL Store. What brands are out there, and what are they known for?

There are lots of good companies manufacturing whole computer systems, and thousands more making individual components. Some are in the United States, some in the Far East. Some sell directly to consumers by mail, and some sell through retail stores exclusively. The big names today have been in business for a number of years, and the oldest aren't necessarily the best. The notables are:

- Desktop Computers—IBM, Micron, Dell, Gateway 2000, Digital, Compaq, Packard Bell, Hewlett Packard

- Laptop Computers—IBM, Toshiba, Hitachi, Fujitsu, Hewlett Packard

- Apple Macintosh PCs—Apple Computer is the only maker of Macs. There were clone makers for a while, but they are fading rapidly because Apple no longer plans to license the operating system to other companies.

- Monitors—Sony, NEC, Motorola, Hyundai, Panasonic, Viewsonic, Shamrock, Magnavox, Samsung, CTX

- Printers—Hewlett Packard, Epson, Alps, Canon, Lexmark

- CD-ROM drives—Phillips, Creative Labs, Samsung, Goldstar

- Sound Cards—Creative Labs, Yamaha, Voyetra

- Modems—U.S. Robotics, Zoom, Hayes, MaxTech, Best Data, Boca Research

- Hard Drives—Seagate, Western Digital, Quantum

- CPUs, Motherboards—Intel, Advanced Micro Devices (AMD), Cyrix, Digital Equipment Corp. (DEC), Motorola, IBM, Evergreen

- Floppy drives—Teac, Sony, Fujitsu, Mitsuni, Toshiba

- Floppies, backup tape, and other media—3M, Imation, Sony, Memorex

- Video cards—Diamond, Trident, Matrox, ATI

- Keyboards, mice, input devices—Logitech, Microsoft

- Mass storage drives—Iomega, Syquest, Ricoh

- Software—Microsoft, Netscape, Borland, Symantec, Autocad, IBM, Corel, Adobe

This list is by no means comprehensive. There are hundreds of manufacturers of whole systems, and many manufacturers produce a broad spectrum of products. Also, the market is constantly changing, and the major producer today is tomorrow's has-been.

Naturally, the AOL service has a site listing plenty of the major computer companies (keyword: **Companies**), shown in figure 7.10. You can search for a particular company, check out Hewlett Packard Online Support, or go to CMPNet, an online listing of 45,000 high-tech firms.

Speed

When buying a new system, you need to know that the speeds of the components don't matter unless they are compatible with each other. That brings us back to the interoperability issue again. It's unimportant how fast your processor or your video card or your hard drive is, for example, if the output you get comes out slowly due to poor bus speed. Any one of the components can create a bottleneck, and mismatching components is a sure way to lower overall performance.

277

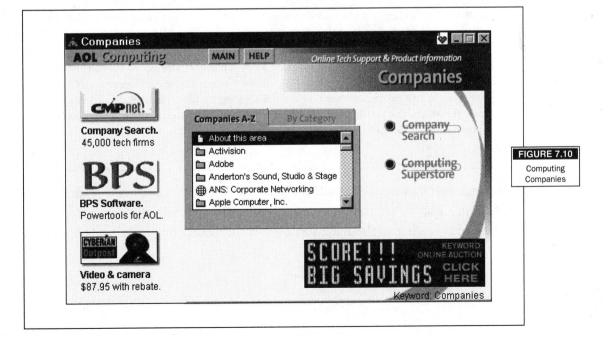

FIGURE 7.10
Computing Companies

MORE USES FOR COMPUTERS

The most common jobs for computers today are data processing functions: applications such as spreadsheets, word processors, and databases. That's great if you're working, but you can use computers for thousands of other tasks, some of which have little or nothing to do with office work.

- *Home security.* Your computer can be the basis for home security systems. For instance, if you want to program all the electrical devices in your home, attach combination sensor/switches to each device and wire them together to an input device on your computer. You can buy the sensors and input device at your local hardware store, along with the software needed to program and control the entire system.

- *Video production.* If you want to produce movies or video, you can buy video capture and output equipment and connect it to your computer. The software will allow you to record, edit, and output whatever video you like, in broadcast quality. You'll need a high-powered computer, of course, but as we've seen, prices for such a system have come down dramatically in recent years.

- *Stargazing.* Amateur astronomers have long known the power of computers for conducting astronomical research, and most telescopes now come with connectors that can plug directly into your computer's ports. The computer can control the direction and speed of the telescope, as well as the image exposure and capture.

- *Surveying.* Surveyors and contractors routinely use computers to capture important data about geography, terrain, facilities, construction, and materials while out in the field. The handheld tape measure and manual surveying equipment are rapidly giving way to laser rangefinders, laser levels, and Global Positioning System (GPS) data capture via computers. You can purchase CD-ROMs that hold lots of information on medical facts, interactive cookbooks, 3-D floor plans, health, photographs, and family trees

In short, if there's a task being done by hand, it's only a matter of time before someone invents a device that will capture and digitize the data, then transfer it to a computer. And someone else will program software to take the drudgery and time out of processing the data. Think of a job or function that is especially tedious, time-consuming, repetitive, or boring, and you've just thought of a new application for a computer—and possibly a gold mine of an opportunity for yourself.

Computer manufacturers, especially the larger brand-name makers, take pride in engineering their systems for maximum performance. They carefully check the components they include in each model to make sure you get the most performance for your money.

I want to buy a system that will process graphics at high speed. What should I look for?

Anytime you're dealing with graphics, video, audio, or 3-D animation, you are using large file sizes and processor-video intensive operations. You want to get the fastest CPU you can find, and you should perhaps even consider a motherboard with room for more than one processor. Intel's 300MHz Pentium II is a good place to start, and so are 333MHz processors. There are 400MHz processors available now. Another high-end processor is the DEC Alpha, made by Digital Equipment Corp., which runs at speeds up to 533MHz.

If you're using Windows 95, you may want to consider a switch in operating systems, depending on the volume of your work and how important it is to your business. Both the Pentium II and the Alpha can run Windows NT, the most common operating system for non-UNIX workstations. Intergraph workstations, such as the TDZ-2000, are among the best of the Windows NT–based workstations, although Dell's products are gaining ground. Dell produces the Dell Workstation 400MT, with a 300MHz Pentium II CPU, 256MB of RAM, a 9GB SCSI hard drive, a 20-inch monitor and high-end video card, with Windows NT 4.0, for under $9,000.

Size

You're not alone if size (or capacity) looms large in your thinking about new computer systems. How big should my monitor be? How much should my hard drive hold? How much room for expansion should my case (or motherboard) have? These are all commonly asked questions about size.

The answer is always changing. Each year, a new standard seems to emerge for the sizes of all typical computer components. In 1998, the standards are 32MB to 64MB of RAM, 2GB to 3GB of hard drive space, 512KB of cache, and a 17-inch monitor. Next year, the standard will change again.

Bundled Suites

Did you know that software comes included with every computer? The basic input/output system (BIOS) comes with every system, even motherboards. Another standard piece of software is the operating system. If you're buying a Wintel PC—a

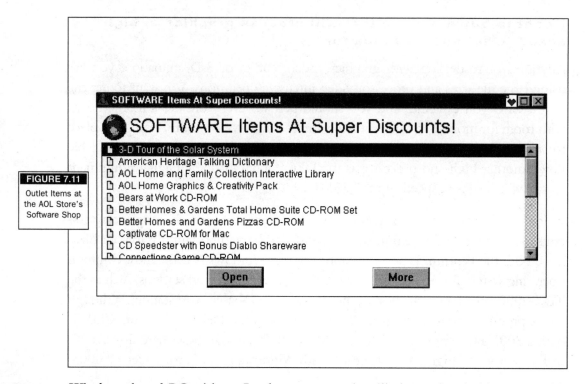

FIGURE 7.11

Outlet Items at the AOL Store's Software Shop

280

Windows-based PC with an Intel processor— it will almost inevitably come with Microsoft Windows 95—or Windows 98 by the time you read this.

Actually, consumers now expect to see these basic software products in whatever system they buy, so it's really not appropriate to consider them part of the "bundled" software. What the term "bundled software" usually refers to is applications programs such as Money, Quicken, Microsoft Works or Office, and CD-ROM games, encyclopedias, and utility packages.

As an example, the advertisement for one computer system especially designed for gamers offers Windows 95 for the operating system—no surprises there. It goes on to provide Descent II—Destination Quartzon, Whiplash, VR Soccer, Mech Warrior, and Hyperblade. Also included are trial versions of Scorched Planet, Tomb Raider, Hellbender, and Monster Truck Madness, and bonus versions of Decathlon, Captain Quazar, You Don't Know Jack, Diablo, The Neverhood, Road Rash, Fire Fight, Ravage D.C.X., Flight Unlimited, War Wind, Free Interprize, and Death Drome. This is all great if you're a gamer, but useless or worse for the office computer.

You can make a good evaluation of what software you're getting by looking for in-depth information about the software bundled with your system. The AOL Store's Software Shop (keyword: **Software Shop**) carries the major software packages. The

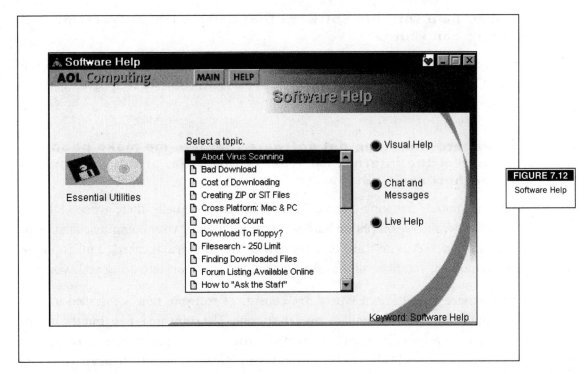

FIGURE 7.12

Software Help

specs and the contents for each package are listed, as well as minimum system requirements. (For some good deals, check out the featured Outlet Items, shown in figure 7.11.)

One of the systems I'm looking at comes bundled with Microsoft Works. Would you say this is a pretty good deal, if the price is similar to another system without it?

Anything you get for free with your system, assuming it's identical in other respects, should be a plus, but there are some things to watch out for. One is that Microsoft Works is essentially a "lite" version of Microsoft Office. It's all many people need, but it has some limitations.

You can find good, working versions of quite a few software programs as shareware or freeware on the Internet that you just download and use. Sometimes, you'll get bundled software that is really just the promotional version, not the full software program. This doesn't mean it's bad. On the contrary, freeware or shareware can be some of the best software you can get, especially considering the price. Just don't pay too much extra for a system with lots of titles, unless the titles are the full-blown versions of the software you were going to buy anyway.

I need help with the software that came with my system. Where can I turn?

Read the online Help files that came with the software, or search for the company on AOL. You can also look for assistance at the AOL Software Help area, shown in figure 7.12.

I've heard that I can get software that lets me make phone calls over the Internet for free. Is this true, and if so, what is it and how can I get it?

Ah, the famous "free long-distance" on the Internet. Actually, there are several ways you can save money on phone bills using the Internet or your computer. First of all, since most new systems these days come with a sound card, speakers, a microphone, and a modem, you have all the gear you need to communicate using your voice.

One service, called Phone Miser SE, consists of software that is installed in your computer and updated regularly over the phone. The software is free, but the update service costs $4.95 per month. It works by routing your phone calls through your PC, meaning your PC has to be on and your phone connected whenever you make a long-distance call.

When you make a phone call, the software checks the area code you're dialing against a list of long-distance service providers and selects the cheapest provider for that specific call at that time of day—something you'd do for yourself if it wasn't so much of a headache. Then it redials the call using the access number of the lowest rate carrier. Voilà—instant savings!

There's another way to obtain nearly free long-distance service using the Internet. It's called Internet telephony. Basically, you make a communications connection with someone else who's online at the time, and the software digitizes your voices and sends them across the Internet as data packets, just like any other data. The voice quality is not very good, but for the price, it's a great deal. Several companies are working on schemes that would let you use the Internet to make calls to regular phones, not just to other PCs with Internet telephony software. But those efforts depend on creating agreements with other countries. The more expensive the call the more attractive the Internet becomes, since the charge to use it isn't based on distance. Calling Singapore over the Internet, at least in theory, costs the same as calling the corner store.

Several companies make software for Internet telephony, including Dialogic, Netspeak, Voxware, and Vocaltec. To find out more, visit the Web site of the VON Coalition (Voice on the Net) at www.von.org, which has a list of the companies involved in the field.

8

YOUR COMPUTER AS YOUR PERSONAL ASSISTANT: MAKING SOFTWARE WORK FOR YOU

As you probably know, there's a vast cornucopia of software out there. Computer stores feature aisle after aisle of attractively packaged wares all claiming to be what you need. Meanwhile, prices are dropping so fast that it's hard not to wonder what the software is really "worth." And how you're going to choose among all these contenders. Or whether purchasing any new software even makes sense.

So, first things first. Do you need to buy any software at all now? It's easy to talk yourself into buying software for the wrong reasons. It sounds cool. Your friends have it and they seem to like it. Your company just got it at work. The software company sent you an upgrade card and you feel obligated to use it.

But there's really only one good reason to buy new software: to take care of some job, function, or need that your current software can't handle adequately for you. Since the software industry is driven in large part by a kind of planned obsolescence, you need to tune out the hype and focus exclusively on your own situation.

For example, before you shell out for a new word processing program, take a close look at your current word processor. Make a list of any functions it doesn't perform well enough for you. And then rate each of the listed items according to importance. And what do you have? If it's just a few relatively minor refinements, nothing really major, then you probably don't need a replacement. But if you've written down several highly-rated functions or features that your current word processing program won't do for you, then an upgrade is probably the best move.

The same drill applies for your database, spreadsheet, and other programs like these, which are the bread-and-butter functions of your PC. Of course, different rules apply for entertainment software. If you buy Origen's newest role-playing game for your son because he really wants it, that's usually reason enough.

Whether you use commercial software packages or shareware, if you're evaluating whether to buy more software, this chapter will be of great use. It describes various software options, explains what each can help you accomplish, and suggests areas on AOL where you can find even more information.

Understanding Software Suites on Windows 95

A software suite is a single, integrated package that comprises a group of "essential" programs—usually some combination of word processor, spreadsheet, database, drawing package, presentation software, communications manager, and personal information manager (PIM). Web authoring tools are starting to be included as well. (The Buyer's Guide Internet Suites section is shown in figure 8.1.)

These suites offer several advantages. One is cost: Their price is a fraction of what you'd pay for all the separate programs. Another advantage is that the component programs look and work alike. This is great because once you've mastered the word processing program you already know a lot about how the spreadsheet, database, and other programs work.

And a big advantage is that because they're integrated, you never have problems with compatibility. You can take information or files from one module and "import" it to another without a glitch.

I use word processing, spreadsheet, presentation, and database programs. Are there packages that have all these programs rolled into one? And which should I buy?

Those applications you listed are all core functions of the office suite packages, and there are lots of products to choose from. Your choice will depend on criteria such as price and range of features. But in terms of one revealing criterion—market share— Microsoft Office 97 is far and away the leader of the pack. This suite comprises five programs, rolled into one:

1. Word (word processor)

2. Excel (spreadsheet)

3. PowerPoint (presentation)

4. Access (relational database)

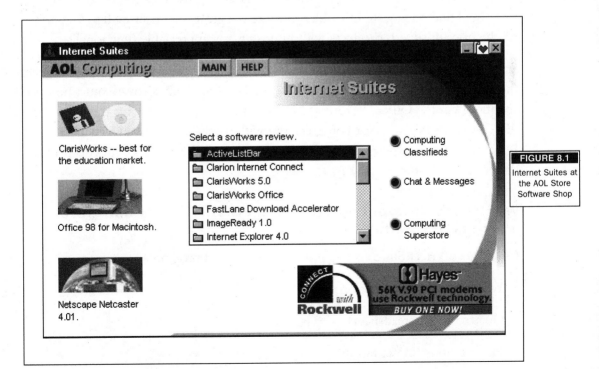

FIGURE 8.1
Internet Suites at the AOL Store Software Shop

5. Outlook (personal information manager)

Go to the AOL Store Software Shop (keyword **Software Shop**), shown in figure 8.1, or the Cyberian Outpost at (www.outpost.com) to get a good deal on Office 97.

Is Microsoft Office 97 worth $500?

Good question. It's hard to say if anything on a little shiny disk is really worth $500. Office 97 is an outstanding software suite, and if you're looking for an all-in-one package, it's an excellent candidate. The only serious competition with Microsoft at the moment is Corel with its WordPerfect Suite 8.0. And this costs significantly less. So there are some alternatives to paying $500.

First, see if you qualify for the competitive upgrade. If you have any legitimate copy of a word processing program, database, or spreadsheet, you probably do. Check with your local software store about what they require in terms of proof of ownership for the competitive upgrade.

Another option is to go with Office 95 instead. Because this is one generation older, you'll find you can get it for a song. If you have trouble finding Office 95, check the AOL Classifieds (keyword: **Classifieds**) for *Computer Shopper Magazine* (available in most computer, book, or grocery stores) for listings of used computer software outlets. You'll find buying slightly older software is a great way to slice 80 to 90 percent off the price of superb products without losing any appreciable functionality.

Sometimes it will require you to make some special arrangements. In this instance, the one hassle is that most documents created on Office 97 software must be saved specifically in the Office 95 format for you to open and work with them in Office 95. This is simple with Word or Excel, but with database files it can be a little tricky. But this is a minor tradeoff for the sake of getting full MS Office functionality for the price of a shareware package.

What's the difference between Microsoft Office and Corel WordPerfect Suite?

Corel WordPerfect Suite also comprises five essential programs:

1. WordPerfect (word processor)

2. Quattro Pro (spreadsheet)

3. Presentations (presentation)

4. CorelDraw (drawing)

5. dBASE (relational database)

So the difference is that Corel has a drawing program, whereas Microsoft comes with a personal information manager.

A friend of mine uses SmartSuite for spreadsheets. What exactly is SmartSuite?

The SmartSuite package comes from Lotus Development Corp., and it consists of three major programs from that company:

1. WordPro (word processor)

2. 1-2-3 (spreadsheet)

3. Freelance Graphics (drawing)

What do you think of MS Works 4.0?

Works 4.0 is the first version of the program designed expressly for Windows 95, and it's very good technology. Some people think of MS Works as "MS Office lite," offering trimmed-down versions of Word, Excel, and Access all in one. But this can be an ideal choice for nonprofessional users who'd find the vast functionality of Office 97 to be overkill.

You can get more info about MS Works on AOL any time at keyword: **WP**. And if you check in at the message board at the PC Word Processing Resources (keyword: **WP**), you can find out what other AOL members think of MS Works 4.0.

What is a common user interface?

Without getting overly technical, let's just say the "user interface" is the look and feel of a program—that is, the features that govern how you interact with a computer when it runs that program. When programs share a *common* user interface, it means they have the same look and work the same way. Virtually all software suites have a common user interface, so each module might have similar commands on the menu bar, tools in the toolbars, and elements in the document window.

Think of the user interface as a car's dashboard. If you borrow a friend's car and it's the same or a very similar model, you know exactly where all the controls are and how to use them: air conditioning, trunk latch, rear-windshield wiper, and so forth. You could say these cars have a common user interface. But if you try to drive a different manufacturer's vehicle, you'll need to pay attention at first to where some controls are located and how they work. The user interfaces are similar but not quite "common"— just as it will probably take you a day or two to become accustomed to, say, a new word processing package.

What is GUI?

GUI stands for Graphical User Interface. Essentially, it's a "mousable" user interface that features visual elements: pull-down menus, toolbars, dialog boxes, check boxes, radio buttons, and other pictorial icons that resemble the concepts they represent. A mousable interface responds to mouse input for such functions as selecting text, choosing commands from menus, and scrolling the screen.

A GUI makes computer software easier to use because people "read" visual representations faster than words or phrases. Examples of icons are a picture of a disk to represent a diskette inserted in a drive, a trash can or a recycle bin to represent the place to discard unwanted files, or a file folder to represent a subdirectory.

290

What's the difference between Windows suites and other,

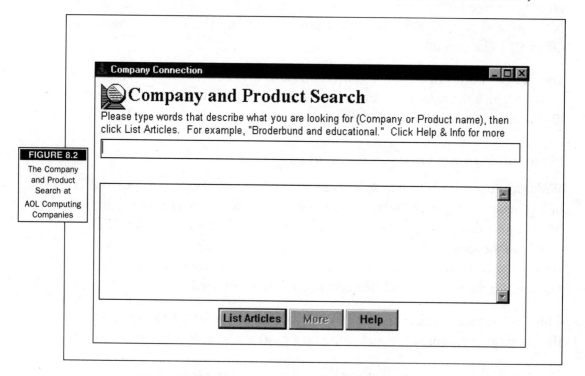

FIGURE 8.2

The Company and Product Search at AOL Computing Companies

lower-priced packages?

The low-priced suites usually don't contain the software manufacturer's most recent products. Instead, they often include several programs that have been around a while and are no longer selling well. This does not mean that they lack anything essential. It's more likely that they lack some hot-shot features or ornamental touches that you may not need. Also, these programs are virtually bug-free and easy to support.

Windows suites are designed so the applications work only with the specific component's GUI. These GUIs are very attractive, and the programs supplied with Windows suites are quite impressive.

If you're a computer neophyte who's tight on money and has a low-end, older-generation, or used computer, and you have no other software, a low-priced suite may work for you. If you've just bought a used machine, you may find some software on the hard drive that will duplicate some suite functions. Unless you have the software manuals and user licenses for the installed software, it's often best to simply delete those files. You can buy an uninstall program from the AOL Store Software Shop (keyword: **Software Shop**).

Finding Compatible Software

Of the factors you need to consider when you choose a specific software package, compatibility should rank pretty high. You may find two or more packages all offering the features you require and within the same price range. In that case, choose the package that is most compatible with your existing software environment.

This environment obviously includes the software already on your computer. But it also means the packages used by your friends, the ones your kids use at school, and your workplace software. It's wise to consider this issue *before* you buy, so make sure to check which packages these people use.

The safest move when upgrading is to stick with what you're familiar with. If you are currently a Word user, stick with Word. If you use WordPerfect, stay with that one.

How can I tell if my existing software is compatible with the software I'm about to buy?

Let's use a word processing program as an example. You'll definitely want access to all your existing letters and documents after you upgrade or buy a new program. So make a list of the formats your current software will "export" to, and take that list with you to the software store. Make sure the package you buy will handle *at least* one of the formats on the list. Remember that if the only common link is ASCII (i.e., plain text) or RTF (rich text format), you'll lose most of your formatting, such as bold, italics, line spacing, and so on.

Should I buy only software that's compatible with what my friends, kids, or office colleagues use?

This is something of a judgment call. Definitely take a look at what software these people use. And pay special attention to people with whom you frequently trade documents. If the program you plan to buy isn't the same version as others', then make sure there's at least one common format that will allow you to share files with them.

Installing Software

Installing software can be a tedious job, but someone has to do it. Most of today's software comes in one of two formats: floppies or CD-ROM.

How do I install software from floppies?

For the most part, it's a cinch. Always read the installation instructions in the software documentation *before* you install any software. Customarily, a "Getting Started" or "User's Guide" manual will give you the step-by-step installation instructions. Another important thing is to check the amount of disk space you have available on your hard drive. We'll talk about that soon.

The larger the program, the more floppies will come with it—even 20 isn't uncommon. Sometimes the initial installing instructions to get you started are printed on the label of the first floppy, usually labeled Disk 1. After you insert Disk 1 in your floppy drive and press enter (if that's what you're told to do), the software shows a setup screen with instructions for the software installation. You'll be prompted to enter some information about yourself (your name or company), the serial number of the software, and specify which directory (folder) you want to store the program in.

The setup program will prompt you to remove Disk 1 and insert the next disk, and so on. Just follow the on-screen prompts.

With some of today's sophisticated software, you can choose the type of installation you want. For example, a typical installation includes all of a program's essential features. This is the recommended installation. A custom installation allows you to pick and choose the features you want to install. Sometimes you're offered a laptop installation option that lets you install a trimmed-down version of the program to conserve your laptop's space.

If the software you're installing is a simple, bare-bones program or old software, the setup program might also ask you some questions about your computer and printer, and perhaps other peripherals. The setup programs on most newer and more sophisticated packages can automatically identify your computer model and detect what's connected to it, so you probably won't have to answer such questions during the installing process.

After you finish installing the software, setup may restart Windows to complete the setup process, depending on whether your AUTOEXEC.BAT file needs to be updated by the new program you just installed. An AUTOEXEC.BAT file is a file that runs automatically when you start or restart the system. This file tells DOS where to find application programs and the names of system configuration programs that set up your computer for use with a printer and a mouse. In some cases, setup will give you the opportunity to register your program online.

How do I install software from a CD-ROM?

The process is nearly identical to installing from floppies. (See the instructions above.) The main difference is that you'll have to load only the one CD (in rare cases, more than one disc is required) into your CD-ROM drive, rather than go through a series of floppies. Virtually all the CD-ROM setup programs will automatically identify your computer and detect what's connected to it, allow you to choose the type of installation you want, and ask you if you want to register online.

How do I know if I have enough space on my hard drive for the software I'm going to install?

Check the space on your hard drive by going into your Windows Explorer, and read the amount of free disk space that shows up at the bottom of the Exploring window.

As for the software you want to install, most products indicate somewhere how much room they take. If not, you can call the software manufacturer.

If you don't have enough space, start deleting unwanted folders and files that you never or rarely use. Or compress the programs you don't use often.

Should I register the software?

Yes. That way you'll be on the software company's mailing list. You'll be entitled to all kinds of special offers, upgrade announcements, and free technical support (if it's available), and you'll be eligible to subscribe to a support package. If you have a modem, feel free to register online rather than fill out a registration card and mail it. It takes just a few minutes.

Downloading Software

The AOL Download Software area (keyword: **Download Software**) is where you go to download shareware. As a recap, with these programs, you can download the files for free, then try them out for a certain amount of time—usually 10 to 30 days. You pay for them only if you decide to keep them. The range of shareware programs is vast, covering all the tasks you can imagine and tons of games.

First, you'll probably want to look through the list of shareware that AOL offers. You can do that in the Download Software area. After you choose some shareware you want to download, just go ahead and start hauling it into your hard drive. Your only constraint is the amount of available disk space on your computer. Once you've installed the programs, make sure to give them all a solid test-drive in the allotted time. During this period, you can use them to your heart's content.

You'll probably find some shareware programs you want to hold on to and others you don't like or need. Make sure to honor your side of the "virtual handshake" by paying for those you keep. You can remove the others from your hard drive simply by going to your Windows Explorer and deleting the program files. This way you won't clutter up your drive with unused programs.

Every day you'll see a new shareware offer in the Daily Download area in the AOL Computing channel. If you want to download the software AOL picked for that day, just click on the Daily Download button and start downloading the program files.

What is the difference between "download" and "upload"?

Like most techno-jargon, these terms are pretty straightforward once you know what they mean. *Downloading* transfers files from a computer, usually a server somewhere on the Internet to your computer. *Uploading* transfers files from your computer to a different computer. These and other computing terms are defined in this book's Glossary.

I want to download database software, but I'm not sure which file I need, or where it is. How can I find it?

You can search for it first with the AOL Find Software feature, shown in figure 8.3.

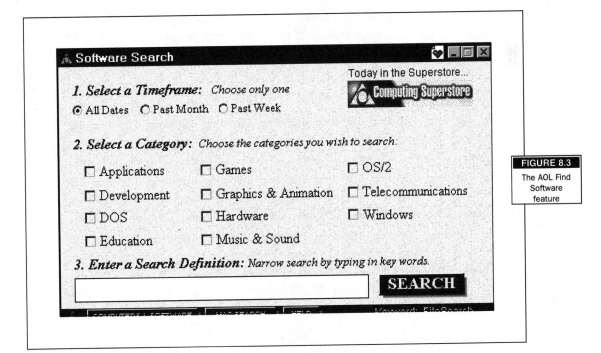

FIGURE 8.3

The AOL Find Software feature

Choose Find on the toolbar and then choose Software from the Find menu. AOL has a searchable database that contains all the files available for downloading on AOL.

I searched for software using its filename and AOL couldn't find it. Why?

When a program's version number changes, so does the filename. So unless you're absolutely sure of the software's filename for the latest version, AOL doesn't recommend searching for files using the filename.

What search methods should I use instead?

There are several ways to do it. You can search for files by using the author's last name or Uploader name, or by using search words that relate to or describe the file. The File Search Utility is not case-sensitive, meaning that it doesn't matter whether the words or phrases have capital letters or not.

How can I do a more focused search for a file or files on AOL?

You can use the words **AND** and **OR** in your search criteria, and you can use them more than once. If you enter two subjects joined by **AND**, you'll find files that contain both sets of words. For instance, you can look for **browser AND internet**. All the files displayed in the window will relate to browsing and to the Internet. You can also use **OR** to broaden your search. If you look for **browser OR internet**, AOL will find files that relate either to browsers or to the Internet.

How can I restrict a file search on AOL?

The way to do this is by using the word **NOT** in your search criteria. For example, entering **browse NOT internet** will show you files on browsing but exclude files related to the Internet.

Another way to narrow your search is to check one of the options in the Software Search form, such as Past Week, Past Month, or All Dates. The first two options will limit the search to files that have been uploaded during the specified time frame.

Also, you can control your search by choosing one or more of the boxes on the Software Search form that pertain to the category in which you think a file is located. If you're not sure about the category, just check All Categories.

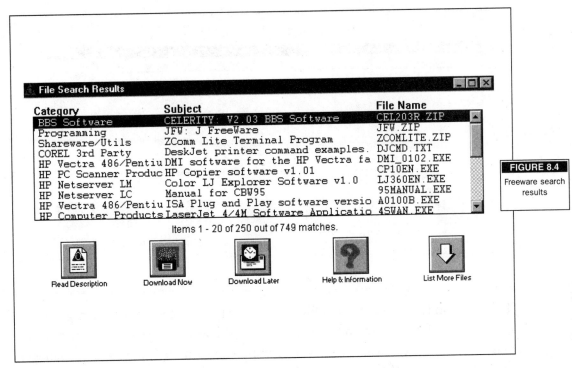

FIGURE 8.4

Freeware search results

A great way to keep tabs on all the hot new software prospects in a field that interests you is to use the Past Week search in combination with one of the categories. You could do this to search for all Windows files that have been added in the past week, for instance.

Can I browse files offline with AOL?

By using Automatic AOL you can download your e-mail, news articles, message boards, and newsgroups and then read them offline.

Where can I download totally free software on AOL?

To locate totally free software, called Freeware, go to the Software Search area (keyword: **Filesearch**) and enter freeware as your search term. Figure 8.4 shows the results of a freeware search.

How can I keep track of files that I want to download?

Use the AOL Download Manager, shown in figure 8.5, which can help you download, upload, and say where and when you want the files to be located on your computer. You can download files with the Download Manager whether you're offline or online.

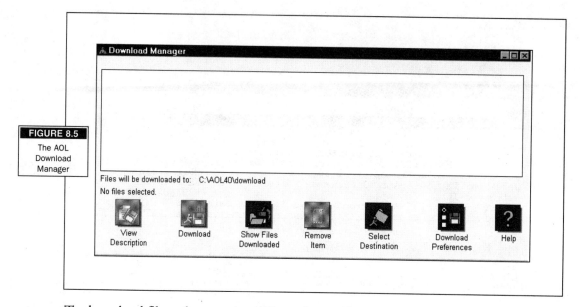

FIGURE 8.5

The AOL
Download
Manager

To download files when you're offline, choose My Files, Download Manager. Click on the Show Files Downloaded button to see the files you've already downloaded and find out where they reside on your computer. Open the Windows File Manager, expand the "AOL 4.0" folder, and open the "Download" folder to see the files you downloaded. Then you can move the files to whatever disk drive or folder you want.

When you're online, and you've found the file(s) you want to download using the Find command or a software library, click on the Download Later button. This adds the selected file to your download list. Click on OK. Repeat the previous steps for each file you want to download. Click on the Download Manager button on the AOL toolbar. A list of the files you selected appears in the Download Manager window. Click on the Start Download button to begin.

The length of time a file transfer will take depends on the file's size and the speed of your modem. AOL gives you the approximate time it takes to download your file(s) in the File Transfer dialog box. If the download is long, feel free to check the Sign Off After Transfer option in the File Transfer dialog box. Then you can move along to other matters. AOL automatically downloads your files, signs off, and extracts files from any compressed files.

Is the estimated time it takes to download a file accurate?

The actual time it takes to download a file may differ from the estimate you see in the File Description, but usually not by too much.

Why does it take so long to download?

There are two factors that might reduce the speed at which you can download files: peak hour traffic and excessive line noise.

AOL's "prime time" is in the evening and on weekends, when hundreds of thousands of members are signed on to America Online at the same time. After school is also a busy time. Huge quantities of information are going back and forth between members' computers and the America Online host computers. Sometimes this causes backlogs for the AOL computers, and it may take a bit longer to download files.

Excessive line noise—basically, static over your phone connection—can cause the AOL computers to have to resend the same data several times. This slows down the overall download speed.

What can I do to avoid peak hour traffic when I need to download a file?

Schedule an Automatic AOL FlashSession to download your files in the middle of the night or early in the morning. Just click the Mail Center icon on the toolbar, choose Set up Automatic AOL (Flashsessions), and choose Schedule Automatic AOL. Then pick all the days of the week when you want Automatic AOL to run, the starting time, and how often. Be sure to keep America Online open when you've scheduled Automatic AOL.

Is there anything I can do about excessive line noise when downloading a file?

Try signing off and signing on again to get a clearer connection. If the problem persists, you may want to ask your phone company to check your telephone line for excessive line noise.

Why can't I get the RealAudio file for the program to download?

You're probably trying to download a file when the host computer is very busy processing requests from other RealAudio downloaders. (RealAudio is a program that can play streaming audio with broadcast-quality sound.) During peak usage times, which is 8 p.m. to 1 a.m., the host computer is slow to respond when sending information to your computer. If these delays are long enough, your AOL software will abort the download.

You can resolve the problem by logging on at another time to download RealAudio.

Can my computer be infected with a virus from shareware?

If you are careful to obtain your shareware from reputable sources on the Web or on the AOL service, your chances of picking up a virus are negligible. Shareware libraries, online services, and bulletin boards that distribute shareware take painstaking precautions to ensure that infected files and disks aren't disseminated. If you're concerned, read more about virus protection programs in the AOL Virus Information center, at keyword: **Virus**. Viruses are also discussed in chapter 2.

Upgrading Software

Upgrading your existing software is the way to go unless there's a compelling reason to migrate to a new program. If you have WordPerfect, then you might as well stay with it. It's sometimes more expensive and time-consuming to switch to a new program.

How do I know when there's an upgrade to my software?

If you're a registered user of the software, you'll get upgrade offers in the mail from the software company. Be sure to check the retail price of the off-the-shelf version. Sometimes discount software stores charge less for the upgrade than the company does.

The AOL Store's Software Shop (keyword: **Software Shop**) sells software upgrades, and the Buyer's Guide (keyword: **Buyer's Guide**) provides advice and reviews on software upgrades.

Do I really have to upgrade software when the manufacturer offers it?

Not always. Make sure the upgrade is substantial enough to make it worth your investment in time and money. Read about the upgrade in the AOL Buyer's Guide to get the scoop.

How do I upgrade my software?

After you buy your upgrade package, follow the installation instructions provided in the software documentation. Be sure to check how much free disk space you have and back up all the important documents you created with the old version of the software you intend to upgrade.

Install the software and read the on-screen prompts. Software upgrades usually don't take very long to install. The new program files will overwrite and update the old program files and add any new files necessary for the upgrade.

Does my anti-virus software need to be upgraded, too?

With anti-virus software, it's an especially good idea to upgrade it whenever a new version comes out. That way, your software can protect you from the latest viruses.

At the AOL PC Virus Information Center (keyword: **Virus**), you'll find more information on upgrading anti-virus software and updating virus files. Look into the Virus Information Center Software Libraries (shown in figure 8.6) to see what information and protection software is available.

How do I update my virus file?

McAfee VirusScan (www.nai.com/download/updates/updates.asp) and Dr. Solomon's Antivirus are the two most popular anti-virus software programs. Both

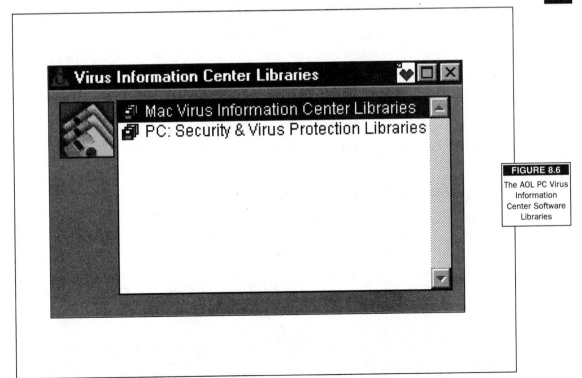

FIGURE 8.6

The AOL PC Virus Information Center Software Libraries

are available through the AOL Store's Software Shop (keyword: **Software Shop**). They provide online updates to virus files monthly. Just go to the McAfee or Symantec Web site and download the virus file of the month.

If you use a different program, the AOL PC Virus Information Center can give you the lowdown on viruses and updating virus files (keyword: **Virus**).

For more information on upgrades, see chapter 6.

What You Can Accomplish

Here's where to find out how to use software to accomplish important tasks and functions at work or home. This section is fact-packed with the best features of each kind of software available today. The basic functionality of word processing includes creating, editing, formatting, and printing documents. You should also be able to read files and images of many types. Word processing applications can be created in word processing programs available to you through AOL's Software Shop.

I saw a database program on sale. Exactly what is a database program and what can it do for me?

A database program manages lists of information—clients, friends, relatives, or any collection of names in your office or home. Common examples of databases are the phone book or your address book.

With a database program, you can find information quickly. For example, you can find out which clients bought products from you last month, or which ones live in a particular ZIP code, or which ones named Fred who live in that ZIP code bought from you last month. All that's done through sorting the database.

Database management software also lets you organize your list quickly, view the list in various ways, and even create reports.

There are two types of database programs: flat-file and relational. A flat-file database is usually limited to information stored in a single file. You can work with one flat-file database at a time. Some of these databases can look up information in other database files but cannot modify those files.

This type of database program is ideal for tracking vast amounts of text-based information such as phone directories. A flat-file database can also easily handle simple catalogs of data, such as shopping lists, invitation lists, to-do lists, and so on.

A relational database, however, allows you to store information in separate files and grab related pieces to use together as you wish. You link relational databases so a transaction in one database will update all the linked (related) databases. For example, a corporation can keep track of international banking transactions in a relational database. The corporate database may have separate files for sales, inventory, and manufacturing. The sales database would automatically open the inventory database and decrease the total of its products by one for each item sold. Similarly, it would add a product to the manufacturing database.

What is the difference between a database program and other programs such as word processing and spreadsheets on my computer?

You probably keep lists of addresses and phone numbers, household chores to do, recipes to make, and groceries to buy. Well, a database program helps you manage these lists.

Word processing programs such as Microsoft Word and Corel WordPerfect manage words. Spreadsheet programs such as Microsoft Excel and Lotus 1-2-3 manage numbers. And database programs such as Microsoft Access, Lotus Approach, and Borland's Paradox manage lists or databases.

What are the top-selling database programs?

Among database programs that are easy to use but limited in power and sophistication are 3 flat-file types: Alpha Four, Approach, and Q&A. Of the relational database managers that give you all the

GOOD RELATIONAL DATABASES

Here are some good relational database managers:

- Access (Microsoft)
- dBASE IV (Borland International)
- FoxPro for Windows (Microsoft)
- Microsoft SQL Server (Microsoft)
- Paradox for Windows (Borland International)

303

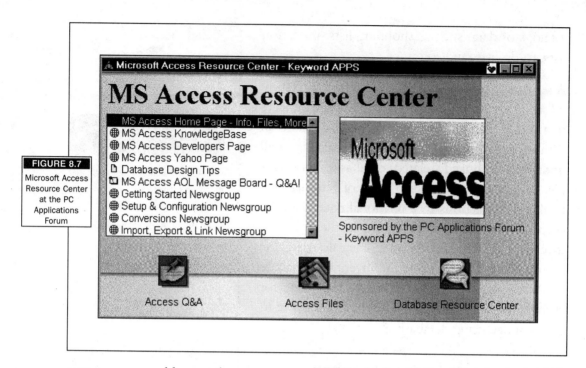

FIGURE 8.7

Microsoft Access
Resource Center
at the PC
Applications
Forum

304

power you could want but are more difficult to learn, the best-sellers include Microsoft Access, dBASE, FoxPro, and Paradox.

Go to the Database AOL (keyword: **Database**) or the PC Applications Forums (keyword: **APPS**) (see figure 8.7) to get more information on database programs. The Buyer's Guide (keyword: **Buyer's Guide**) offers good advice and helpful reviews on the top-selling database programs.

I was surprised to find how very expensive database software is. Are there any Windows-based shareware programs for me, or other good budget programs?

Some low-cost personal data managers, such as FileMaker Pro Resource Center (keyword: **Filemaker**), shown in figure 8.8, offer limited relational database capabilities. But such programs are essentially flat-file database managers, so they offer much less relational capability than the full-featured behemoths. If you opt for a flat-file database, you'll need to examine any prospective package carefully to see if it can link files the way you want them linked.

Other inexpensive database programs you might want to explore are Alpha Four, Approach, and Q&A.

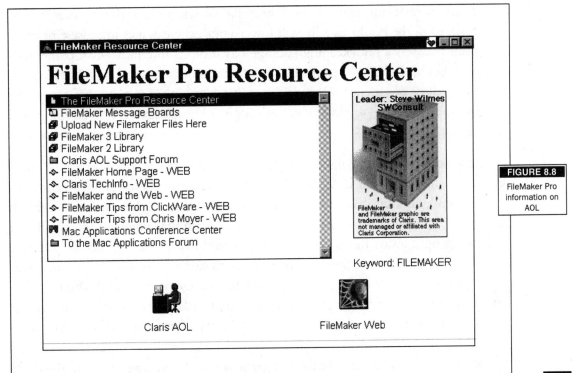

FIGURE 8.8

FileMaker Pro information on AOL

305

I supervise an accounting department at a law firm, and I need to collect monthly data on each employee's number of mistakes, then present the data graphically. Should I use MS Excel or MS Access for collecting data and creating pie charts?

A spreadsheet program such as Excel is easier to learn than a database program. However, Excel and Access can input and import data from a wide range of sources, in many different formats.

If you have a lot of text-based information to store, go with Access. If your data is mostly numerical, or if you plan on using it for calculations, use Excel.

Both Excel and Access create beautiful charts, but it you want the best of both worlds, Excel can read your Access-created files.

My husband has a gourmet catering business, and I'm in charge of billing his 100 or so clients. Can you recommend a user-friendly program?

There are several inexpensive bookkeeping programs on the market today. Computerizing the books usually will lower your expenses and increase efficiency. You want to assess a bookkeeping package based on its interface. Most contemporary packages have GUI-like controls. You often run them intuitively, with the menu bar and pull-down menus. Well-designed bookkeeping programs offer separate interfaces, one for those who have little or no knowledge of bookkeeping and another for experts.

QuickBooks by Intuit (see figure 8.9) is good for business accounting needs, and a shareware alternative called ATREX is also fine (keyword: **Quickfind**). After you go to Quickfind, choose Shareware, and type **Atrex** in the search box. Enter a search definition. This will take you to the Atrex shareware that you can download and start using right away. But if your husband would like a catering-specific package, they're out there. The nice thing about going with such a customized solution is that it will incorporate accounting, invoicing, client management, and scheduling, all in one program. To find a listing of companies that make catering programs, try the keyword: **Quickfind**, then choose Shareware, and type **Catering** as the search word.

What features should I look for in a good bookkeeping program?

A bookkeeping program should have these essential modules:

- General ledger

- Billing

- Accounts payable

- Accounts receivable

- Purchasing

- Budgeting

If you run a service-oriented business, you'll also want time-billing, project-tracking, and job-costing features in your bookkeeping program. Inventory-based retail businesses can use point-of-sale and multistore control features. Wholesalers and telemarketers should look for order-entry and multiwarehouse support.

The bookkeeping software should have other components such as automatic check writing, reconciliation, report generation, and the flexibility to use either laser-generated or preprinted forms.

FIGURE 8.9

Intuit area on AOL

307

Whatever type of business you run, you can find customized software solutions on AOL. Just post a message in the appropriate AOL forum for other AOL members' ideas and opinions.

What types of home finance programs are available?

There are several broad categories of home finance programs: general, taxes, and electronic banking services.

What do general home finance programs offer?

General home finance software can include one, many, or all of the following features:

BOOKKEEPERS' PARADISE

You'll find information about these popular bookkeeping software packages on AOL by using the company name for the keyword or going to the Companies area on the Computing channel (keyword: **Companies**):

- ACCPAC BPI Integrated Accounting (Computer Associates)
- Complete Accounting (Peachtree Software)
- QuickBooks (Intuit)

Basic functions of good bookkeeping software:

- General ledger
- Accounts payable and receivable
- Inventory
- Payroll

What you can do with a bookkeeping program:

- Compare individual job costs with revenues to identify profitable jobs immediately.
- Track back orders as well as partial and drop shipments
- Fill in familiar forms onscreen, such as checks and invoices
- Calculates sales taxes
- Record income, payroll, and sales taxes
- Calculate payroll earnings and deductions
- Pay and file taxes

- Banking—checking, savings, and credit card tracking

- Budgeting

- Debt reduction

- Credit repair

- Investment tracking—stocks, bonds, mutual funds, and the like

- Net worth

- Financial planning

- Mortgage calculation and amortization

- Insurance

What's the difference between a shareware and a commercial home finance program?

Shareware finance programs often focus on only one of the general home finance functions, whereas most commercial programs will cover all the functions.

Where can I go to find out about shareware home finance programs on AOL?

To browse through shareware home finance programs, use the keyword: **Quickfind**. Enter a search word that describes your area of interest. For example, enter any of the following search words:

- Banking

- Checking

- Check print

- Budget

- Debt

- Cash flow

- Invest

- Stock

- Bond

- Mutual fund

- Mortgage

- Amortize

- Loan

Is a home finance program worth the trouble?

The advantage of using a home finance program to track your budget, expenses, savings, and investments is that you have a solid record of your transactions. This can come in handy for tax purposes. Another advantage is that you'll gain a heightened awareness of where your money is going.

What is tax software, and how can it help me prepare my taxes?

Tax software such as Quicken or Andrew Tobias' tax program is another type of home finance program. It helps you prepare your taxes, offers you online support, and sometimes even gives you tax advice and electronic filing capabilities. Many commercial tax programs provide state tax forms for most states, with automatic transfer of information between state and federal forms.

The IRS says that the most common errors on tax forms are mathematical ones. By using a tax prepa-

309

These popular commercial tax-preparation programs will help you organize and set up your tax information:

- Kiplinger Tax Cut (Block Financial)
- Tax Edge (Parson's Technology)
- Turbotax (Intuit)

Features to look for in Tax Preparation Programs:

- Audit feature that warns of potentially troublesome entries
- The ability to import data files in the widely supported TXF (tax exchange format)
- Help menu or manual with information on IRS instructions, tax tips, commonly asked questions, instructions on using the package
- Videos to guide you through some of the more difficult tax decisions
- Allocation of mortgage interest and other expenses between the business and your itemized deductions on Schedule A
- Backup worksheets for any data entry line

ration program, you eliminate that threat. You also get some rollover of information from one year to the next, which reduces data entry. If you're thinking about buying a tax program, consider product compatibility with your general home finance program. You'll want a tax preparation program that can import data directly from your general home finance program.

I'm trying to save money on preparing my taxes. Are there any shareware tax programs available on AOL?

There are two shareware tax program favorites: AM-TAX by AM Software and Bammel STAX. Shareware tax programs will help you figure your federal income tax.

Do I need electronic banking service software?

If you want an electronic bill-paying service so that you can pay bills without writing hard-copy checks, then an electronic banking service is for you. The most popular services are Checkfree (www.checkfree.com) and BillPay USA. You can access them through major online services or as a standalone service in some areas. You can log on to the service and "write checks," so to speak, or you can schedule automatic bill payment at given times. Fees for this service vary, depending on the number of checks written. Call your bank to find out more about how to bank online or go to the AOL Personal Finance area (keyword: **Banking**).

What is a personal information manager?

A personal information manager (PIM) is a collec-

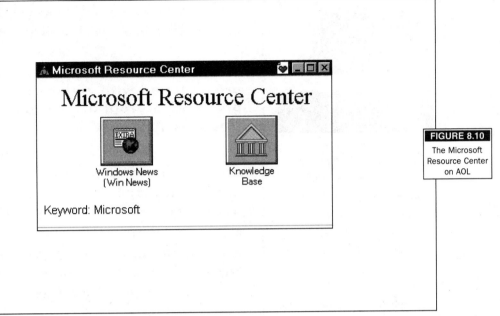

FIGURE 8.10

The Microsoft Resource Center on AOL

tion of desktop utilities such as appointment calendar, notepad, and phone list with a built-in auto-dialer. You'll find quite a few PIMs that offer an interesting combination of functions, and many single-purpose desktop utilities. Some have as many functions as a 12-speed blender, while other specialize in calendar or dialing features. Go to the Microsoft Resource Center (keyword: **Microsoft**), shown in figure 8.10, to find out about Outlook 97, a very powerful PIM that comes with e-mail, a calendar, a weekly planner, a content list, sticky notes, a project manager, and a journal for recording your actions in Microsoft Office applications.

What is presentation software?

Basically, presentation software is a tool that enables you to easily design sophisticated, professional-looking presentations. The razzle-dazzle effect that used to cost many thousands of dollars is now within the grasp of any PC user. Your final product may comprise slides with bulleted lists, charts, clip art, drawings, spreadsheets, and much more. And you can use your presentation data to make beautiful 35mm slides, flip charts, overhead transparencies, and even animation with sounds.

Presentation software is easy to learn and produces visual aids very quickly.

Each slide you create (sometimes called a page) is integrated within the whole presentation.

I can already make some slides for a presentation with my powerful word processing program. So what benefits does presentation software offer?

This type of software dramatically expands the scope of what you can accomplish. With presentation software you can choose a design for the entire slide show you create, organize the information in an outline, create the slides, enhance the slides, and create the output. The output can consist of overhead transparencies, 35mm slides, flip charts, electronic presentations, handouts for your audience, and speaker notes.

To check out Adobe Persuasion, an excellent presentation package, go to the Adobe Online site (www.adobe.com), shown in figure 8.11.

My computer came with some software, including a spreadsheet program. What would I use this for?

Spreadsheets are not just for financial number crunching. They can be of use to anyone from bookkeepers to beekeepers to bookies. Everyone, at some point, has to keep track of numbers. Some of the things you can do with spreadsheets include balancing your checkbook, tracking inventory, computing profit, calculating your taxes, as well as doing mathematical and scientific calculations.

Today's spreadsheet programs are capable, feature-rich, and easy to use. Some even offer integrated databases. Several spreadsheet programs now offer three-dimensional performance—in other words, worksheets can have multiple pages.

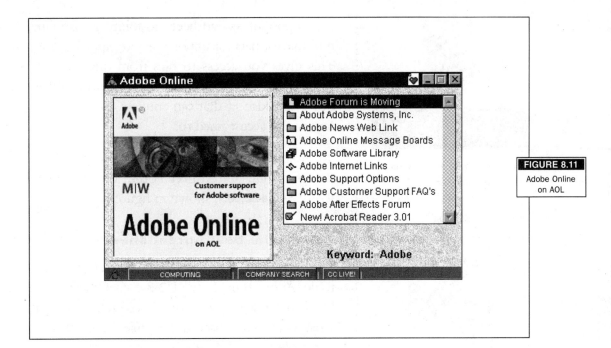

FIGURE 8.11

Adobe Online on AOL

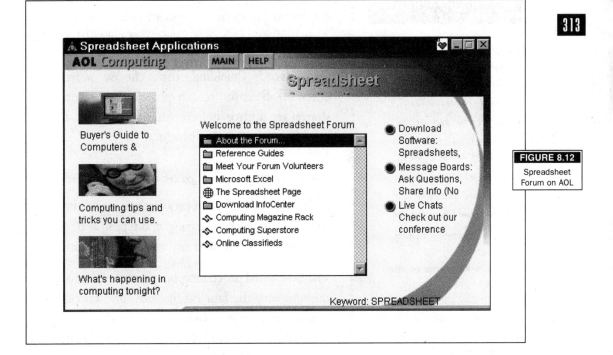

FIGURE 8.12

Spreadsheet Forum on AOL

An important spreadsheet capability is handling multiple formats for importing and exporting files. This gives you access to files from other spreadsheet and database programs. It's also helpful to buy a spreadsheet that can emulate the user interface you're accustomed to.

To explore the spreadsheets available on the market, go to the Spreadsheet Forum on AOL (keyword: **Spreadsheet**), shown in figure 8.12.

What's the best spreadsheet?

The answer, of course, depends on what you need to do. At one time, Lotus 1-2-3 owned the market, but it no longer does. You should take a look at what your office uses if you need compatibility with colleagues. If you'll be using the spreadsheet program exclusively for home use, consider Microsoft Excel or the spreadsheet in MS Works. Also available is a nice shareware spreadsheet that offers compatibility with MS Excel. To find it, go to keyword: **Quickfind**, then choose Search and enter **SDSS** as the search phrase. The spreadsheet shareware author is here online and does a good job of supporting this product.

What can a word processor do for me?

Everyone needs a word processor at some time. Pen and paper won't do the trick, and typing and retyping on typewriters is time-consuming and frustrating.

The best word processing program is not necessarily the one with the fanciest features. Sometimes those features just get in your way. The ideal word processor does everything you need it to do and makes you feel comfortable doing it. It should be compatible with the program you use at your office or school.

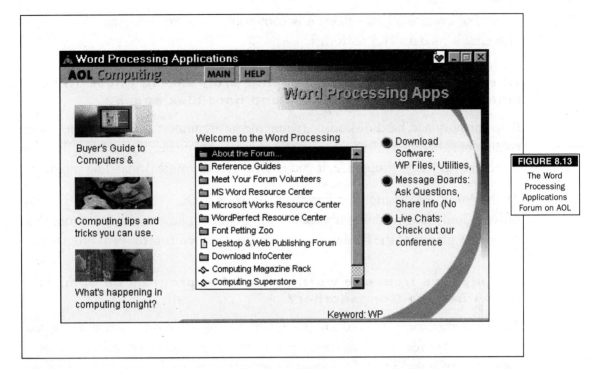

FIGURE 8.13

The Word Processing Applications Forum on AOL

Don't miss the Word Processing Applications Forum on AOL (keyword: **WP**), shown in figure 8.13. It can provide useful information on word processing programs and their capabilities.

What standard features should I look for in a word processing program?

The features that used to be considered extras or options are now standard features. These include the following:

- Spell checker

- Thesaurus

- Macros

- Fonts

The quality of these features varies from program to program. See how many words are covered by the spell checker and thesaurus—the more the better. Macros offer simple and quick ways to automate routine tasks. For example, you could set up a macro that types in your full address, just by hitting a function key. Fonts are type styles. For example, Times Roman is commonly used for newspaper body copy. Helvetica is used for IRS tax forms.

When I choose a word processing program, do I need to consider my computer's memory and hard disk space?

Both memory and hard disk space requirements are important. If you don't have enough of either for a full installation of a certain word processing package, find one that demands less. (Or upgrade, if you really prefer the more demanding program.)

At the Word Processing Applications Forum on AOL (keyword: **WP**) and the Buyer's Guide (keyword: **Buyer's Guide**), you'll find out how to choose a word processing program and the hardware and software requirements for each program.

Will my files from one word processing program be compatible with those from another?

This is another consideration, and potentially an important one. Almost every program can create files in ASCII (plain text) format in addition to its native format. A native format is the default file format an application program uses to store data on. But ASCII files lose important formatting information, such as bold, italics, line spacing, and so on. If you import an ASCII file into another word processing program, it may take a lot of time and effort to reformat it. You might want to seriously consider a word processing program with the ability to export files in various formats.

Stop by the AOL Word Processing Applications Forum to get information on compatibility among word processing programs.

Can I mix text and graphics in a word processing program?

Yes, using its graphic formats. A good word processing program comes with graphic filter files that allow you to import graphics into a word processing document. These files let you import DCX, BMP, TIP, and other graphic file formats. Be sure that any such program you think about buying can use files in PCX, BMP, and TIF graphic formats.

Can I test-drive a word processing program before buying it?

The best way to determine whether you like a word processing program is to use it for a while. Some retail computer stores have installed word processing packages on computers for you to try. Software companies let you evaluate trial versions of their packages. These are obtainable either by phone or by download at the company's Web site. This package usually has all the same features as the regular software package. You can install the package and take it out for a spin. See how you like it. You might find that some packages have a time limit on them and will no longer run after a specified period of time. If this happens, you'll need to uninstall the software so that it doesn't take up space. The software may come with an uninstall file that you double-click on in the folder where the software is stored. If you're using Windows Explorer, use the add/remove feature in the control panels to remove the software.

If you decide to buy the full-blown software package, you can order it at the AOL Store Software Shop (keyword: **Software Shop**) and get some good buys. The software company will ship the word processing package directly to you. You install the package and register online so that you can get all the product, upgrade, and software company information you need to stay informed about the word processing program. If you decide that you don't want the package after all, some software companies offer a money-back guarantee. And you should take them up on it.

Should I expect technical support for a word processing package?

While you are trying out a word processing product, make sure to test the software company's technical support, too. See if technical support representatives are available at hours convenient to you.

Here are some relevant questions to ask yourself:

- How long does it take you to reach the support line?

- How long do you have to hold after reaching it?

- Do you pay for the call, or is a toll-free number available? Do you pay by the minute by dialing a 900-prefix phone number?

- Are the technical support representatives actually able to help you with common or tricky questions?

What is a desktop publisher?

Nowadays it's hard to distinguish between high-end word processing and desktop publishing programs. Old desktop publishing programs let you control things like fonts, scaling, line spacing, kerning, and wrapping text around graphics. You took your completed word processing files to a desktop publisher and graphic artist to turn them into attractive documents. Back then, desktop publishing programs were the only way you could combine text and graphics—although they couldn't handle text very well. The new desktop publishing programs give you powerful word processing features, such as global search and replace, spell checkers, and thesauruses.

Today's word processing programs can automatically index, lock illustrations to paragraphs or pages, and captions and page numbers. They can also take care of fonts, scaling, line spacing, kerning, and wrapping text around graphics. You can churn out brochures, flyers, newsletters, and bulletins with mixed text and graphics in color in a snap.

The AOL Desktop Publishing Forum (keyword: **DTP**) offers a lot of information on desktop publishing programs, applications, and message boards.

Since I already have a powerful word processing program, why would I want a desktop publisher?

The reasons you might want to purchase a desktop publishing package are convenience and document size. For convenience, some desktop publishing packages provide many ready-to-use templates for a broad range of documents. And as for document size, it's far easier to produce long documents with a desktop publishing program than with a word processing program.

What should I look for when I go to purchase a desktop publishing package?

First, make sure that its video drivers work satisfactorily with your monitor and video card. Second, look at the back of the software box for minimum and recommended hardware requirements. Make sure your computer qualifies under "recommended" and not merely "minimum." Be sure that the program supports both your printer and a PostScript printer. That way you will be able to send PostScript output to a service bureau so they can print high-quality output on any type of paper, card stock, envelopes, or whatever you want to print on.

Also, make sure the program you select can import and export the text and graphic formats you use. It should also supply templates for the types of documents you want to produce. Look for a wide selection of high-quality clip art supplied with the program. You should be able to edit or embellish art with the program's drawing tools. Several scalable fonts should come with the program, and it also should accommodate third-party fonts. A scalable font is a font you can enlarge or reduce to any size available in the font program.

What is a font manager?

A font manager is a program that helps you organize and use your fonts. If you publish newsletters, design brochures, or require a variety of fonts in your business, then you'll need a font manager program. A good font manager program is FontMinder by Ares Software Corp. There are hundreds of thousands of fonts you can buy to get a varied library of fonts with examples from all the

DESKTOP PUBLISHING PROGRAMS

These are some of the best desktop publishing programs on the market:

- Adobe PageMaker (Adobe Systems)
- CorelDraw (Corel Corp.)
- FrameMaker (Frame Technology Corp.)
- DoDOT (Halcyon Software)
- Info Publisher (Adobe Systems)
- Microsoft Publisher (Microsoft)
- QuarkXPress (Quark)

What Desktop Publishing Programs can do for you:

- Rearrange a paper page into a screen page
- Move text and graphics and size them proportionately
- Build documents that are complex or that require different elements for different locales, languages, or formats
- Create layouts you can reuse
- Import and export HTML files, complete with in-line graphics and links
- Customize the Tool palette by rearranging and hiding tools
- Set preferences to show the true look of the document as you drag, resize, or reshape (observe correct text flow and item stacking)

319

major font families. Check out the many fonts offered by the font designer company Bitstream. Consider buying a kerning editor to manage the way your fonts look. Kerning controls the amount of space between characters (letters and numbers). A good kerning editor to check out is LetrTuck by EDCO Services.

I want to use the fonts that I downloaded from AOL. My computer expert friend told me to set up the fonts in Windows Font Manager. How do I do that?

What you'll need to do is open the Windows Control Panel and choose Fonts. In the Fonts window, choose File, Install New Font. Choose the folder where you downloaded the fonts from AOL, and choose the fonts you want to use. Click on OK, and Windows copies the fonts to your Font Manager. Now the fonts are ready to use with any Windows program.

What is graphics software?

Graphics software comes in many flavors: drawing packages, CAD (computer-aided design), image editing and painting, clip art, and digitized stock photos. Take your pick.

A good place on AOL to learn more about digital images and pictures is the Pictures area (keyword: **Pictures**). There's information on digital cameras, scanners, graphics formats, and image editing. This site also enables you to share your photos with others. You'll find out how to build your own Web page and share images via e-mail. There's even a link to the Barnes and Noble (keyword: **barnesandnoble**) site, where you can purchase books on graphics software.

What is a drawing program?

Drawing programs let you create geometric shapes. For example, you can create a circle and easily change the size or colors of the circle.

What is CAD?

CAD stands for computer-aided design and is an essential tool for draftspeople, architects, and technical illustrators. A CAD program such as AutoCad allows objects to "remember" their width, height, and depth. AutoCad is the most popular CAD program. It has a nationwide authorized training center and hundreds of add-on programs by third-party software companies. This sophisticated drawing program costs thousands of dollars, but allows you to truly work in three dimensions.

What are image editing and paint programs?

Let's start with defining image—specifically, digital image. A digital image is made up of many little dots or pictures elements, called pixels. When you scan a photo into your computer, or when you create a photo-realistic image with your image software, you're working with millions of little dots (pixels). That's why scanned images require a lot of disk space, and that's why printing a photograph correctly is tricky. Manipulating and controlling all those pixels is a big challenge.

To manipulate and control the pixels that make up photographs, you use image editing and paint programs. These offer precision controls for handling full-color and grayscale images. You've probably seen "morphing" on MTV or television commercials, which involves special effects that transplant one person's head onto another's body, turn a sunny day into a thunderstorm, and so on. The best features of an image editing and paint program are the controls that let you render and print images with the highest possible exactness.

The AOL Pictures area (keyword: **Pictures**) provides helpful information on image editing.

What is clip art?

Clip art consists of drawings and digitized stock photos that are "canned" and usually free. Clip art provides collections of visuals for nonartists who need graphics for their publications. Clip art can be commercial drawings scanned from pre-computer

Here are the most popular drawing programs:

- CorelDraw (Corel)
- Adobe Illustrator (Adobe Systems)
- Visio (Visio Corp.)
- Canvas (Deneba Software)
- AutoCAD (Autodesk)

What a good Drawing Program can do for you:

- Select colors using RGB (red, green, and blue–the color system of the Web)
- Create both client-side and server-side image maps to act as links on your pages
- Smooth the edges on exported GIF and JPEG images
- Assemble illustrations and diagrams by dragging and dropping objects created from stencils
- Develop complex interactive illustrations

Other features to look for in a drawing program:

- Consistently exacting and flexible drawing tools
- Image-editing, page-layout, presentation, and design tools
- Clip-art library

322

clip art collections. There's also very beautiful clip art—not just drawings but patterns, textures, and scanned photographs.

The clip art that came with my software program is too generic for my company's newsletter, which I edit. Where can I purchase more unusual clip art?

Certain versions of CorelDraw contain massive quantities of clip art. You can also find clip art in Microsoft Office 97 and WordPerfect 8, and the AOL GraphicSuite program (keyword: **GraphicsSuite**).

At the AOL Pictures area (keyword: **Pictures**), there are beautiful and unusual clip art and graphics formats.

What are digitized stock photos?

Digitized stock photos are stock photo collections on CD that contain tens of thousands of images. Buying these stock photos gives you whole photo albums chock full of photographs that you can use on your computer. You might want to insert a photo into a greeting card, bulletin, newsletter, or the like to spice up a document.

Agencies license stock photos. Keep in mind that your license to use them is usually more restrictive than the wide-open policies that apply to regular clip art. In other words, you might not be able to use a particular photo in a commercial publication without paying a separate licensing fee.

Corel Corporation sells a rapidly growing collection of photos on CD. Kodak's Photo CD format has become a standard.

Go to the Pictures area (keyword: **Pictures**) on AOL, where you'll find collections of photographs that you can download. This site also enables you to share your photos with others via e-mail. Also, check out MasterClips in the AOL Store Software Shop (keyword: **Software Shop**).

What is a Web building program?

You can create a home page on the Web that other people can visit. First, check out AOL's easy-to-use Personal Publisher program (keyword: **Personal Publisher**). It makes creating your own site a breeze and lets you incorporate text and graphics. Once you create a Web site, you can upload it to the Web, and make changes to it whenever you want.

America Online members get 2MB of free Web space per screen name for your Web site. This is enough space for many pages of text or several pages of text and graphics.

The Pictures area (keyword: **Pictures**) can help you learn how to incorporate pictures into your Web pages.

What is a domain?

A domain is a unique name that identifies an Internet entity. For example, aol.com, where com is the domain that stands for company, and the Internet entity is America Online; whitehouse.gov where gov stand for government and the White House is the Internet entity; npr.org where org stands for organization and National Public Radio is the Internet entity.

I would like to build a business Web site. How can I do this?

PrimeHost (keyword: **PRIMEHOST**) lets you create your own domain name for your business. Instead of having the naming convention http://members.aol.com/screen-name, you can have your own domain name. For example, http://www.mybiz.com. The domain name for your business allows you to use a familiar name rather than an Internet addresses. This way, you'll put your business on the Web and get it noticed.

PrimeHost also offers member services where you can enroll in classes about developing you Web site, use tools to build a site, promote your Web site, and get customer service for your site. You can also get templates from which you can build your Web site to achieve a certain look. PrimeHost will also inform you of other Web sites that will help you create your own site.

What software would you recommend to build a personal Web site?

Personal Publisher (keyword: **Personal Publisher**) is an extremely easy Web page creation program. What's nice about Personal Publisher is that you don't have to know anything about HTML (hypertext markup language), which is the language that Web pages are written in. Personal Publisher asks you simple questions about what text you want, how it should look, and what multimedia elements you want, such as sound or graphics. You just have to answer the questions in plain English. This Web building program does all the work for you and even publishes your pages on the Web.

If you want to change the page later, you can easily edit it, add to it, and modify what you have there. There is no fee for creating a page using Personal Publisher. Remember, you get 2MB of Web space for each screen name on your America Online account. Start to design a Web page today—it's free and it's easy.

My graphics don't show up on my Web page. What can I do to fix this?

Here are four things you can check on to ensure that the graphics do show up on your Web page:

1. View your graphics offline. Open your graphics files in a word processing or drawing program or use a graphic viewer to make sure they display properly.

2. Be sure your graphics files have the correct filename extensions: GIF or JPEG. Check to see that you've uploaded your graphics at My Place.

3. Check to see that the filenames and locations of your graphics files match exactly the names that you used in your HTML document. The graphics filenames must match in case and location.

3. Check to make sure your Web browser is set to display graphics. To do so, choose Members from the top menu, then choose Preferences, and WWW.

The changes I made to my Web page don't show up. What next?

There are three things you can do to ensure that any changes you made to your Web page show up:

1. Make sure that you have properly updated your Web page by either using the Edit feature in Personal Publisher, or by uploading to My Place.

2. Wait a few minutes. The changes might show up automatically.

3. View your Web page in your browser by clicking on the Reload button. This forces your browser to reread your Web page from the Web rather than calling up an older version of your page from your Web cache.

My page looks like a text file or directory listing. Help!

Be sure you have named your Web page with the HTM extension. This is how your browser identifies it as a Web page. If your browser cannot find a Web page, it will show you a directory (folder) listing of your Web page instead. If you forgot to include the HTM extension on your Web page filename, just rename your page and upload it again to My Place. Once everything is working again, you can delete the old Web page (the one without the HTM extension). Use the Utilities icon in My Place.

I can't get to my Web page. Where do I go now?

Sometimes traffic on the Web or system problems can make it difficult to access your Web page either for editing in Personal Publisher or for viewing in your Web browser. When this happens, you can do the following to correct the situation:

- Check the system status at keyword: **Personal Publisher**.

- Report any problems at keyword: **System Response**.

- Try again later or the next time you log on. Problems can clear up with just a little patience and time.

The Publish to Web feature in my HTML program doesn't work. What can I do?

If you use an HTML program such as Microsoft Publisher or Microsoft FrontPage, you have the Publish Wizard that automatically uploads your page to their Web server space. Other HTML programs might have this automatic publishing feature, too.

I created a Web page using Microsoft FrontPage. What's my next step?

Check to see if the latest version of Personal Publisher supports FrontPage filename extensions. If not, you can always manually upload your Web page to My Place, and it should work fairly well.

Is there any software that can help me easily publish my personal Web site on the Web?

To build your first Web site, use an easy program like Personal Publisher. It may well serve all your needs. If you're ready to try something more complex, then use your own HTML editor, such as HotDog or Microsoft FrontPage. After you create your Web site using any Web building program your heart desires, then go to My Place on AOL (keyword: **My Place**). From there you can upload your Web pages and any support files, such as GIFs, WAVs, or MIDIs. My Place publishes your Web page on the web at the following Web site: http://members.aol.com/yourscreenname/. There is no extra charge for creating Web pages and uploading them to My Place.

Here are some helpful hints for you when uploading your Web pages to My Place:

- It's a good idea to name your main page index.htm. The name index.htm will show up automatically when someone browses your Web directory.

- Remember to use the HTM extension when naming your HTML pages.

- You have 2MB of Web space for each screen name on your account. This translates to enough space for several hundred pages of text or several pages of text and graphics.

- Get your creative juices going and enjoy the process of building a Web page.

- If you need some help putting your Web page together, AOL can help you at keyword **On the Net**.

What is encryption software?

Most people never think about PC security until someone sneaks in and copies a confidential file, or reads a private love letter. You can use a file encryption utility to password-protect the file you're concerned about. The encryption software turns the file into hieroglyphic gibberish. Anyone who knows the password can restore it to its original form.

What is backup software?

Backup software is an essential safety feature. Eventually, every hard drive fails, and unless you have a recent backup, you lose your data. Some good Windows backup programs include

- Norton Desktop for Windows

- PC Tools Pro

- PC Tools for Windows

For more information on backups, see chapter 5.

Is there any software that will detect software problems on my PC?

Well, "diagnostic software" is supposed to detect software and operating system problems by testing every nook and cranny of your computer. But even when a computer is acting flaky, some diagnostic packages fail to identify anything wrong.

But Norton Utilities and PC Tools for Windows do have an effective Windows resource/crash monitor diagnostic. This gives you a constant readout of free memory and hard disk space. An alarm sounds if resources sink too low and your computer is about to crash.

Norton Utilities also has a Windows diagnostic for INI file analysis and advice. It helps you fine-tune your WIN.INI and SYSTEM.INI files, the two most complicated things about configuring Windows. This diagnostic software keeps a log of the changes you have made or the software you installed, which can be helpful when tracking problems on your PC.

Is there software that will detect hardware problems on my PC?

Some hardware diagnostic programs such as PC Tools Pro and Norton Utilities offer a very comprehensive series of tests for tracking down a hardware problem. Norton Utilities hardware diagnostics is very thorough because it actually tests for software interrupt conflicts, and can solve some convoluted configuration problems. And First Aid is a good one for Windows95 users.

Stop by the Windows Forum on AOL (keyword: **WIN**), or the Windows 95 Forum (keyword: **WIN95**), or the Mac Utilities (keyword: **MUT**), or the AOL Store Software Shop (keyword: **Software Shop**) for more information on the right diagnostic software for your computer.

Special Software for Kids and Parents

Here today, gone tomorrow. There are great entertainment and education games that have fallen by the wayside, and new ones have quickly stepped up to replace them. This happens quite a bit, so it's a good idea to check out the Games Forum on AOL (keyword: **Games**) to keep up with the most current education and entertainment PC games. By the way, when setting up that home computer, put it in a central location to maximize the chances that everyone will be inclined to use it.

What kind of education software packages should I buy for my kids?

You can choose from math, reading, spelling, geography, and history games. Some educational programs simply tutor and others teach while they entertain.

For preschoolers, take a look at Broderbund Putt-Putt Joins the Parade. It doesn't teach basic skills like naming colors and counting, labeling shapes, and rattling off the alphabet. However, it's one of the best ways to keep a preschooler in front of the computer for more than 30 seconds. Putt-Putt is a kiddy adventure starring a happy-go-lucky car. There are no wrong turns, and it rewards kids for exploring everything they see.

If you have a CD-ROM drive—and having one is an especially good idea for parents—you can buy your preschooler a "living book." Broderbund Living Books, a four-story series, is part passive read-along and part interactive exploration. Grandma & Me is a 12-screen talking story about Critter's trip to the beach with Grandma. The narrator can even read in one of three languages. Each word is highlighted as the narrator reads the story. Your child can turn the page to move on, go back for another look, or just sit back and listen to the music and dialogue.

My kids have asked about KidPix. What is it?

328

KidPix is a must-have for your home learning library. It's a paint program by Broderbund that looks unassuming enough on the surface, but underneath is a fun digital canvas. You hear sound effects that explode from the speakers when your kids paint, erase, or draw, and lots of cute noise-emitting stickers can be stamped on the screen.

My child's best friend uses KidCuts. Exactly what is it?

Broderbund KidCuts is the companion program to KidPix. This edutainment (education and entertainment) game lets kids make masks, stage puppet shows with scenery, and print paper dolls.

What types of game programs are there for kids?

There are all kinds of good games out there for kids. Starting with PC role-playing games—called RPGs by Dungeon junkies— your child can rely on fantasy as a backdrop and player involvement as a hook. In an RPG, you run a group of characters on a heroic quest through a world where magic reigns and advanced armament means a sharp sword. Role-playing games share several traits. Human and nonhuman characters battle a blend of bizarre creatures like orcs, mages, and assorted mutants and monsters. Another trait is a good-versus-evil plot line, where you fight to right a wrong. Also, puzzle-like problems and a long play time means your kids' engagement in RPGs can be measured in dozens of hours. You should steer clear of role-playing games unless you're a game vet, or extremely patient.

Like most PC games, RPGs come and go. It's a good bet that some of the newest will stick around. You can think of them as the best dungeons in the neighborhood.

What are some good role-playing games for older kids?

Origin Ultima Underworld is a good one. There are two versions. This game has first-person, 3-D perspective features, where you see castle corridors and dank hallways as if through the main character's eyes.

In Ultima Underworld II: Labyrinth of Worlds, you must defeat the Guardian, an evildoer, by finding a black gem as you make your way out of a complex prison. It has fairly standard plot, but the wonderful graphics make it special.

329

What recommendations would you make for building a good children's software library?

When it comes to building a good children's software library, you can't judge quality by looking at the pretty boxes. There is a Web site called Children's Software (www.childrenssoftware.com) that discusses the latest releases. A good software library provides access to the Internet and reference CDs and games that support school subjects. It's smart to evaluate the software for both educational and entertainment value. Also listen carefully to what other families have to say. Before you make any purchases, however, make sure your computer can run the software. The AOL Store Software Shop (keyword: **Software Shop**) has Kids Only Games and Entertainment aisles.

My kids use our home computer more than I do. Is there any particular printer I should buy for them?

Get a color ink-jet printer. The kids will love it!

How should I set up my home computer so that it's easy for my kids to use?

Use a sturdy chair that puts the keyboard at your child's elbow level, and set the computer monitor at eye level for your shortest child. For toddlers, your lap works great.

My children are having all the fun on our home computer. Are there computer games parents can enjoy, too?

The graphic adventure games are basically comic books for grown-ups. Graphic adventures are related to RPGs, but they're more like grown-up comic books than morality plays. Adventures put you in the shoes of a single character heading through a set story line. Branching plots move you toward a fixed ending. Adventures are often funny, and can be like gritty cop dramas, science fiction scenarios, and tales of intrigue and mystery. Another feature of a good adventure is that it can be completed quickly. Adventures are good for first-time PC game players. These are interactive programs that entertain you for as long as you want.

Indiana Jones and the Fate of Atlantis by LucasArts features Harrison Ford. This interactive program takes you around the world in a race against Nazis for a strange and powerful metal once used by the inhabitants of the Lost Continent. You can play without typing a stroke or clicking on icons to talk, grab objects, or move. The

CD-ROM version is all-talk.

My adult neighbors play Leisure Suit Larry, and now my husband wants it. What kind of game is that?

Sierra Leisure Suit Larry is one of the longest-running and strangest graphic adventure programs for parents. Larry Laffer is the star, an inept make-out man who goes through adventures that have lots of guy-stuff comedy. There are five Larry adventures, enough to keep you busy for two solid days.

What adventure games are good for parents?

Sierra, who makes Leisure Suit Larry, specializes in the graphic adventures category. You might want to check out Space Quest, Police Quest, and King's Quest. Sierra's titles provide a wide variety of stories and settings. You're bound to find something in the Sierra line that you'll like.

I would like to screen programs, Internet sites, and other important files on my home computer, which my kids use. Is there a way to do it?

Absolutely. The Net Nanny acts as an invisible monitor between the Internet and your family. With the help of a site list, it operates quietly in the background, carefully screening out sites, words, phrases, and content that you have determined are inappropriate. You can download this list for free from the Larry Magid Web site. Net Nanny is the only program that allows you to monitor, screen, and block access to anything residing on, or running in, out, or through your PC, online or off. It's a two-way screening in real time. Net Nanny gives you full control of your kids' access to:

- WWW URLs

- Newsgroups

- IRC (Internet Relay Chat) Channels

- FTPs (File Transfer Protocols)

- E-mail

- Non-Internet BBSs (Bulletin Board Systems)

- Words

- Phrases

- Personal information—address, credit card number, and so on.

It operates on the Internet, AOL, and CompuServe, and all local applications running on your PC.

There are no monthly site update subscription fees for Net Nanny.

How can I ensure a safe online experience for my family and me?

The AOL Neighborhood Watch (keyword: **Neighborhood Watch**) is a great area to visit because it provides tools and tips for a safe online experience. With Neighborhood Watch you can customize AOL to suit your needs. For example, you can set parental controls, stop junk e-mail, and protect your computer from viruses. This area also lets you notify AOL of any bad experiences you had online, shop and do your banking safely online, and get safeguard suggestions.

My 10-year-old loves to explore AOL. How can I monitor what she's up to?

AOL Parental Controls let you take charge of your children's online experience in many ways. First, you need to give your children their own screen names. (Parental controls work by screen name.) Next, choose the My AOL icon on the AOL toolbar. Choose Parental Controls and then click Set Parental Control Now. You can specify different levels of access for each child.

For children ages 12 and under, you should assign the Kids Only category to your children's accounts. You'll discover how safe, fun, educational, and enriching the Kids Only channel on AOL (keyword: **Kids Only**) is for your kids. The restrictions on a Kids Only account include the following:

- Cannot send or receive Instant Messages

- Cannot enter member-created chat room

- Cannot use premium services

- Can only send and receive text-only e-mail with no file attachments or embedded pictures

There is no extra fee for accessing the Kids Only area.

I have two teenagers, 15 and 17. I would like to limit their access to certain places on AOL and the Internet. How would I do that?

For teenagers ages 13 to 15, you should choose the Young Teen category. For teenagers ages 16 to 17, choose the Mature Teen category. The limitations on these types of accounts are:

- Young Teens may visit some chat rooms, but not member-created chat rooms or private rooms

- They're restricted to Web sites appropriate for 13- to 15-year-olds

- They can't use premium services

- They're blocked from Internet newsgroups that allow file attachments

The 18+ category gives a teenager unrestricted access to all features on AOL and the Internet.

The parental control restrictions are just guidelines. It is up to you to choose the right level of access for your child. For instance, you may consider your 15-year-old a "mature teen," while other parents may want the "young teen" setting for a boy or girl of the same age.

After you set a parental control, you can tweak the settings by using the Custom Controls feature. These parental controls enable you to adjust specific activities, depending on your child's needs. For example, you can control chat, the Web, e-mail, newsgroups, and file downloads.

You can alter the categories for your child at any time. That way, you can adjust your children's access so that it's best suited to their maturity level or special needs.

Where can I find parents' and kids' computing news articles?

The best place to find news articles on any computing topic is at the Larry Magid Show area on AOL (keyword: **Larry Magid**). At this site, choose Chat & Archives, Larry's Archives, and then Hardware or Software. These articles are written by computer columnist and child online safety expert Larry Magid. Larry is a great source for interesting computing articles.

APPENDIX I

QUESTIONS MOST FREQUENTLY ASKED OF AOL MEMBER SERVICES

The following are the questions AOL Member Services staff answer most often.

How do I install the AOL software?

Installing AOL is as easy as 1, 2, 3:

1. Insert the AOL disk into your computer.

2. *Windows 95 users:* Click on Start on the taskbar. *Windows 3.x users:* Click on the File menu of your Windows Program Manager, then select Run. Type A:SETUP, B:SETUP, or D:SETUP, depending on which drive the AOL disk is on, and click on OK.

3. Follow the easy instructions and you'll be online in minutes.

How do I uninstall the AOL software?

AOL 3.0 for Windows 95:

1. Click on the Windows 95 Start button.

2. Select Settings and then Control Panel.

3. In the Control Panel window, double-click on the Add/Remove Programs icon.

4. In the Add/Remove Programs window, highlight America Online, then click on Add/Remove.

5. In the America Online for Windows Uninstall window, remove the check from the Fast Mode box, then click on OK. The uninstall program will search for all copies of the AOL software on the hard drive. All copies that are found on the hard drive are then listed.

6. Highlight the AOL3.0 directory, then click on Delete. During the uninstall process, you have the option to save downloaded files, which are stored in the C:\TEMP\AOL30 directory. You are notified after the AOL software is removed from the computer.

AOL 3.0 for Windows 3.x:

1. Double-click on the Main Program Group.

2. Double-click on File Manager.

3. Within File Manager, locate the AOL directory. By default it's C:\AOL30.

4. Click on the AOL directory name so that it is highlighted.

5. Press the DEL (Delete) key on the keyboard.

6. Close the File Manger.

7. Close the Main Program Group.

8. Locate the AOL Program Group

9. Highlight the AOL program group by clicking on it once.

336

10. Press the DEL key.

11. Click on OK.

AOL 3.0 for Macintosh

1. From the Macintosh Desktop, double-click on the Hard Drive icon.

2. Locate the AOL folder. If multiple AOL folders exist, make sure the correct one is selected.

3. Drag the AOL folder to the Macintosh TrashCan.

4. Click on Empty Trash from the Special Menu.

How can I reinstall the AOL software?

The process of reinstalling the AOL software is the same as for the original installation. The only difference is that you must decide whether you want the old AOL information copied to the new version. This option is only available if you already have existing AOL software installed on your computer. This option is not available if you want to install AOL on a new machine that does not already have AOL software installed.

Upgrades from existing AOL software will copy your screen names, stored passwords, preference settings, access numbers, and AOL artwork. This makes it convenient for you to quickly sign back on to the AOL service.

During installation, you will want to upgrade to a newer version of the AOL software, if available. For assistance with reinstalling the AOL software, go to the AOL Help Files offline, or go to keyword: **upgrade** online.

How do I set up my modem or change my modem speed?

America Online needs to communicate smoothly with your modem. To do so, it uses a modem profile, a piece of software that explains what your modem means by each signal it sends and receives. Since each modem is a little different, AOL includes a long list of modem profiles. You just have to choose yours from the list.

How to Set Up America Online to Work with Your Modem

1. Sign off from America Online.

2. In the Sign On window, click on Setup. A dialog box appears.

3. Click on Setup Modem.

4. Highlight your modem from the Choose Modem listbox.

Note: If your modem is not listed, try using one of the generic Hayes-compatible modem profiles, or you can find additional modem profiles online at keyword **Modem** in the Modem Profile Library.

How to Change Your Modem Speed for AOL 3.0

1. Sign off from America Online.

2. Click on the Setup button in the Setup and Sign On window.

3. Choose the location that you want to change.

4. Click on Edit Location.

5. At Next Modem Speed click on the pulldown arrow and select the desired speed. Do this twice.

6. Click on Save.

Note: The instructions for changing your modem speed for AOL 4.0 are likely to be similar but were not available at the time of this writing.

How is the connection from my computer to AOL made?

Connection to AOL is a multistep process that requires very little action from you. Most of the steps are handled automatically by your computer and modem and the access modem. All you have to do is enter your password and click on Sign On to initialize the modem. Here's what automatically happens after you take that easy step:

- Your computer initializes the modem, and the phone line receives a dial tone and begins dialing.

- After the number has been dialed, the modem "shakes hands" with the modem at the access node and establishes the connect speed. This is usually where the modem makes the screeching noise.

- Once the connection is established, the connect speed appears in the window and the access node sends communication to the server to ask for attention.

- At that point, the server tells the modem that it will accept communications with your computer. Your computer now has an established connection with the host. The host obtains your connect speed and your software version.

- Finally, the network verifies your AOL password and the connection is established and ready.

What is a TCP/IP connection and how do I use it?

TCP/IP stands for Transmission Control Protocol/Internet Protocol. It is a communications format for transferring data on a network. America Online's software lets you use TCP/IP (if it is available on your computer) instead of your modem to connect to AOL at no extra charge. Connecting to AOL with TCP/IP is often faster than the usual modem-based connection process, and it will not interfere with your use of other TCP/IP software such as Netscape Navigator.

System Requirements

To connect to AOL through TCP/IP or a SLIP or PPP account, you will need the following:

- America Online for Windows version 2.5 or higher.

- WINSOCK.DLL version 1.1 (comes with AOL version 3.0).

- A direct Internet connection via TCP/IP, or a P or PPP connection.

- If you are using a SLIP or PPP, you will need a program such as Trumpet Winsock, which you can download from our file libraries. Go to keyword **Quickfind**, click on Shareware, then type Trumpet Winsock as your search word.

1. Establish your SLIP or PPP connection, if necessary, by connecting to your ISP or other Internet service provider.

2. In the Sign On window, click on the Setup button.

3. Click on the Create Location button.

4. Select TCP/IP from the Network dropdown box.

5. Click on Save.

6. Click on OK to return to the Sign On window.

7. Click on Sign On and you will connect to AOL over the TCP/IP connection.

What can I do if I receive a busy signal when attempting to connect to AOL?

Occasionally the traffic on the AOL system gets extremely busy. When this happens you may get a busy signal from the access number you are dialing. America Online has an Autodialer program that will continue to attempt to connect when a busy signal is encountered. The Autodialer will redial two different numbers up to 18 times. The Autodialer can be downloaded at keyword: **Autodialer**.

How can I get local access in my area?

At America Online we have spent a significant amount of time and money increasing the capacity of our service. We have installed additional modems, created additional access numbers, and added higher-speed modems all across the country. The best ways to find out if we have increased or added capacity or connect speeds in your area is to go to keyword: **Access** on AOL.

How can I get a faster access number in my area?

To request faster access to AOL, you can fill out a request form at keyword ACCESS. Another option is to use the AOLnet 800 or 888 numbers to connect to AOL at speeds of up to 56K. The numbers are 1-888-245-0113 or 1-800-716-0023 and are surcharged at $6 per hour or 10 cents a minute.

What are the possible reasons for receiving the message "Received no carrier from modem"?

A "no carrier" message can happen either when you are trying to sign on or when you are online and get disconnected. The modem may not be configured properly. Sometimes you might get a "No carrier" or "P3 packet reflected" error message when you're on the AOL service. As a result, you will be disconnected from the service. The possible causes for this particular problem are the same as being bumped offline. This error can also be generated if you disconnect the phone line from the modem while on the AOL service.

The following are other possible reasons you may have received the "no carrier" message, and possible solutions.

Possible Cause: Your modem has misdialed and therefore the access node will not answer.
Solution: If no high-pitched screeching sound was heard upon connection, then check the number being dialed.

Possible Cause: You have Call Waiting on your phone line and an incoming call broke the connection.
Solution: Disable Call Waiting in the AOL setup. Call Waiting will automatically be enabled when you sign off from AOL.

Possible Cause: The connection was broken when another extension on the phone line was picked up.
Solution: Sign on to AOL again.

Possible Cause: You are using the wrong modem profile.
Solution: Change the modem profile in your setup.

Possible Cause: There may be noise on your phone line.
Solution: To check for noise on your household phone line, listen for static after dialing a single digit. If you hear anything, contact your local telephone company for help.

Possible Cause: If you are running the Windows operating system, you may have an RPI modem.
Solution: See What Is an RPI Modem? and the information at keyword: **RPI Help** to determine whether your modem could be causing the problem, and how to solve it.

Possible Cause: In Windows, you are attempting to connect at 28.8K and your external modem has an older UART chip.

Solution: Upgrade to an I/O card with a 16650 UART, or connect at a maximum speed of 14.4K.

How to Determine What UART Chip Your Modem Uses (Windows 95)

1. On the Windows 95 Start menu, point to Settings and click on Control Panel.

2. In the Control Panel window, double-click on the Modems icon.

3. In the Modems Properties window, click on the Diagnostics tab.

4. Highlight the COM port that your modem is using, and click on More Info.

5. Look for information about your UART chip in the Port Selection section of the More Info window.

How to Determine What UART Chip Your Modem Uses (Windows 3.*x*)

1. Exit Windows.

2. Type MSD at the DOS prompt.

3. Type C for information about your COM ports.

4. Look for information about your UART chip.

What can I do when I receive the error message "Open failed for COMX" or "Unable to initialize your modem" upon signing on to America Online?

There are three possible scenarios.

1. The modem is being used by another program. *Windows 3.x users:* Use the Task List to exit all programs that are currently using the modem, such as fax programs, phone answering software, and the Windows program Terminal. *Windows 95 users:* Use the Task List to exit all programs that are currently using the modem, such as fax programs, phone answering software, and the Windows program HyperTerminal. Disable the Caller Access function within the Dial-up

Networking area.

2. The modem used with a laptop isn't turned on. Look for a program or control panel that controls the modem power for the laptop.

3. The modem selection is incorrect. The AOL software may be sending incorrect commands to the modem. Determine what modem model is installed, then:

- Launch the AOL software.

- Click on Setup in the Sign On window.

- Click on Setup Modem.

- Select the modem model from the huge list of modems.

- Click on OK.

What could it mean when I receive the message that my account is already signed on?

Since each account has the ability to have five screen names, there is the possibility that someone else could be signed on to your AOL account from a different location. The Guest feature on AOL lets you or anyone else in your family sign on to AOL from any computer that has the AOL software and necessary components for signing on.

If it is not possible for anyone else to be signed on to your AOL account, then there is the possibility that your account is being used by an unauthorized person. If that is the case, it is best to call our Billing Department at 1-800-827-6364 to discuss the situation.

Another possibility is that the connection to the AOL server has not been disconnected. When you connect to AOL, the connection is not a direct connection to our server. Your modem dials an access number. From that access number you are then connected to the AOL server. If you cannot determine a cause for the message from these descriptions, you may need to contact our technical support group at 1-888-265-8006 (for Windows) or 1-888-265-8007 (for Macintosh).

What is a General Protection Fault (GPF), and how can I fix it when I get one?

This error message is generated by Windows whenever an application or program tries to load something into memory that is already occupied by another program. Since two programs can't reside in the same location, Windows is forced to generate an error message. You can try the following solutions, in order of listing, to resolve the illegal operations or GPFs in AOL.

- Close AOL, then launch AOL again.

- Close all applications, including AOL, then restart the computer.

- Go to keyword: **upgrade** to see if you can use a newer version of AOL.

- Reinstall the AOL software, including copying over your data, then delete the old version.

If a GPF continues to occur, write down the affected module and memory address and contact a Technical Representative.

When I was attempting to access the Internet, the site that I was looking for would not open. What are the possible reasons?

If you are unable to connect to a specified Web site, it is probably because the browser cannot find the server or computer that holds the Web page you specified. The Web address you entered may be incorrect, the server on which the Web page is located may be shut down or busy, or the Web page may no longer exist.

Tips for Connecting to Web Sites

Make sure the Web address you entered exactly matches the Web address you were given. Spelling or punctuation errors can prevent the browser from finding the server.

If you believe the Web address is correct, the problem may be with the computer or server that stores it. The server may be offline for maintenance, or too many people may be trying to access the server at once. Wait a moment and click on the Reload button to try again.

If neither of these approaches resolves the problem, the Web page may no longer exist. The Web is growing and changing rapidly. Web pages come and go—a page available yesterday simply may not be there today.

Note: AOL does not censor any Web sites or information available on them, with the exception of AOL-affiliated Web sites (i.e., member home pages). At no time will AOL restrict your ability to access a Web site that may contain adult information. Of course, as a parent you can exert Parental Controls to keep this stuff away from your children.

How do I run a third-party Internet application over AOL?

America Online is capable of running third-party applications, such as Netscape Navigator, over the AOL connection. We have a special version of Netscape Navigator (keyword: **Netscape**) designed to be 100 percent compatible with AOL. Microsoft Internet Explorer is now included with the AOL software.

What are ways to improve the speed of the AOL service?

One way to ensure that AOL operates as fast as possible is to make sure the modem speed setting matches your modem's capabilities. You can set the modem speed by clicking on Setup in the Setup and Sign On window. Another option is to upgrade to the latest version of America Online (keyword: **upgrade**). Other housekeeping can be performed, such as compacting the Personal Filing Cabinet and purging the Web cache to prevent slowness on the Web. We'll discuss purging the cache shortly.

How do I increase the speed of my browser?

Sometimes going out on the World Wide Web can be time-consuming. Occasionally the problems you encounter are on the end of the site you're visiting itself, but more often a combination of factors are at work. You can speed things up at your end by streamlining your browser, a program that displays Web pages.

One thing you can do to streamline your browser is to turn images off. Sometimes it's hard to get around a Web site if the images are turned off, because buttons are usually images. But if you're looking for a specific piece of text, you can save search time by turning images off.

How to Turn Images Off If You Are Using AOL for Windows 95 (32-bit)

1. From the Members menu, click on Preferences. The Preferences window appears.

2. Click on the WWW button. The WWW Preferences window appears.

3. Click on the General tab.

4. Uncheck the Show Pictures check box.

5. Click on the OK button. Your Web browser will now draw pages with generic image icons where Web images would normally download. If you want to see one of the images behind the generic image icon, simply double-click on it.

How to Turn Images Off If You Are Using AOL for Windows 3.x (16-bit):

1. From the Members menu, click on Preferences. The Preferences window appears.

2. Click on the WWW button. The WWW Preferences window appears.

3. Uncheck the Show Images check box. Your Web browser will now draw pages with generic image icons where Web images would normally download. If you want to see one of the images behind the generic image icon, simply click on it.

What is the Web cache? How can I purge the Web cache?

Cache files are copies of Web pages and graphics that your Web browser stores on your computer when you visit a Web site. When you go to that site again, it will check the cache to see if it has been there before. If it has, it will load the site from your cache and display it. This speeds up the loading of the Web page and reduces the burden on the network.

You should clear (or "purge") your disk cache regularly, especially if you are having problems seeing Web pages. While a healthy cache can speed up your Web surfing, you might start to have problems when the cache begins to fill up.

The procedure for clearing your disk cache will depend on your Web browser.

If you are using Microsoft Internet Explorer as your Web browser, click on Options and select the Advanced tab. Then find the "Temporary Internet Files" section, and click on the Settings button. Finally, click on the Empty Folder button.

If your AOL software does not use Microsoft Internet Explorer, click on Preferences under the Members menu at the top of the window, then click on WWW, then the Advanced button. Finally, click on the Purge Cache button.

How to Empty Your Browser's Cache
If You Are Using AOL for Windows 95 (32-bit)

1. From the Members menu, click on Preferences. The Preferences window appears.

2. Click on the WWW button. The WWW Preferences window appears.

3. Click on the Advanced tab.

4. Under Temporary Internet Files, click on Settings.

5. Click on the Empty Folder button. A dialog box asking if you want to delete all your temporary Internet files appears.

6. Click on Yes.

7. Click on OK. The Settings window disappears.

8. Click on OK. The AOL Internet Properties window disappears.

9. Close the Preferences window.

How to Empty Your Browser's Cache
If You Are Using AOL for Windows 3.x (16-bit)

1. From the Members menu, click on Preferences. The Preferences window appears.

2. Click on the WWW button. The WWW Preferences window appears.

3. Click on the Advanced button.

4. Click on the Purge Cache button. Your hard drive will erase all of the files in its cache.

What is the download directory? Where is it located? Why is it the default folder for downloads?

When you download a file, you move it from AOL's computers onto your own computer. So, once a file is downloaded, you'll need to go to your computer's hard drive (usually the C:\ drive) to find it. The download directory located inside your AOL3.0 (or 4.0) directory is the default directory on your computer where AOL places most files that you download.

Note: Whenever you download files, you should make a note of the directory you're downloading the file to as well as the filename. Writing down that information will keep you from opening every folder on your computer to find the file. It's also a good idea to download all files to the same directory.

How to Find a File You've Downloaded

1. From the File menu, click on Download Manager. You may do this online or offline.

2. Click on Show Files Downloaded.

3. Select the file you're having trouble finding.

4. Click on Show Status to see where the file was placed.

What is a TOD, and why is it downloading on my computer?

A TOD is a Tool on Demand. Tools on Demand are additions to the current AOL software that were not included in the original software version. Recent TODs improved security features for the Microsoft Internet Explorer, updated the Welcome and Channels windows, and added charting features to the Portfolio area.

Occasionally, America Online will send out TOD updates to improve your AOL software's functionality, or to add new features to the service. The download is automatic and will occur either upon sign-off or when you access a new feature on the service that the software currently doesn't support. They usually don't take much time at all, and there's never a charge.

How do I attach a file to e-mail?

With AOL, you can attach any file—word processing documents, spreadsheets, graphics, photographs, even sounds—to an e-mail message and send it to another AOL member or any Internet e-mail address. This is great for sending baby photos to Grandma or delivering a top-priority project or proposal to your out-of-town customer—faster than overnight.

How to Attach a File to Your E-mail Message

1. In the Compose Mail window, click on the Attach button. The Attach File window appears.

2. Browse your hard drive or floppy drive directory for the file you want to attach.

3. Highlight the filename, and click on Open. The Attach File window will close, and you'll see the filename listed on your e-mail form. If you change your mind and decide not to send the file, click on the Detach File button.

4. Fill in the address, subject, and body of your e-mail as usual. Even if your attachment contains your primary information, it's customary to include some kind of "cover letter" in the e-mail message box.

5. Click on the Send button. You'll see a blue status bar indicating that your attachment is being sent with the e-mail.

If you want to send more than one file with your mail, you'll need special compression software to turn several files into one file.

Note: The recipient must have software that is compatible with your file to open the attachment. For example, if you send someone a WordPerfect file, your recipient must have either WordPerfect or a word processing program capable of opening WordPerfect files. Also make sure the file is compatible with your recipient's computer—a Macintosh machine may not be able to read some Windows files, and vice versa.

349

Currently, there is a size limit of 17MB for attached files. Members will not be able to attach or send files larger than the limit. But with AOL 4.0, members can easily include pictures *within* their e-mail messages (not as separate attachments).

Can I limit the amount of junk e-mail I receive?

Not only can you limit the junk e-mail, but you can also decide who is allowed to send mail to your mailbox. AOL has set up mail controls at keyword: **Mail Controls** so you can take control of junk e-mail.

Can I limit the areas of the service that my family uses?

The Master Screen Name has the availability of Parental Controls at keyword: **Parental Controls**. The Master Screen Name may choose one of several options, including 18+, Mature Teen, Young Teen, or Kids Only, or you may customize the Parental Controls. By customizing the Parental Controls, you can limit the areas that are visited by each screen name online. Each time that you create a new screen name, you will be asked to set Parental Controls on that screen name.

How does your service compare to an Internet service provider (ISP)?

AOL is a complete service. There is no need to separately configure different applications for browsing the Web, e-mail, plug-ins, and so on. Here are the benefits of AOL compared to an ISP:

Easier Set-Up and Learning Curve

- Easier e-mail

- Seamlessly integrated

- Easy-to-use Address Book

- Easy document attachment

- Drag-and-drop hyperlinks

- Color, italicize, underline, etc.

Easier to Find What You're Looking For

- Content channels for all member interests

- Find feature and keywords

- "Match Your Interests" help at keyword **QuickStart**

Easier Navigation

- Content is organized by familiar subjects.

- Our programming department places the most relevant content at the top level of each channel.

- Easy-to-understand toolbar icons get you places immediately.

Customer Service

- Connect to a live person via phone or online help 24 hours a day, 7 days a week.

- Extensive Help documentation available online, too (keyword: **Quick Reference** or **Help**).

- Free!!—Even the call is toll-free.

Unique Ways to Communicate with People

- E-mail with color, font enhancements, and hyperlinks

- Searchable Member Directory—even tells you who's online now

- Member Profiles

- Buddy Lists

- Instant Messages with color, font enhancements, and hyperlinks—You can communicate via e-mail on the Net, but real-time communication requires IRC or Internet Telephony software, neither of which is as good or as easy to use as what's available on AOL.

- Most popular and easiest chat—over 12 million people to chat with

- Personal Publishing

- Parental Controls

Safety

- Virus-screened software—All files available for download in software libraries have been thoroughly screened for viruses.

- Shopping guarantees—Merchandise purchased online is guaranteed by the respective retailer.

- Guarantees against credit card fraud

- AOL provides a set of community standards and enforcement mechanisms, Community Guidelines and Terms of Service (keyword: **TOS**)— The Internet relies on an unwritten code of behavior that is frequently violated and doesn't extend far enough.

- People are available online when trouble arises (Guides and CAT reps)

- Privacy controls allow you to control the distribution of your private information.

Everything on the Internet and More

- Fully integrated software for all your Internet needs, Mail Center, Web, FTP, gopher, and newsgroups. AOL makes it easy to use your favorite browser or other Internet software so you can choose how you use the Internet.

Flexibility

- Personal Publisher—Create your own home page in minutes for free.

- Software Libraries for free downloads

- Keep multiple windows open and viewable at the same time.

- Automatic AOL and offline reading of e-mail and newsgroups let you manage your online time more efficiently.

- File Grabber lets you download and decode multiple newsgroup files—no messing with cumbersome decoding programs.

AOL Extras

- Up to 5 screen names per AOL account, allowing family members, roommates, and others to have their own sub-account, or you can have several different types of sub-accounts for your own use such as business vs. fun.

- Better organized content, more live programming, more useful, more efficient, more community, more interaction, more chat, more personalization, more safety, easier e-mail

- Major brands like *Newsweek*, ABC, MTV, Nickelodeon, and *Rolling Stone*

- AOLPress—free Web publishing software

- Over 100 magazines/newspapers free on AOL

- Affordable pricing

- Largest access network in the country (great for travelers!)—local access numbers available nationwide

- Access from over 75 countries at International Access

Parental Controls

- Parental Controls empower parents to make AOL safer for their kids.

- Special "safe" areas for kids and teens

- Branded content created specifically for kids

- Vast educational resources and tools for your kids, including Homework Help

More Efficient Money Management

- Easily set up and track your stock portfolios.

- Maintain multiple portfolios.

- Improve your investing performance with the wealth of information available in the Company Research area and Motley Fool Forum.

How can AOL save me money?

AOL has services that can actually save you money. For example:

- Do online banking.

- Sign on a friend.

- Use AOL instead of the library for research.

- Send and receive e-mail.

- Get news from AOL.

- Let AOL be your "at home" mall.

- Do online shopping.

- Read newspapers online (and save on subscription costs).

- Find bargains online (Classified Ads).

- Make travel plans.

- Send attached files.

- Read Consumer Reports.

- Get stock quotes.

What are your billing policies?

AOL offers various billing plans to suit your individual needs. For $21.95 per month you can have unlimited access to AOL on the Standard Unlimited Plan and you won't have to worry about hourly charges. Another option is the One Year Plan which costs $239.40 for one year of service, which is equivalent to $19.95 per month. If you are a light user you may prefer the Limited Plan which costs $9.95 per month for 5 hours, $2.95 for each additional hour or the Light Usage Plan which costs $4.95 per month for 3 hours, $2.50 for each additional hour. If you would like to access AOL through an Internet Service Provider you can sign up for the BYOA (Bring Your Own Access) Plan. This plan costs $9.95 per month.

During your first 30 days with AOL, your membership fee is waived. You are responsible for any other charges during your trial membership (AOL Store charges, connect charges, Premium area charges). Additional time over the trial offer will be billed by the minute, and the rates can be checked at keyword BILLING. After the first 30 days you are billed a membership fee plus any other charges incurred during the previous billing cycle.

Can I change my billing date for America Online?

From the date when you first set up your AOL account, you are given a 30-day free trial membership. After the 30-day period, you are billed for your monthly membership fee and your billing date is established. The billing date cannot be changed.

Can I change my master screen name?

When you open an America Online account, you are asked to choose a Master Screen Name. The Master Screen name cannot be changed because it is used to identify the account for our records. The Master Screen Name is the only screen name that can create new screen names, set Parental Controls, and change billing information. Fortunately, there are four additional screen names that you can create by going to keyword: **Names** and selecting the Create a Screen Name option.

If I am on the unlimited plan, is everything covered by the monthly membership fee?

The unlimited monthly fee covers unlimited usage of the AOL service only. The fee does not cover use of Premium areas, such as Premium Games, nor does it cover communication surcharges, long-distance phone charges, AOL Store charges, or any charges other than use of the service.

What are the rates for Premium Games and other things not covered by the monthly membership fee?

These are the additional charges:

- Premium Games are surcharged at $1.99 per hour. Charges may be incurred in other Premium areas. Upon entering a Premium area, the user is informed of the charges that will be incurred.

- Usage of the AOLNet 800 or 888 numbers for U.S. members is 10 cents a minute or $6 per hour.

- AOL Store charges may also be charged to your AOL bill.

- In addition, members who are not on the unlimited plan will be charged for use above and beyond what their billing plan provides. For example, members on the $9.95 limited plan get up to 5 hours of online time per month. Members who use more than 5 hours during the month are charged $2.95 per hour. Unused hours will not be carried over to the next month.

- Members who bill their AOL account to a checking account will be charged a monthly $5 fee in addition to their membership fee.

How can I keep the cost of the service down?

There are several ways to keep the cost of AOL to a minimum.

- You can restrict any screen name from going into Premium areas or from making purchases online by going to keyword: **Parental Controls.**

- In addition, we offer lower pricing options such as the Limited Plan described above. This is the plan of choice for infrequent users.

- We also offer the Light Usage plan for $4.95 a month, with 3 free hours monthly and $2.50 per hour for time over the allotted 3 hours.

For members on the hourly plans who wish to keep the costs down, we offer some features that you can do offline. For example:

- E-mail can be composed offline and saved for later delivery.

- Members can also go into "free" areas online such as keywords **Member Services** and **Billing.** Time spent in free areas does not deplete the monthly free hours bank.

Automatic AOL is another feature that saves time and money. You can find more information at keyword **Automatic AOL**.

What are the ways that I can pay for my America Online account?

There are several options for paying your America Online account.

- AOL Visa, Visa, MasterCard, Discover, and American Express are all available credit card options to members in the United States.

- Or you may have your AOL bill electronically debited from a checking account or debit card. America Online charges a $5 handling fee for members who bill to checking accounts. Members who have chosen to be billed by debit card are not charged the $5 fee.

If I close my AOL account, can I reactivate the account if I decide to use the service again?

When you close your America Online account, the cancellation takes place immediately and you will not be able to sign on to the service again. A cancellation letter is sent to AOL members from the United States and arrives within 7 to 10 business days. Our records are kept on file and you may call at any time within 6 months to reactivate your account. After 6 months your account information is no longer available and it will be necessary for you to create a new account.

Are there reasons AOL may close my account?

Occasionally there are instances where AOL may close your account in accordance with the Terms of Service, which are outlined at keyword: **TOS**. There are a variety of reasons your account may be closed, including an inability of AOL to collect fees accrued on the account or activity on your account that violates the Terms of Service (e.g., transfer of pornographic files, password solicitation).

Who can get information on my AOL account?

The only person who can get information on your account is the person responsible for paying for your AOL account. America Online has established a privacy policy that safeguards your personal information, and is committed to protecting its confidentiality. All of the billing information that you provide is kept secure. You can access information on your account by going to keyword: **Billing**, where you can also modify your billing information or update your address.

357

APPENDIX II

PC COMPUTER PREVENTIVE MAINTENANCE CLASS

The following is a transcript of an online class held at the AOL PC Hardware Forum on November 26, 1997. The instructor was Chuck Smith (screen name PC Chuck). Computing classes are a great way to widen your knowledge of PCs. Try one sometime.

Welcome, everyone! :) I am Chuck Smith, AOL's PC Hardware Forum leader (keyword: **PC Hardware** or **PHW**). Tonight I'd like to give you a good overview on how to keep your equipment working at its best, as well as making sure you have a good working plan to keep your valuable programs and data protected and backed up.

At the end (or in about 45 minutes), we'll have time to take some questions, and like all of our classes here, if we don't have time to get to your question or it's a more detailed problem/question, I'd like to invite you to send me an e-mail at screen name PC Chuck and/or visit our weekly conferences (live chats) in the PC Hardware Forum (keyword: **PC Hardware** or **PHW**).

Okay, let's get started. Remember to watch the top screen for what I'm saying, and if you miss something, don't worry. You can stop back here tomorrow and find the transcript for tonight's class to read/print.

I'd like to start with surge protectors or surge-protected power strips. These are devices you plug computer equipment (or other electronics, like stereos, TVs, etc.) into. The device, in turn, plugs into an electrical outlet in the wall.

In an ideal scenario, should you have a power surge from an electrical storm or possible construction in your area, which may cause a sudden drop and surge of power on the electric lines, the surge-protected power strip will first attempt to absorb the surge or release it through your electrical ground lines. If it can't, as a last resort the surge-protected power strip will actually open up the circuit and keep all power from coming to your equipment. As with most things you buy for your computer, you are going to find varying quality and features with these types of power strips. And in most cases, the better ones are going to cost more but be well worth it in the long (and short) run.

You can also find models that let you protect your computer's modem, by offering surge protection to the incoming phone line which goes to your computer's modem. Phone line surges damage modems, answering machines, cordless phones, and just about any of the newer, more delicate communications equipment we enjoy today. Phone line surge-protected power strips are probably one of the most overlooked things you can get to protect your computer. I've seen damage done to computers, including the motherboard and other components inside, due to electrical surges that came from the phone lines. So it's something worth looking into, especially if this type of electrical surge is a problem in your area.

Another type of power protection for your computer comes in the form of a power line conditioner, which is good for areas in which "brown-outs" and power drops happen at times, such as smaller, rural areas or even larger cities in summertime when everyone turns on their air conditioners at the same time. These devices connect between your computer and the electrical outlet, and monitor the voltages coming in from outside. Some also offer surge protection. If the power drops (or rises) beyond normal ranges, these devices will compensate one way or another.

If your computer is required to be on at all times, such as a business computer, or even a home computer that you rely on to be up and running at certain times, you may want to look into a backup power supply. In most cases, this is a set of very powerful batteries that are constantly being charged, so that whatever equipment you have connected to the backup power supply (which, in turn, is connected to your power outlet on the wall) will continue to run even if you lose electrical power to your home or business building.

Backup power supplies come in two general types. The first type is for people who need to be able to cleanly shut down their computer system and the software they are running, should power be lost. These give you between 5 and 15 minutes to shut down so that you won't lose any valuable data that is in the computer's memory and hasn't been saved yet. The other type is more expensive, but can give you up to several hours of continuous hours of power, so you can keep on using the computer, even if outside power to your building is completely cut off for an extended period of time.

Speaking of power, I know we'll have this question later if I don't address it now, so I'll get it out of the way. And the question is... "Should I turn my computer off or keep it running?" Well, if you see a storm coming, or you're going to be away (on vacation for a week, for example), it is a good idea to disconnect your computer's power strip from the wall, since that is the best protection from surges, as you can imagine. As far as turning it off during the day, my feeling is that just going to lunch or leaving the room isn't reason enough to warrant powering off the computer.

However, the end of the day is a good time to close out your applications (software), shut down Windows, and power off all your equipment. I liken powering the computer off and on excessively to turning a lightbulb on and off. I don't know about you, but I can't remember the last time I saw a lightbulb burn out while it was in use. Usually it burns out the next time you turn on the light switch or lamp. Your computer, its power supply, and other components heat up and cool down like a lightbulb. I think this adds some stress to the electric components, which are affected as much, if not more, by the heating up and cooling down process.

Okay, moving on to keeping your computer and other components around your computer clean and in good working order. Let's start with your keyboard. (I'm not going to mention any names, but I'm sure we can find some interesting things in just about any of our keyboards if we try. There are a few simple, inexpensive ways to keep your computer's keyboard clean and protected.

First of all, if you use it in an environment that is dusty or dirty (or if you have kids and your computer is located around a main living area, like me, then use a clear plastic cover. They're great, trust me, and for the $20 for the new keyboard and $10 (or less) for the cover, your total investment will pay for itself if it saves you from buying several keyboards over a year or two.

If you have an existing keyboard that needs to be cleaned, you'll find that small vacuum cleaners designed for cleaning keyboards, printers, and small office equipment work well. They usually do a good job of getting between the keys without having to apply any liquid cleaners, or removing the key caps (tops on the keys). If you want to save some money, stop by a local hardware store or office/art supply store, and pick up a small paintbrush, like one used to paint small lettering on signs. You'll be surprised at what a good job those paintbrushes can do.

The key is to keep up with cleaning and prevent dirt/dust from building up and getting sticky between the keys so you have to take more drastic actions to get the keys clean.

Canned air is another option. But with the price of even a small can being over $5 in most stores, buy yourself a couple of paintbrushes instead, or invest in a small keyboard vacuum.

If you need to clean the tops of the keys and around the edges, you can use a very lightly dampened soft paper towel or cloth (lint free, if possible) without getting any cleaner between the keys. You'll have pretty good luck using a mild window cleaner, general purpose (non-abrasive) cleaners, or even rubbing alcohol.

If your mouse or trackball is acting up, you'll find rubbing alcohol and a Q-tip will work pretty well. To get inside the mouse, remove the little access door, then clean the rollers and inside to keep the ball moving freely and smoothly. If your mousepad is getting dirty or worn, just replace it. Lint and other dirt on a mousepad not only builds up inside the mouse where the roller ball is, but also interferes with traction so that the mouse does not move easily across the mousepad.

For cleaning monitors, remember to always power off the monitor first. A light, good-quality glass cleaner on a soft cloth will work pretty well for cleaning both the glass surface and the case, keeping it clean and looking good. You can also do the same with the outside of the computer and things like your printer, scanner, and external drive cases.

Cleaning your computer is hard to do, I know, but cleaning on a regular basis takes a lot less time in the long run, compared to doing a major cleanup later. :)

Besides keeping your computer clean, and protecting it from power surges and problems with power conditions, something that's even more important is to make sure you have (and use regularly!) a good backup system for your valuable programs and data on your computer's hard drive. This is probably one of the most overlooked areas in computing, and it affects new and experienced computer users alike.

Years ago, when computers first offered hard drives instead of having to insert floppy diskettes to run programs and store data, backing up to floppies wasn't a bad way to make backups of your important and most commonly used data files and programs on the hard drive. Today, with hard drives being thousands of times larger than floppies, attempting to make backups to floppies is pretty impractical, to say the least.

Tape backup drives were developed, ranging from early models which backed up 40 megabytes to today's, which can back up well over 2 or 3 gigabytes of data and files. They're commonplace in business, but are still slow. And using them usually means more work, especially when you need to retrieve the few files that have been lost or accidentally erased from your hard drive.

Removable cartridge drives, such as Iomega Zip and Jaz drives and those by Syquest, offer the advantage of speeding backup. They are also accessible like a floppy drive, but they hold much bigger files, so you can not only back up but also copy files to and from cartridges easily. And moving data with cartridge drives is easier than with other parallel port-based backup devices, which connect to the back of your desktop or laptop PC where you'd rather have your printer connected.

Removable cartridge drives come in internal models for those who want to save the desk space, as well as external ones, which may either be connected to a SCSI controller card (inside your computer) or via the parallel printer port. Any way you go, just making sure you are creating backups on a regular basis—that is, as often as you cannot afford to lose the information—is a definite step in the right direction. In fact, cartridge drives that connect to the printer port will even allow you to connect your printer to the back of them, so you can keep your printer connected at all times.

As I promised, we have some time for some questions, if anyone has something related to tonight's topic. :)

Question: A program that will make a file-for-file mirror copy of my hard drive to Zip disks?

Answer: There are several programs, and more coming out all the time—supporting Windows 95, too (which is a little more involved in backing up than DOS/Windows 3.1). These programs will allow you to span a complete "image" of the hard drive (Windows 95, programs, data, etc.) across several removable cartridges—like the Zip or Jaz ones, so when you restore it, you get back close to, if not exactly, what you started with. Or, you can just copy files to the removable Zip cartridges like you would to a floppy, just you have much more room to do so with 100 Megs vs. 1.44 Megs.

Question: What kind of Zip drive do you recommend?

Answer: Most people do well with the parallel port-type Zip drives.

Question: Price range of phone surge protectors? Where to obtain them?

Answer: They range from $12 to $50 (if included with the power strip), and are available at most computer and office supply stores, as well as mail-order dealers.

Question: How to restore my hard drive if I crash without using a canned restore application?

Answer: Here's a common scenario: You have a bunch of documents, accounting files, etc. on your hard drive, and you've been keeping backup of the files by copying them onto the Zip disks on a regular basis. Suddenly you have to reformat your hard drive and reinstall Windows and your applications (software programs). If you do that, you can simply copy the data files back into the recreated (by reinstalling the software) directories, and you'll be back up and running again. If you want to go to a greater extreme, you can do a complete backup of everything on the hard drive, so you can format and make the hard drive bootable, install the Zip software (or use the GUEST program to get a drive letter for the Zip drive assigned and accessible), then restore the backup files from the Zip disks. I still would consider keeping the files copied onto the Zip disks, too, such as documents, etc., so if you don't need to do a complete restore, you can just get access to and/or copy back the needed files.

Question: Surge protector minimum ratings?

Answer: Generally, the most common ratings and differences with surge protectors come in the measurement of Joules ratings and the speed in which they can stop the incoming surge, which is referred to as the "clamping rate." If you look at the $15 to $50 power strips in stores and catalogs, you'll see those standing out the most, as well as the warranty and equipment insurance policies.

Question: Do you have a preference between Zip and Jaz and why?

Answer: Zip drives are still very popular, and the prices for the Zip disks are now under $10 each when you buy in quantity, so compared to Jaz cartridges, which are usually between $80 and $90, it's a little easier on the budget, especially if you want to keep files on separate disks, and can't fit them all on one or a couple of Zip disks. Jaz drives are nice if you want to do that more complete backup of the entire (or most of the) hard drive. To be honest, I wish I could just get more of my customers to simply copy some of their important documents and data files onto Zip disks, so that if they need to reinstall Windows and their programs, they have the really important stuff secured and available to put back.

Question: Are power conditioners also useful for short-term power outage?

Answer: Not really. They are really for keeping the power clean and consistent. Backup power supplies will let you close your application and do a clean shut down, in the event of a total power loss, and you can get uninterruptible power supplies that will give you up to several hours of operating time, even if you lose all power.

Question: What types of combo units are available? Prices?

Answer: Telephone/power surge protectors should be in the range of $100 to $300, depending on how good they are, and the company that backs them—sometimes even offering a mini insurance plan that, in the event that they don't do what they are supposed to, your equipment repair/replacement costs are partially or completely covered up to a certain dollar amount.

Question: What is the mid-range price of a backup power supply that allows a 5-minute backup before shut down?

Answer: Most likely under $150. :)

Question: Can a techie tell if the damage is from frying?

Answer: Sometimes, but I don't get involved in that at my shop, personally, as I figure it's a no-win situation getting in between the customer and the insurance company. (If I wasn't there to see the surge or lightning storm, I'm better off just saying what needs to be replaced, period, and not trying to determine the cause.) Know what I mean? :)

Okay, so is everyone here clear on (and committed to) making good, routine backups? Thanks, everyone, for coming to tonight's class, and all the really good questions, and I'll see you in two weeks—same time, same place! :)

Glossary

accelerator board. An expansion board that increases computing speed by adding a faster CPU (central processing unit).

access number. A phone number (usually local) used to connect to an online service.

access time. The rate at which a computer finds data.

America Online. The world's largest Internet online service. As of this writing, AOL has 12 million members.

analog. Describing data that is represented continuously rather than in intervals. A clock with a minute and an hour hand is an analog device.

antivirus program. Software that detects and eliminates computer viruses.

AOL Fax Center. An AOL service that allows members to send faxes online.

AOL NetFind. The AOL search engine used to search the Web and newsgroups, not the AOL service.

AOL Post Office. An AOL service that allows members to send paper mail online.

AOLNet. America Online's high-speed data network.

application. A computer program that performs a specific task. Word processing and database programs are examples of types of applications.

ASCII (American Standard Code for Information Interchange). The standard used by most computers to represent text.

ATA (AT Attachment). A data transfer interface.

AT bus. (See **ISA (Industry Standard Architecture) bus.**)

ATX. State-of-the-art motherboard configuration.

Automatic AOL. Formerly called Flashsessions, Automatic AOL is a feature members can use to handle certain online tasks at pre-determined times. For example, through Automatic AOL members can sign on to AOL, send and retrieve mail, download files, and automatically sign off.

bandwidth. The amount of information a piece of hardware can transfer during a given time period, measured in bits per second (bps).

BaseT. The speed of data transfer within a computer network, measured in Mbps.

baud rate. A measurement of data transmission speed between modems, or the number of bits per second that are transferred between modems. Lower speeds are usually expressed in baud rate, whereas higher speeds may be expressed in bps, or bits per second.

BBS (bulletin board system). Online sources of interactive information such as games, messages, public domain software, and shareware, usually devoted to a specific subject or interest group.

beta. A test version of new software.

beta-testing. The practice of sending software to volunteer users who try out the product and report problems.

BIOS (basic input/output system). Software built into the motherboard that contains the written instructions for what the computer can do. The BIOS on most personal computers contains the operating instructions for the keyboard, display screen, disk drives and other basic functions.

bit. The smallest measurement of data storage; eight bits equal one byte.

bit-map. A grid that represents the bits dictating how a picture is displayed on a computer screen. A black-and-white picture, for example, is made up of bits that are either on (expressed in code as 1) or off (expressed in code as 0). The computer processes the information provided by a bit map into pixels that comprise the picture.

BMP. The Windows graphics format.

bookmark. A browser feature that allows a user to identify a document or Web site to visit it another time.

boot. To start a computer's operating system.

bps (bits per second). A measurement of data transmission speed. The higher the bps rate, the faster the speed. For example, a modem that operates at 57,600 bps is considered fast, while a 9,600 bps modem is considered slow.

browser. An application that provides access to Internet sites (especially World Wide Web sites).

Buddy Lists. An AOL feature that allows members to create a list of screen names and be notified when a name on that list comes online.

bus. The wires inside a computer that send data from one place to another in the machine.

bus speed. The rate at which a computer's components swap information.

byte. A unit that measures hard disk storage space. One alphabet character takes up one byte of space (or eight bits).

cable modem. A modem that operates at about 10 Mbps.

cache. A high-speed mechanism on a computer that allows it to hold and retain frequently used data. A cache may be either a special section of the computer's main memory or a special high speed storage area.

CAD (computer aided design) system. Software used primarily by engineers and architects that allows them to view a design from any angle or distance.

capacitor. An internal energy storage device that is recharged each time the computer draws power, and discharged during the period when power is not being drawn.

cartridge drive. Portable data storage medium used for backing up data. Some cartridge drives can hold up to one gigabyte.

case. The part of a computer that holds the power supply, the hard, floppy, and CD–ROM drives, and the motherboard.

CCD (charge-coupled device). A semiconductor used in a digital camera.

CD–ROM (compact disc read-only memory). A type of storage disk that can hold large amounts of data, including sound, video and graphics applications.

CD–ROM writer. A CD–ROM drive that reads CD–ROM disks and also records data on them.

CD-RW drive. A CD drive that reads CD–ROM disks, records data on them, and allows a user to reuse them.

Center Stage. An AOL area that features live conferences with guest stars.

Channels. The way AOL organizes its content. Numerous subject-specific channels can be found on the Channels table of contents screen.

chat. An AOL feature that allows more than two members to communicate with one another in real time online.

CISC (Complex Instruction Set Computing). A type of computer chip technology that preceded the RISC chip technology.

clip art. Illustrations that may be inserted into documents. Commercially available clip art packages contain pictures in several different file formats that may be cut and pasted into numerous word-processing programs. Copyright restrictions do not usually apply to clip art.

clock speed. The rate at which a computer processes information.

clone. A knockoff of a major company's hardware or software.

cluster. A segment or partition of files, grouped and numbered for tracking and memory purposes by a computer's operating system.

COBOL (common business-oriented language). An early programming language that has been superseded by more sophisticated languages.

color depth. The number of colors that can be displayed, measured in bits.

commercial online service. A company that provides online information and content as well as Internet access.

COM port: The port on the processor where external communications peripherals, such as printers and modems, are connected.

compressed files. Documents that have been decreased in size so they take less time to download.

CompuServe. A leading online service, specializing in the business and professsional markets. CompuServe is owned by AOL, and is operated as a separate brand.

conference room. An AOL chat room that can hold more than 23 people.

consolidation. A spreadsheet feature that allows the user to combine cell values from several spreadsheets into a separate summary sheet.

cooling fan: A small fan attatched to the heat sink that serves to absorb and dissipate heat from the CPU.

CPU (central processing unit). The part of a computer that stores, processes, and controls the system.

CRT (cathode-ray tube) monitor.. A monitor that works by directing a stream of electrons across the back of the screen. Most TVs and computer monitors use CRT technology.

database. A collection of information in machine-readable form. Database programs enable users to manipulate this information.

data transfer rate. The amount of time it takes to load data into RAM.

defragmentation. A computer housekeeping chore that should be performed once a month to keep a system operating at peak performance. It can be executed by accessing Programs/Accessories/System from the Start Menu. (See also **fragmentation.**)

desktop. 1) The graphic elements on a computer screen that display icons portraying folders and documents; 2) A type of computer that sits on a desk.

desktop publishers. Programs that are capable of creating documents with different typefaces, margins, and justifications and that enable the user to insert graphics into the text.

digital. Describing data that is measured at discrete intervals. An example of a digital device is a clock that displays time as numerals rather than using hour and minute hands.

digital camera. A camera that stores the pictures you take as computer data files.

digital imaging. The process that allows graphics, including photographs, to be stored in a computer.

DIMM (dual in-line memory module). A group of memory chips on a small circuit board that can be installed one at a time. (SIMMs need to be installed two at a time.)

disk defragmenter. A procedure which improves disk speed by rewriting files so that all parts of each file are written to consecutive sectors. Files tend to become fragmented with use which slows down performance during retrieval operations. (See also **defragmentation**)

DMA (direct memory access). A system that transfers data from main memory directly to a device, bypassing the CPU.

domain. The part of a URL that describes a group of computers administered as a unit.

download directory. The AOL default directory for files downloaded from the AOL service.

DOS. The operating system that preceded the first version of Windows.

dot-matrix printer. A printer that produces closely spaced dots to compose letters, words, and pictures by striking pins against an ink ribbon.

dot pitch. The distance between the dots that make up images on a screen. The smaller the dot pitch, the crisper the images.

download. To receive files from another computer.

371

dpi (dots per inch). A measurement of screen resolution. The lower the dpi, the sharper the image.

DRAM (dynamical random access memory). The generic name for all RAM memory modules. The data on DRAM chips disappear when power is turned off.

drawing program. A software application that enables the user to create geometric shapes.

driver. An interface program that translates instructions from an operating system to peripheral devices, into commands the peripherals can understand.

DVDROM disc. A CD–ROM disc that holds at least 4.7 gigabytes, the equivalent of six regular CD–ROM discs.

DVDROM drive. A CD–ROM drive that reads very high storage capacity discs.

EDO RAM (extended data out random access memory). A specially manufactured chip that performs better than common RAM.

e-mail. An online method of communication that sends messages and attached files electronically.

encryption. A process of scrambling messages so that only those who have the decoding key can read them.

ENERGY STAR. Energy-saving guidelines for PCs and monitors established by the EPA (Environmental Protection Agency).

EPS (Encapsulated PostScript) file. A PostScript program that has a header describing the width and height of the image and how to place the image on the page.

.EXE (executable) file. An executable file or a file that may be run; an application file for PCs

expansion board. A printed circuit board, such as a video adapter, graphics accelerator, sound card, or internal modem, that adds capabilities to a computer.

expansion slot. The opening into which a circuit board is inserted.

FAT (file allocation table). A system used by the computer to keep track of files.

Favorite Places. The AOL bookmark feature that enables AOL members to quickly go to sites on the AOL service or the Internet.

finger-pointing. The practice of a tech support representative blaming a piece of software other than the one manufactured by his or her company.

firmware. Software that is permanently encoded onto computer chips.

Flash BIOS. An upgradable BIOS system.

Flash EPROMs. Reprogrammable read-only memory chips.

Flashsessions. (See **Automatic AOL.**)

flatbed scanner. A type of scanner that captures an image by passing a high-intensity light over the face of the object to be scanned.

floppy disk. A magnetic-coated 3.5-inch plastic device that holds up to 1.4MB of data.

floppy drive. The part of the computer that accepts floppy disks.

forum. A discussion group devoted to a particular topic. Typically, forums include an online message board on which participants can post questions and answers; a file library containing topic-relevant applications and downloadable text files; and a conference or chat area for real-time dialog, interviews, and guest appearances.

fragmentation. A term that describes the condition of a disk that has scattered pieces of files stored in different places. Fragmentation causes a slowdown in a computer's performance, as the disk searches for the various parts of the file. (See **defragmentation.**)

freeware. Downloadable software available at no charge.

FTP (file transfer protocol). The system used for dowloading files from the Internet.

GIF (graphics interchange format). A file format that specifies how graphic images are compressed for use online. GIF is used mostly for less sophisticated artwork such as cartoon and line drawings, rather than photographs, which display better in the JPEG format.

gigabyte. A measurement of data storage equal to 1,024 megabytes.

glare filter. A transparent screen that fits over a monitor to reduce glare and reflections.

glidepad. An input device controlled by sliding a finger around a pad.

gopher. An Internet application that searches for information via a series of menus. As each menu is displayed, the user selects an item, which leads to another menu, until a document appears on the screen. Gopher was one of the earliest Internet information retrieval tools, and has now been largely supplanted by the Web.

GPF (general protection fault). A Windows error message that occurs when one application tries to use memory that is in use by or already assigned to another application, causing a Windows application to crash.

GPS (Global Positioning System). A constellation of 24 satellites developed and operated by the U.S. Department of Defense which is used for navigation and precise geodetic position measurements. GPS permits land, sea, and airborne users to determine their three dimensional position, velocity, and time.

GUI (graphical user interface). A format that makes use of windows and menus and portrays a desktop on the computer screen. A GUI allows a user to navigate by using a mouse to point and click on pictures and icons rather than using keyboard commands. The AOL service is an example of a GUI application.

handwriting recognition. A technique that allows a computer to read hand-written material.

hard disk space: The area where your applications and files are stored when they're not being used.

hard drive. The part of a computer that reads, writes, and holds data.

hardware. The tangible parts of a computer (disk drives, keyboards, display screens, printers, chips, and so on).

heat sink. A device that absorbs and dissipates heat from the CPU.

HPC (handheld personal computer). (See **palmtop computer**.)

HTML (hypertext markup language). The code used to write Web pages.

hub. A central point used to connect segments of a local area network (LAN).

hyperlink. A graphic element or text in an online document that a user can click on to be taken to a different document.

inkjet printer. A printer that squirts tiny drops of ink onto the paper.

Instant Message. An AOL feature that enables members to communicate with other AOL members and Internet users in real time online on a one-to-one basis.

interlaced monitor. A monitor that displays high resolution but has an increased rate of screen flickering.

Internet. A network of networks that connects groups of computers and enables users to communicate via e-mail, the Web, and commercial online services.

Internet telephony. Technology that facilitates phone calls using the Internet rather than phone lines.

intranet. An internal network navigated similarly to the way the Internet is navigated. Intranets are usually created by organizations and are accessible only to authorized personnel.

I/O (input/output). A term used to describe operations or devices that enter data into or take data out of computers. A printer is an example of an input/output device.

IRQ: IRQ or Interrupt Request refers to the hardware lines used by PC peripherals (such as printers or modems) to communicate to the microprocessor that the device is ready to send or receive data.

ISA (Industry Standard Architecture) bus. A type of bus that can carry 16 bits of data at a time.

ISDN (integrated services digital network) line. A communications format that allows voice, video and data to be sent via digital telephone lines. Most ISDN lines offered by telephone companies provide data rates that are three times as fast as a high speed modem.

ISP (Internet service provider). A company that supplies a user with access to the Internet via a dial-up telephone line.

Jaz drive. A disk drive that accepts removable cartridges that hold up to 2 gigabytes of data.

JPEG (Joint Photographic Experts Group). A relatively high quality format for compressing pictures such as photographs, artwork, and paintings. JPEG compresses color images to about 5 percent of their size with some loss of detail.

jumper. A plastic plug that fits over two pins, used to reconfigure expansion boards.

kerning. Controlling the amount of space between letters and numbers in text.

keyboard. The part of a computer that enables a user to input data with letters, numbers, special characters, and function keys.

keyword. A shortcut that enables AOL members to navigate the service quickly.

kilobit (Kb). A measurement of RAM. Each bit is 1/8 of a byte.

kilobyte (KB). A measurement of data storage equal to 1,024 bytes.

LAN (local area network). A network that connects computers in a small area, such as a building or a group of buildings in close promixity to each other.

laptop. A portable computer small enough to sit on a user's lap. Laptops may also come with a battery pack that must be recharged after several hours. (See also **note-**

book computer.)

laser printer. A printer that uses a laser to form an image on a rolling drum that transfers the image to paper.

LCD (liquid crystal display). The type of display used for digital watches and most PCs.

line printer. A printer that prints one line of text at a time, but no graphics.

lossy technique. A method of file compression often used for video files in which some amount of data is lost.

LPT (line printer terminal) port. A term that originally referred to a line printer and that now refers to any kind of printer.

Macintosh Computer. A computer introduced in 1984 by Apple Computer, and which is known for the graphical user interface that is embedded in its operating system.

MacOS. The operating system used by Apple Macintosh computers.

macros. Small programs that act as shortcuts and make applications run more efficiently.

macro virus. A computer virus that affects all the data files of the same application as the downloaded document infected with the virus.

mainframe. A big computer that can support thousands of users at the same time.

MDRAM (multibank dynamic random access memory). A new fast performance form of random access memory that is currently used in video and graphics accelerators.

megabit (Mb). A measurement of RAM. Each bit is one-eighth of a byte.

megabyte (MB). A measurement of data storage equal to 1,048,576 bytes.

Member Services. An AOL feature that provides a great deal of help and information; it is especially useful to members who are relatively new to the service.

memory effect. A characteristic of nickel cadmium batteries that makes it necessary to drain them completely of power before recharging.

Merced. A new computer chip in development by Hewlett Packard and Intel that works on a different principle from current ones.

message board. A means of online communication that allows users to post new messages, as well as respond to others.

MHz (megahertz). A measurement of processing speed.

MIDI (musical instrument digital interface). A device that allows computers to record sounds created by a synthesizer and produce new sounds.

MIPS R10000. A very fast RISC CPU.

MMX (multimedia extensions). Multimedia technology developed by Intel that processes operations previously handled by sound and video cards.

modem. A device that converts digital signals to analog data and transmits them across phone lines to facilitate Internet and online service connections and faxing.

monitor. The box that contains the display screen that enables a computer user to view data.

Moore's Law. The concept that the number of transistors per square inch on the surface of a processor chip doubles every 18 months.

motherboard. The large internal circuit board that contains the CPU, RAM, cache, and slots for additional circuit cards.

mouse. A device that enables a computer user to navigate screens by pointing and clicking on words or icons.

377

MPEG (Motion Picture Experts Group). A type of video compression technology.

multimedia. Sound, graphics, video, text, and animation presented in an integrated system on the computer. Multimedia applications have huge storage requirements, and so they are most commonly found on CD ROMs.

multitasking. A computer's ability to run more than one program at a time.

My Place. An area on the AOL service where members may upload files, such as those associated with their own web sites.

nanosecond. A measurement of chip speed. One nanosecond equals one-billionth of a second.

netiquette. An informal code that governs the behavior of people online.

newsgroup. Online discussion group in which participants post messages to each other.

NIC (network interface card). An expansion board that allows a computer to connect to a network.

non-interlaced monitor. A monitor that has a screen that displays high-resolution images without much flickering or streaking.

NOS (network operating system). Software that enables computers to connect to a network.

notebook computer. A portable computer, usually small enough to fit inside a briefcase. (See also **laptop**.)

NTSC (National Television System Committee) standard. A TV video signal used by the United States and Japan.

OCR (optical character recognition). The ability of a computer to read words and numbers and translate them into a format that can be edited.

operating system. The program that performs basic computer tasks such as translating input from the keyboard to the screen, keeping track of files and directories, and controlling printers and modems.

overdrive processor. A microprocesser chip that allows an owner of a 486-based PC to upgrade to a faster microprocessor simply by installing the chip

packet. A small chunk of data to be transmitted over a network that contains the target address as well as the information to be sent.

PAL (Phase Alternate Line) standard. The TV video signal used in Europe (except for France).

palmtop computer. A handheld device that looks like a very small notebook computer.

parallel port. A data communication pathway that allows a CPU to work with devices not directly connected by buses and that transmits multiple bits of data simultaneously.

parallel processing. A technology that utilizes multiple CPUs to optimize performance.

parity. A type of error-checking that automatically checks data every time it is read from memory.

partitioning. A process that eliminates wasted disk space by dividing memory or mass storage into separate sections.

PBC (pipeline burst cache). A type of cache that maximizes performance by fetching memory before it's requested. It also accesses memory in the cache while other memory is being fetched.

PCI (peripheral component interconnect) bus. A type of bus that can carry 32 bits.

PCX. A graphics file format used for optical scanners, faxes, and desktop publishing.

PDA (personal digital assistant). A handheld device that uses a stylus or voice recogition rather than a keyboard and provides computer functions, phone, fax, and network connection.

PDF (Portable Document Format). A technique that makes it possible to read transmitted formatted data.

peer-to-peer. A method of networking used mainly in small workgroup situations where each computer communicates directly to the others on the network.

peripheral. An external device such as a printer, scanner, or modem that's attached to a computer.

Personal Filing Cabinet. A feature of the AOL service that allows members to store incoming and outgoing e-mail and message board and newsgroup postings on their computer's hard disk.

Personal Publisher. A feature of the AOL service that allows members to easily create Web home pages.

PIM (personal information manager). Software that has a collection of features such as an appointment calendar, a notepad, a phone list, and a calculator program.

pixels. Horizontal and vertical dots that display images on a monitor.

platform. (See **operating system.**)

plug-and-play. A term that describes a computer's ability to automatically detect the hardware it has and install the appropriate peripheral drivers.

plug-in. Software that is easily installed that expands the capabilities of applications.

post. To enter a message on a forum, BBS, newsgroup, or message board.

PostScript. A language used by desktop publishing programs to create camera-ready copy.

POTS (plain old telephone service). The standard telephone service used in most private homes.

power on. To turn on the power to your computer.

power supply. The device that converts the electricity from the wall outlet to the correct voltage necessary to run the computer.

PPP (point-to-point protocol). The most common Internet communications format.

379

protocol. A pre-arranged format used to transmit data.

RAM (random access memory). The temporary main storage area for program data. RAM is not saved when the computer is turned off.

RealAudio Player. A plug-in that can play streaming audio with broadcast-quality stereo sound.

real time. With practically an indiscernible delay of information transfer. A telephone conversation and an Instant Message conversation both occur in real time.

reboot: To restart your computer. (See also **boot.**)

recycle bin. A Windows 95 temporary storage place on the hard drive for deleted files.

refresh rate. The speed at which a monitor redraws the images displayed. The higher the rate, the less the images flicker.

resolution. The term used to describe how clearly and sharply images appear on a monitor or printed material. The higher the resolution, the sharper the image.

RISC (Reduced Instruction Set Computing) chips. A chip that performs at high speeds because it recognizes, and therefore has to process, a small number of instructions. It's also less expensive to produce because it requires fewer transistors.

ROM (read only memory). A computer's permanent storage area. ROM is saved when the computer is turned off.

router. A device that connects two local area networks (LANs).

RTC (real-time clock). A computer clock that operates on a battery separate from the power supply so that the clock can keep track of time even when the computer is turned off.

RTF (rich text format). A language for formatting documents with features such as fonts, margins, italics, and so on.

scanner. A computer component that can read printed text and illustrations and translate the information into a form that is usable by the computer; a device that can digitize printed images.

scanner resolution. A measurement of how much detail a scanner can reproduce, expressed in dpi.

screen name. The label assigned to each member of an online service that serves as a means of identification. Members of the AOL service choose screen names from between three and ten numbers and/or letters. Each account can have up to five screen names.

screen saver. A program that was originally used to prevent an image from burning into the screen when it was in a fixed position for a long time. Newer monitors have screen safeguards built in, so screen savers are now more commonly used for decoration or amusement.

SCSI (small computer system interface). Pronounced "scuzzy," an interface standard for attaching peripheral devices to computers.

SDRAM. State-of-the-art video card technology.

search engine. A program that enables a user to retrieve information online. A search engine may search the whole Web or a particular site. An example of a search engine is AOL NetFind.

SECAM (Sequential Couleur Avec Memoire) standard. A TV video signal used in France.

seek time. The amount of time it takes a program or device to find data.

serial port. A data communications pathway that allows a CPU to work with devices not directly connected by buses and that transmits data one bit at a time.

server. The computer in a network that runs the operating system.

SGRAM (synchronous graphics random access memory). A fast performance form of random access memory used on video adapters and graphics accelerators.

shareware. Downloadable software that is available for trial use (usually from 10 to 30 days). Users who decide to keep the software are expected to pay a nominal fee to the owner.

SIMM (single in-line memory module). A group of nine memory chips on a small circuit board. SIMMs need to be installed two at a time.

SLIP (Serial Line Internet Protocol). An Internet communications format.

software. The information, data, or instructions that make a computer useful; or anything that may be stored electronically. A word-processing program contains software. The physical disk on which the software is recorded is hardware.

software library. An online repository of downloadable software.

sound card. A device that records audio input and provides audio output to your speakers.

spam. Unsolicited online communication or solicitations.

SRAM (static random access memory). A fast form of RAM.

streaming. A technique that enables data to be displayed before the whole file is transferred. Streaming technology is commonly associated with downloading multimedia files such as music files on RealAudio.

suite. A software package that comes with a group of compatible programs, such as a word processor, spreadsheet, database, drawing package, presentation software, communications manager, and personal information manager.

surge protector. A device that protects a computer from electrical surges.

SVGA (super video graphics adapter). A color graphics adapter card that can display sharp images at 1,028 x 768 pixels, the highest current standard.

swap file. A piece of the hard disk that holds the contents of RAM when there isn't enough memory for all the programs and files open at the same time. The computer can move programs or files into the swap file as needed to free up more main memory.

system disk. The disk that stores the operating system files necessary to start the computer. Most users use a hard drive as their system disk.

T1. A phone line that is capable of transmitting data at a rate of 1.54 million bps.

T3. A phone line that is capable of transmitting data at a rate of 44.75 million bps.

tape backup unit. A data storage medium that uses a cassette cartridge.

TCO (total cost of ownership). A dollar figure that represents how much it costs to own a PC. TCO factors in the original cost of the computer and software, hardware and software upgrades, maintenance, technical support, and training.

TCP/IP (Transmission Control Protocol/Internet Protocol). A communications format for transferring data on a network.

TIFF (tagged image file format). A technique used for storing bit-mapped images.

TOD (Tool on Demand). An AOL addition to the current software that was not included in the original version. Recent examples of TODs are improved security features, updated Welcome and Channels screens, and added charting features to the Portfolio area. AOL members receive TOD downloads automatically.

trackball. A sphere that rests in a fixed base and operates like a mouse.

TSR (terminate-stay resident) program. A program such as a calendar, calculator, spell checker, or dictionary that can be accessed quickly from another application and that always stays in memory.

UART (universal asynchronous receiver-transmitter). Hardware that manages incoming data.

Ultra ATA. State-of-the-art technology that supports fast data transfer rates.

UNIX. An operating system developed in the 1970s, originally characterized by cryptic command names and an overall absence of user-friendly features. UNIX has begun to make more use of GUI.

upload. To send files from one computer to another.

UPS (uninterrupted power supply). A device that contains a battery and sensors that detect problems with the power supply and automatically switch a computer to battery power when necessary.

URL (uniform resource locator). An Internet address.

USB (Universal Serial Bus). A device that allows users to daisy-chain up to 127 other devices off of a single port.

Usenet. A system of Internet newsgroups that cover over 25,000 subjects.

utilities program. Software that performs system-managing tasks such as uninstalling software, fighting computer viruses, backing up files, and encryption.

V.90. An internationally approved standard that addresses the incompatibility of two competing modem technologies, 3COM's X2 and Rockwell Semiconductors' K56 Flex. The two companies have agreed to manufacture new products that will comply with the V.90 standard.

VDOLive Player. A plug-in that produces streaming video with sound.

VGA (video graphics adapter). A graphics display system that provides screen resolutions of up to 640 x 480 pixels.

video accelerator. An adapter that has a processor to increase the speed of rendering and updating images.

video card. The part of a computer that provides video signals to the monitor.

videoconferencing. A technology that uses computer networks to transmit audio and video data to facilitate face-to-face conversations with more than two people at a time.

video driver. Software that runs the video card on a PC.

viewable image size. The largest window size that can be displayed on the screen.

virtual memory. A section of the hard drive set aside for temporary storage to free up more RAM. Virtual memory should be set for 2.5 times the amount of installed RAM.

virtual reality. An artificial environment that mimics the real world through the use of technology.

virus. Software that causes damage to computers and files.

VL-bus. A type of bus used in PCs made prior to 1995. VL-bus technology has been superseded by PCI-bus technology.

voice recognition software. Software that allows a user to speak into a microphone to control computer operations.

VR. See **virtual reality.**

VRAM (video random access memory). A fast performance RAM that displays while new data is being accessed.

VRML (Virtual Reality Modeling Language). The code used to display 3-D on the Web.

WAN (wide area network). A network that spans a large geographical area, made up of two or more LANs.

.wav. Windows sound files.

wavetable synthesis. A technique for reproducing MIDI sound that is more realistic than   FM synthesis.

WebTV. The brand name for one type of set-top box that provides an Internet connection from the TV.

Windows 95. The operating system most commonly used with personal computers.

Windows 98. The most current version of the Windows operating system.

Windows NT. An operating system usually used for computer networks.

Wintel. A term used to describe the close association between industry giants Microsoft and Intel, as when a Windows operating system runs on an Intel microprocessor.

Wireless communication. The new technology of portable, mobile and transportable phones, which transmit signals via low energy radio waves to local antenna sites.

workstation. 1) A kind of computer used for applications such as CAD/CAM, desktop publishing, and software development that require high-resolution graphics and a GUI; 2) a computer connected to a LAN (local area network).

World Wide Web. A part of the Internet that displays graphics, audio, and video, provides links to different documents, and is formatted in HTML.

WRAM (Windows random access memory). A fast performance RAM that allows a video adapter to display memory as new bytes are being added.

X value. The measurement that is determined by how many times faster a drive is than the standard 300K per second data transfer speed. This mainly applies to CD ROM drives.

Y2K (year 2000 problem). Refers to the potential worldwide crisis at the beginning of the year 2000, when computers programmed with dates using only the last two digits (98, 97, and so on) instead of the whole year will be confused, throwing systems into chaos.

ZIF (zero insertion force) socket. A slot that opens by using a lever at the side of the mounting fixture, thereby eliminating the need for special tools to insert and remove chips.

zip drive. A disk drive that accepts disks that can hold up to 100 megabytes of data, used primarily for backing up data and transporting large files.

TROUBLESHOOTING INDEX

KEYWORD INDEX

389

GENERAL INDEX

3M, 276

A & V Forum, 26–29
accelerator board, 69, 70
access numbers, 92, 95, 96, 98, 99, 102
access time, 67, 74, 263
active matrix, 267
add-ons, 31, 54, 86
address books, 54
Adobe, 276, 312, 314, 319, 321, 322
Aladdin Systems, 71
Alps, 247, 276
AM Software, 310
AMD (Advanced Micro Devices), 261, 276
America Online, 1, 4, 5, 7, 8, 26, 58, 75,
   89, 91, 95, 206, 214, 270, 277, 299,
   310, 320–324, 326, 332, 345, 346,
   348, 351
   access numbers, 98, 99, 102, 340, 343,
   353; AOL Live, 111; AOL Store, 2, 4, 9,
   12, 15, 19, 28, 34, 39, 41, 57, 60, 68,
   69, 71, 72, 75, 78, 81, 83, 85, 87, 90,
   98, 138, 139, 144, 150, 155, 156,
   161–163, 165, 167, 171, 173, 178, 180,
   189, 214, 215, 217, 218, 222, 223, 230,
   231, 234, 235, 239, 243, 247–249, 254,
   270, 275, 276, 280, 288, 291, 323, 328,
   330, 354, 355; AOL Computing
   Classifieds, 12; AOL Press, 353;
   Automatic AOL, 2, 113, 124, 125, 128,
   268, 299, 356; billing, 108, 109, 297,
   354–357; Buddy Lists, 129–134, 351;
   chat rooms, 20, 37, 45, 89, 108–112,
   129, 131, 134, 145, 260, 332, 333, 351;
   Computing channel, 2, 8, 11, 17, 138,
   141, 145, 185, 197, 204, 248, 257, 295;
   Computing Newsstand, 9, 248, 258,
   260; Computing Tips, 9; conference
   rooms, 134; connecting to, 90, 92, 95,
   96, 98, 99, 101–103, 253, 338–340;
   Daily Download, 2, 11, 12; Download
   Manager, 127; e-mail, 89, 91, 113–126,
   128, 207, 351, 354, 356; Favorite Places,
   118, 119; fax mail, 120; forums, 3,
   9–11, 26, 32, 34, 36, 37, 45, 53, 64,
   68–70, 73, 82, 84, 97, 359; installing,
   107; Instant Messages, 2, 89, 129,
   131–133, 332, 351; Internet access
   through, 2, 192, 195; keywords, 11, 15;
   long distance phone service, 115;
   Member Directory, 114, 130, 351;
   Member Services, 2, 3, 15, 89, 90,
   105–108, 202, 335, 356; navigating, 12,
   20, 107; NetChannel, 53; Online
   Classroom, 13, 14; NetFind, 26, 197,
   203, 205; Parental Controls, 332, 333,
   345, 350, 352, 353, 355, 356; PC Help
   Desk, 10, 15; PC Virus Information
   Center, 18; Personal Filing Cabinet, 123,
   124; Preferences, 71; software, 91, 196,
   215, 335–337, 339, 342, 343, 345, 347,
   352; Software Shop, 9; technical support,

391

393

diagnostics, 34, 78, 184–187, 194, 327, 328, 342

Dialogic, 282

Diamond, 276

digital imaging, 4, 12, 25, 28, 29, 41, 138, 154, 163–166, 210, 244, 269, 270, 320, 321

DIMMs, 221, 222, 262

disk fragmentation, 70, 183, 189, 228

DMAs (direct memory assistants), 199, 245

domains, 323

DOS, 11, 56, 71, 78, 110, 190, 191, 194, 198, 216, 223–225, 262, 293

dot pitch, 141, 231, 233, 239, 255, 263, 364

downloading, 15, 17, 58, 64, 125, 181, 270, 295–297, 299, 320, 331, 339, 340, 348, 352

AOL Download Manager, 127, 297, 298; audio files, 138, 149; Daily Download, 2, 11, 12, 64, 295; file compression/decompression, 24, 71, 126, 127; files, 91, 92, 103, 107, 124–126, 128; FTP (file transfer protocol), 60; games, 24, 128; software, 1, 7, 8, 11, 12, 17, 18, 20, 22, 23, 27, 29–31, 58, 62, 63, 71, 82, 128, 133, 138, 148, 184, 204, 281, 294, 295; video software, 138

Dr. Solomon's antivirus software, 19

Dragon Systems, 83

DRAM, 236, 260, 264

drivers, 57, 58, 76, 81, 83, 147, 148, 184, 187, 193, 196, 198, 224, 319

DriveSpace, 71

Duplexx Software, 26

DVD, 84, 85, 161, 241, 242, 244

EDCO Services, 320

EDO, 236, 237, 260, 264

EIDE (Enhanced Integrated Drive Electronics), 263

e-mail, 2, 53, 54, 58, 60, 63, 64, 85, 89, 91, 100, 107, 113–126, 128, 131, 148, 154, 164, 165, 178, 179, 181, 207, 208, 211, 297, 320, 323, 331, 332, 348–352, 354, 359

emergency system disk, 191

encryption, 34, 327

Energy Star, 143, 232, 234

EPA (Environmental Protection Agency, 234

Epson, 57, 276

error messages, 107

expansion cards, 54, 65

FAT (file allocation table), 194, 228, 234

Favorite Places, 118, 119

fax, 86, 113, 202

modems, 81, 94, 96, 98, 198, 266

file compression, 24, 71, 120, 126–128

filenames, 225, 226, 296, 324, 325, 348, 349

finger pointing, 203

floppy disks/drives, 48, 50, 55, 56, 67, 73, 74, 173, 217, 236, 240, 241, 260, 262, 263, 273, 276, 292–294, 349, 363, 364

fonts, 82, 319, 320

Ford, Harrison, 330

forums, 9–11, 26, 29, 32, 35, 37, 45, 53, 64, 68–70, 73, 97, 100, 110, 128, 150,

397

399

401

Introducing the
AOL NETBOOK COLLECTION

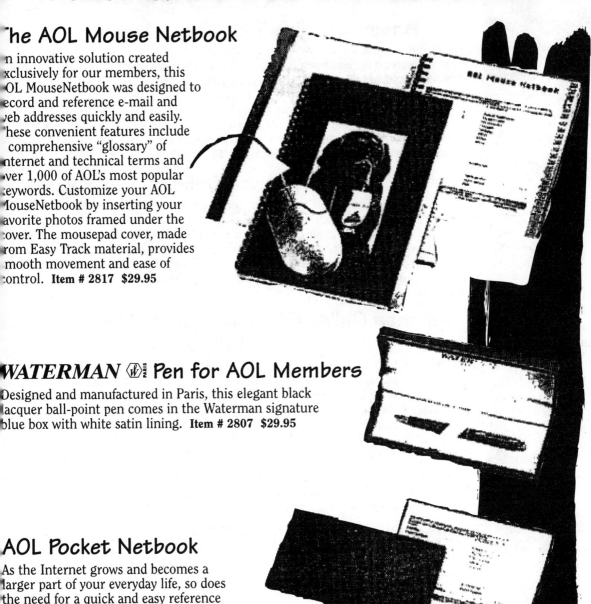

The AOL Mouse Netbook

An innovative solution created exclusively for our members, this AOL MouseNetbook was designed to record and reference e-mail and web addresses quickly and easily. These convenient features include a comprehensive "glossary" of internet and technical terms and over 1,000 of AOL's most popular keywords. Customize your AOL MouseNetbook by inserting your favorite photos framed under the cover. The mousepad cover, made from Easy Track material, provides smooth movement and ease of control. **Item # 2817 $29.95**

WATERMAN PARIS Pen for AOL Members

Designed and manufactured in Paris, this elegant black lacquer ball-point pen comes in the Waterman signature blue box with white satin lining. **Item # 2807 $29.95**

AOL Pocket Netbook

As the Internet grows and becomes a larger part of your everyday life, so does the need for a quick and easy reference guide. This uniquely designed Netbook can be helpful for jotting down your favorite places online and recording names and addresses. **Item # 2809 $15.95**

TO ORDER CALL: 1-800-844-3372 EXT. 1029

The Official AOL BOOK COLLECTION

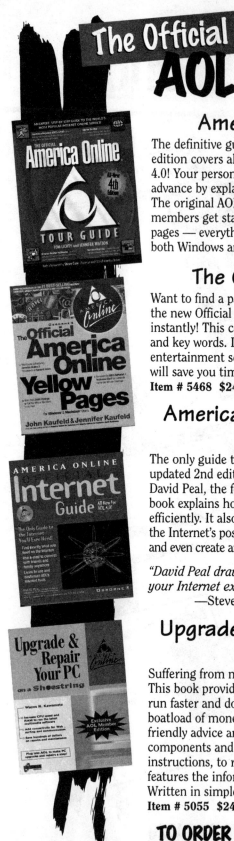

America Online Tour Guide, Version 4.0

The definitive guide for AOL members since its first edition in 1992, This all-new edition covers all the exciting, new, timesaving, fun features of AOL's latest release, AOL 4.0! Your personal tourguide to AOL, it takes you through the basics, then helps you advance by explaining some of the more powerful features that are built into the service. The original AOL guide, author Tom Lichty has helped more than 1 million AOL members get started. You'll appreciate his engaging and humorous style. Over 600 pages — everything you need to know to enhance your online experience with AOL. For both Windows and Macintosh users. **Item # 5053 $24.95**

The Official America Online Yellow Pages

Want to find a particular area on AOL but don't have much time to search? Then let the new Official America Online Yellow Pages help you find what you are looking for instantly! This complete guide covers thousands of AOL sites, providing full descriptions and key words. It makes accessing news, stock quotes, sports stats, and even the latest entertainment scoop, as easy as typing in one word. Organized in Yellow Pages style, it will save you time & money by helping you find what you want on AOL fast!
Item # 5468 $24.95

America Online Official Guide to the Internet, 2nd Edition

The only guide to the Internet officially authorized by America Online. This new and updated 2nd edition has all the details on AOL's latest software — version 4.0. Written by David Peal, the former Editorial Manager of America Online's Internet connection, this book explains how to use AOL's special navigational tools to find information fast and efficiently. It also explains how AOL makes accessing and using the Internet easy. Discover the Internet's possibilities as you learn how to plan a vacation, job hunt, make friends online and even create and post your own website! **Item # 5532 $24.95**

"David Peal draws on his years of working with AOL to share insider tips that can turn your Internet experience into something truly extraordinary"
—Steve Case, Chairman and CEO of America Online.

Upgrade & Repair Your PC on a Shoestring — AOL Members Edition

Suffering from new computer envy? Well don't throw that old computer away just yet! This book provides the solid advice and information you need to make your computer run faster and do the things your want without a Ph.D. in Computer Technology and a boatload of money! Four sections take you through upgrading your PC with lots of friendly advice and encouragement. From determining what you need, to explaining components and what they do, to the Nuts & Bolts with complete illustrations and instructions, to resources on AOL to help you through the process. This book also features the information you need to troubleshoot and make simple repairs yourself. Written in simple, easy to understand language for all computer users.
Item # 5055 $24.95

TO ORDER CALL: 1-800-844-3372 EXT. 1029

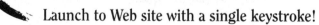

GRAPHICS MADE FUN AND EASY
for the whole family!

Enter the exciting world of digital imaging — no experience necessary!

America Online's GraphicSuite

Now you can produce professional-looking art on your computer even if you've never worked with digital art before. Our AOL exclusive GraphicSuite CD-ROM makes it easy! Ten top-rated user friendly programs on one CD-ROM give you the tools to create, retouch, and organize images, then import them into your documents or post them on a Web site. **Item # 6708 $29.95**

- Turn ordinary photos into dazzling banners, greeting cards and more!
- Add animation and sound to your e-mail!
- Organize your images with drag and drop ease!
- 10,000 ready-to-use clip art photos and images! <u>BONUS</u>

TO ORDER CALL: 1-800-844-3372 EXT. 1029

Order your
Books, CD-ROMs, and AOL Planner Collections Today

To order by phone: 1-800-884-3372 ext. 1029   **To order by fax: 1-800-821-4595**

Item#	Title	Quantity	Unit Price	Total Price
5053	America Online Tour Guide, Version 4.0		$24.95	
5468	The Official America Online Yellow Pages		$24.95	
5532	America Online Official Guide to the Internet, 2nd Edition		$24.95	
5055	Upgrade & Repair Your PC on a Shoestring		$24.95	
5533	You've Got Pictures! AOL's Guide to Digital Imaging		$24.95	
5066	America Online's Creating Cool Web Pages		$24.95	
5065	Genealogy Online, Special AOL Edition		$24.95	
5067	AOL's Students' Guide to the Internet		$19.95	
6894	AOL's Internet AcceleratorSuite		$39.95	
6708	America Online's GraphicSuite		$29.95	
2817	The AOL Mouse Netbook		$29.95	
2807	Watermen Pen for AOL Members		$29.95	
2809	AOL Pocket Netbook		$15.95	

Prices subject to change without notice.

Shipping and Handling:
Under $20.00 = $4.00
$21.00-$30.00 = $4.25
$31.00-40.00 = $4.75
Over $50.00 = $5.00

Subtotal $ _____
Shipping & Handling $ _____
Sales Tax (if applicable) $ _____
Total $ _____

ORDERED BY:

Name _____

Address _____

City _____ State _____ Zip Code _____

Daytime Phone Number (___) ____ - _____

METHOD OF PAYMENT

☐ VISA
☐ MasterCard
☐ Discover
☐ American Express

☐☐☐☐☐☐☐☐☐☐☐☐☐☐☐☐
Account Number
Expiration Date: ☐☐ - ☐☐

SHIP TO: (if different from above)

Name _____

Address _____

City _____ State _____ Zip Code _____

Daytime Phone Number (___) ____ - _____

_____
Signature
(Required for all credit card orders)

Send order form and payment to:
America Online, Inc.
Department 1029
P.O. Box 2530
Kearneysville, WV 25430-9935